SHACKLETON'S
LAST VOYAGE

EYEWITNESS ACCOUNTS

SHACKLETON'S LAST VOYAGE

FRANK WILD

AMBERLEY

To The Boss

First published 1923, this edition 2014

Amberley Publishing
The Hill, Stroud
Gloucestershire, GL5 4EP

www.amberley-books.com

British Library Cataloguing in Publication Data.
A catalogue record for this book is available from the British Library.

ISBN 978 1 4456 3593 4 (print)
ISBN 978 1 4456 3608 5 (ebook)

Typeset in 10pt on 13pt Minion.
Typesetting and Origination by Amberley Publishing.
Printed in the UK.

Contents

Contents

Editor's Note

By the time he wrote his account of the *Quest* expedition, Frank Wild had taken part in five Antarctic expeditions, including Captain Scott's *Discovery* expedition and Shackleton's *Endurance* expedition, now famous as one of the great epics of survival. Cape Wild on Elephant Island, where the men from *Endurance* camped after escaping the Antarctic ice, and where Wild took command while Shackleton went on to South Georgia to seek help, is named after him. Most of Wild's life after the *Quest* expedition, his last trip to the South, was spent in southern and eastern Africa. Although his ashes were interred in Johannesburg, in 2011 they were reburied in Grytviken, South Georgia, at the right hand of Sir Ernest Shackleton.

Although Shackleton died in South Georgia, while the *Quest* was on its way to Antarctica, his presence loomed large for much of the remainder of the expedition. The *Quest* expedition had been organised by Shackleton, who seems to have been bored by life on the lecture circuit in post-war London, and part of the burden that fell on Wild when he took command after Shackleton's death was that Shackleton did not appear to have had a firm idea of what he wanted to achieve in the Antarctic. Wild's experiences on the *Endurance* expedition and the period spent on Elephant Island in particular also loom large, understandably so.

This was the last expedition of the Heroic Age of Antarctic exploration; in the future, explorers would have the benefit of modern technology in their trips to the South.

Editorial interventions have been kept to a minimum and the opinions and attitudes of Shackleton, Wild and their companions are as they were originally written down in 1923.

Preface

Sir Ernest Shackleton died suddenly; so suddenly that he said no word at all with regard to the future of the expedition. But I know that had he foreseen his death and been able to communicate to me his wishes, they would have been summed up in the two words, 'Carry on!'

Perhaps the most difficult part of my task has been the recording of the work of the expedition. It has been to me a very sad duty, and one which I would gladly have avoided had it been possible. The demand, however, for the complete story of Sir Ernest Shackleton's last expedition has been so widespread and insistent that I could no longer withhold it.

In the subsequent pages of this book the reader will find recorded the story of the voyage of the *Quest*, the tight little ship that carried us through over 20,000 miles of stormy ocean and brought us safely back.

I make no claim to literary style, but have endeavoured to set forth a plain and simple narrative.

The writings of explorers vary, but in my opinion they have all one common fault, which is, that they have attempted to combine in one volume the scientific results with the more popular story of the expedition.

This book is for the public. I have sought to eliminate the mass of scientific details with which my journal is filled, to avoid technical terms, and to retain only that which can be easily understood by all.

Of the parts of the narrative that deal with Sir Ernest Shackleton I have passed over very shortly. Pens far more able than mine, notably those of Mr Harold Begbie and Dr Hugh Robert Mill, have written of his life and character.

Though I was his companion on every one of his expeditions, I know little of his life at home. It is a curious thing that men thrown so closely together as those engaged in Polar work should never seek to know anything of each other's 'inside' affairs. But to the 'Explorer' Shackleton I was joined by ties so strongly welded through the many years of common hardship and struggle that to write of him at all is extremely difficult. Nothing I could set down can convey what I feel, and I have a horror of false and wordy sentiment. I trust, therefore, that those readers who may think that I have dealt too lightly with the parts of the story which more intimately concern him will sympathise and respect my feelings in the matter.

I must take this opportunity of acknowledging my deep feeling of gratitude to Mr John Quiller Rowett. What the expedition owes to him no one, not even its individual members, can ever realise. There have been many supporters of enterprises of this nature, but usually they have sought from it some commercial gain. Mr Rowett's support was due solely to his keen interest in scientific research, which he had previously instituted and encouraged in other fields. He bore practically the whole financial burden, and this expedition is almost unique in that it was clear of debt at the time of its return.

But, in addition to this, I owe him much for his kindly encouragement, his clear, sound judgement, and his unfailing assistance whenever I have sought it. Mrs Rowett has given me invaluable assistance throughout the preparation of the book and has corrected the proofs. For her kindly hospitality I owe more than I can say, for to myself and others of the expedition her house has ever been open, and we have received always the most kindly welcome. In this connexion I could say a great deal, but it would be inadequate to convey what I feel.

The expedition owes also a debt of gratitude to Sir Frederick Becker, for his encouraging assistance was rendered early in its inception.

To the many public-spirited firms who came forward with offers of assistance to what was considered a national enterprise I must make my acknowledgements. It is regrettable that many of the smaller suppliers of the expedition seized the chance of a cheap advertisement at the time of our departure, but a number of the more reputable firms made no stipulation of any sort, but presented us with goods as a free gift. I can assure them that I do not lightly regard their share in helping on the work, for we were thus enabled to carry in our food stores only the best of products, Sir Ernest Shackleton rigidly eliminating all goods which he felt unable to trust.

To Mr James A. Cook I owe much for the hard work he has done at all times and for the help which he rendered while the expedition was away from England.

To my many other friends who have at one time and another been of assistance I tender my grateful acknowledgements, knowing full well that they will realise how impossible it is for me to thank them all by name.

I must thank Dr Macklin for the care he took in keeping the official diary of the expedition. This and his own private journal, from which I have freely quoted, have both been invaluable to me.

To 'The Boys', those who stood by me and gave me their loyal service throughout an arduous and trying period, I say nothing – for they know how I feel.

Frank Wild

CHAPTER 1

Inception

After the finish of the Great War, which had employed every able-bodied man in the country in one way or another, Sir Ernest Shackleton returned to London and wrote his famous epic *South*, the story of the Imperial Trans-Antarctic Expedition. Before it was finished he had again felt the call of the ice, and concluded his book with the following sentence: 'Though some have gone, there are enough to rally round and form a nucleus for the next expedition, when troublous times are over, and scientific exploration can once more be legitimately undertaken.'

For many years he had had an inclination to take an expedition into the Arctic and compare the two ice zones. He felt, too, a keen desire to pit himself against the American and Norwegian explorers who of recent years had held the foremost position in Arctic exploration, to win for the British flag a further renown, and to add to the sum of British achievements in the frozen North.

There is still, in spite of the long and unremitting siege which has gradually tinted the uncoloured portions of the map and brought within our ken section after section of the unexplored areas, a large blank space comprising what is known as the Beaufort Sea, approximately in the centre of which is the point called by Stefansson the 'centre of the zone of inaccessibility'. It was the exploration of this area that Sir Ernest made his aim. In addition he felt a strong desire to clear up the mystery of the North Pole, and for ever settle the Peary-Cook controversy, which did so much to alienate public sympathy from Polar enterprise.

It is characteristic of him that before proceeding with any part of the organisation he wrote first to Mr Stefansson, the Canadian explorer, to ask if the new expedition would interfere with any plan of his. He received in reply a letter saying that not only did it not interfere in any way, but that he (Stefansson) would be glad to afford any help that lay in his power and put at his disposal any information which might prove valuable.

Sir Ernest's plans were the result of several years of hard work with careful reference to the records of previous explorers, and his organisation was remarkable for its completeness and detail.

The proposed expedition had an added interest in that the whole of his Polar experience was gained in the Antarctic. It met with instant recognition from the leading scientists and geographers of this country, who saw in it far-reaching and valuable results. The Council of the Royal Geographical Society sent a letter which showed their appreciation of the importance of the work, and expressed their approval of himself as commander and of the names he had submitted as those of men eminently qualified to make a strong personnel for the expedition.

Sir Ernest Shackleton was fortunate in securing the active co-operation in the working out of his plans of Dr H. R. Mill, the greatest living authority on Polar regions.

The scheme, however, was an ambitious one, and was likely to prove costly.

The period following the end of the war was perhaps not a suitable one in many ways to commence an undertaking of this nature, for Sir Ernest had the greatest difficulty in raising the necessary funds. In this country he received the support of Mr John Quiller Rowett and Sir Frederick Becker.

Feeling that the work of exploration and the possible discovery of new lands in what may be called the Canadian sector of the Arctic was likely to be of interest to the Canadian Government, he visited Ottawa, where he was in close touch with many of the leading members of the Canadian House of Commons. He returned to this country well pleased with his visit, and stated that he had obtained the active co-operation of several prominent Canadians and received from the Canadian Government the promise of a grant of money.

He was now in a position to start work, and immediately threw himself into the preparation of the expedition. He got together a small nucleus of men well known to him, including some who had accompanied him on the *Endurance* expedition, designed and ordered a quantity of special stores and equipment, and bought a ship which cost as an initial outlay £11,000. Dr Macklin was sent to Canada to buy and collect together at some suitable spot a hundred good sledge-dogs of the 'Husky' type.

It would be impossible to convey an accurate idea of the closely detailed work which is involved in the preparation for a Polar expedition. Much of the equipment is of a highly technical nature and requires to be specially manufactured. Everything must be carried and nothing must be forgotten, for once away the most trivial article cannot be obtained. Everything also must be of good quality and sound design; and each article, whatever it may be, must function properly when actually put into use.

At what was almost the last moment, while preparations were in full swing, the Canadian Government, being more or less committed to a policy of retrenchment, discovered that they were not in a position to advance funds for this purpose, and withdrew their support. This was a great blow, for it made impossible the continuance of the scheme.

In the meantime the bulk of the personnel had been collected, some of the men having come from far distant parts of the world to join in the adventure, abandoning their businesses to do so. Some of us, knowing of the scheme, had waited for two years, putting aside permanent employment so that we might be free to join when required; for such is the extraordinary attraction of Polar exploration to those who have once engaged in it, that they will give up much, often all they have, to pit themselves once more against the ice and gamble with their lives in this greatest of all games of chance. Yet if you were to ask what is the attraction or where the fascination of it lies, probably not one could give you an answer.

Sir Ernest Shackleton received the blow with outward equanimity, which was not shaken when, with the decision of the Canadian Government, the more timorous of his supporters also withdrew. Always seen at his best in adverse circumstances, he wasted no time in useless complainings, but started even at this eleventh hour to remodel his plans.

Nevertheless, the situation was a very difficult one. He had committed himself to heavy expenditure, and what weighed not least with him at this time was his consideration for the men who had come to join the enterprise. At this critical point Mr John Quiller Rowett came forward to bear an active part in the work, and took upon his shoulders practically the whole financial responsibility of the expedition. The importance of this action cannot be too much emphasised, for without it the carrying on of the work would have been impossible.

Mr Rowett had a wide outlook which enabled him to take a keen interest in all scientific affairs. Previous to this he had helped to found the Rowett Institute for Agricultural Research at Aberdeen, and had prompted and given practical support to researches in medicine, chemistry and several other branches of science. His many interests included geographical discovery, and he saw clearly the important bearing which conditions in the Polar regions have upon the temperate zones. He saw also the possible economic value of the observations and data which would be collected.

His name must therefore rank among the great supporters of Polar exploration, such as the brothers Enderby, Sir George Newnes and Mr A. C. Harmsworth (afterwards Lord Northcliffe).

Mr Rowett's generous action is the more remarkable in that he was fully aware in giving this support to the expedition that there was no prospect of financial return. What he did was done purely out of friendship to Shackleton and in the interests of science. The new expedition was named the Shackleton-Rowett Expedition, and announcement of it was received by the public with the greatest interest.

As it was now too late to catch the Arctic open season, the northern expedition was cancelled, and Sir Ernest reverted to one of his old schemes for scientific research in the South, which again met with the approval of the chief scientific bodies.

This change of plans threw an enormous burden of work not only upon Sir Ernest, but also upon those of us who formed his staff at this period, for we had little time in which to complete the preparations. Dr Macklin was recalled from Canada, for under the new scheme sledge-dogs were not required.

The programme did not aim at the attainment of the Pole or include any prolonged land journey, but made its main object the taking of observations and the collection of scientific data in Antarctic and sub-Antarctic areas.

The proposed route led to the following places: St Paul's Rocks on the Equator, South Trinidad Island, Tristan da Cunha, Inaccessible Island, Nightingale and Middle Islands, Diego Alvarez or Gough Island, and thence to Cape Town.

Cape Town was to be the base for operations in the ice, and a depot of stores for that part of the journey would be formed there. The route led eastward from there to Marion, Crozet and Heard Islands, and then into the ice, where the track to be followed was, of course, problematical, but would lead westwards, to emerge again at South Georgia.

From South Georgia it led to Bouvet Island, and back to Cape Town to refit. From Cape Town, the second time, the route included New Zealand, Raratonga, Tuanaki (the 'Lost Island'), Dougherty Island, the Birdwood Bank, and home via the Atlantic.

The scientific work included the taking of meteorological observations, including air and sea temperatures, kite and balloon work, magnetic observations, hydrographical and oceanographical work, including an extensive series of soundings, and the mapping and careful charting of little-known islands. Search was to be made for lands marked on the map as 'doubtful'. A collection of natural history specimens would be made, and a geological survey and examination carried out in all the places visited. Ice observations would be carried on in the South, and an attempt made to reach and map out new land in the Enderby Quadrant. Photography was made a special feature, and a large and expensive outfit of cameras, cinematograph machines and general photographic appliances acquired.

The Admiralty and the Air Ministry co-operated and materially assisted by lending much of the scientific apparatus. Lt-Com. R. T. Gould, of the Hydrographic Department, provided us with books and reports of previous explorers concerning the little-known parts of our route, and his information, gleaned from all sources and collected together for our use, proved of the greatest value.

It was decided to carry an aeroplane or seaplane to assist in aerial observations and to be used as the 'eyes' of the expedition in the South. Flying machines had never before been used in Polar exploration, and there were obvious difficulties in the way of extreme cold and lack of adequate accommodation, but after consultation with the Air Ministry it was thought possible to overcome them. The machine ultimately selected was a 'Baby' seaplane, designed and manufactured by the Avro Company.

One of the first things done by Sir Ernest Shackleton in preparing for the northern expedition had been the purchase of a small wooden vessel of 125 tons, named the *Foca I*. She was built in Norway, fitted with auxiliary steam engines of compound type and 125 horse-power. She was originally designed for sealing in Arctic waters, the hull was strongly made, and the timbers were supported by wooden beams with natural bends of enormous strength. The bow was of solid oak sheathed with steel. Her length was 111 feet, beam 23 feet, and her sides were 2 feet thick. Her draught was 9 feet forward and 14 feet aft. She was ketch-rigged, and was reputed to be able to steam at 7 knots in still water and to do the same with sail only in favourable winds.

At the happy suggestion of Lady Shackleton she was re-named the *Quest*.

Sir Ernest received what he considered the greatest honour of his life. The *Quest* as his yacht was elected to the Royal Yacht Squadron. Perhaps a more ugly, businesslike little 'yacht' never flew the burgee, and her appearance must have contrasted strangely with the beautiful and shapely lines of her more aristocratic sisters.

She was brought to Southampton in March 1921, and placed in the shipyards for extensive alterations. The work was greatly impeded by the strike of ship workers, the general coal strike which occurred at that time, and by difficulties generally with labour, which was then passing through a very critical period.

It had been intended to take out the steam engines and substitute an internal-combustion motor of the diesel type, but owing to the difficulties mentioned this had to be abandoned, and on the advice of the surveying engineer in charge of the work the old engines were retained. The bunker space was readjusted at the expense of the fore-hold, allowing a carrying capacity of 120 tons of coal, and giving a steaming radius which, with economy and use of sail, was estimated at from 4,000 to 5,000 miles.

This work was in process when it became necessary to alter the plans of the expedition, and Sir Ernest realised that the *Quest*, which had been considered eminently suitable for the northern scheme, was not so well adapted for the long cruise in southern waters. It was impossible at this stage to change the ship, but further alterations were made on deck and in the rigging generally to adapt her for the new conditions.

Two yards were fitted, a topsail yard, 39 feet in length, and a foreyard to carry a large square sail, 44 feet in length. The mizen-mast was lengthened to give a greater clearance to the wireless aerials. The existing bridge was enlarged, carried across the full breadth of the ship and completely enclosed with windows of Triplex glass. The roof formed an upper bridge open to the air. To improve the accommodation, which was inadequate, a deck-house, 12 feet by 20 feet, was erected on the foredeck. It contained five rooms: four small cabins, and a room for housing hydrographical and meteorological instruments. New canvas and running gear was fitted throughout, and no expense spared to make her sound and seaworthy. Mr Rowett was absolutely insistent that everything about the ship must be such as to ensure her safety and the safety of all on board in so far as it was humanly possible. To everything in connexion with the ship herself Sir Ernest, as an experienced seaman, gave his personal attention. The work of the engine-room, which, as he was not an engineer, he was not able to supervise directly, was entrusted to a consulting engineer.

The *Quest*, though strong and well equipped, was small, and consequently accommodation generally was limited and living quarters were somewhat cramped. The forecastle was fitted as a small biological laboratory and geological workroom. In it were a bench for the naturalist and numerous cupboards for the storing of specimens. Leading from it on one side was a small cabin with two bunks for the naturalist and photographer respectively, and on the other was the photographic dark room.

The amount of gear placed aboard the ship was large, and the greatest ingenuity was required to stow it satisfactorily.

Two wireless transmitting and receiving sets, of naval pattern, were installed under the immediate supervision of a wireless expert, kindly lent to us by the Admiralty. The current for them was supplied by two generators, one a steam dynamo producing 220 volts, and a smaller paraffin internal-combustion motor producing 110 volts. The *Quest* being a wooden vessel, there was great difficulty in providing suitable 'earthing'. For this purpose two copper plates were attached to either side of the ship below the water-line.

The more powerful of these sets was never very satisfactory, and we ultimately abandoned its use. The smaller proved entirely satisfactory for transmitting at distances up to 250 miles. The receiving apparatus was chiefly of value in obtaining time signals, which are sent out nightly from nearly all the large wireless stations, and which we received at distances up to 3,000 miles. By this means we were frequently able, while in the South, to check our chronometers; but atmospheric conditions in those regions were very bad, and by producing loud adventitious noises in the ear-pieces interfered so much with the clarity of sounds that the obtaining of accurate signals was generally impossible.

A Sperry gyroscopic compass was installed, the gyroscopic apparatus being placed in the deck-house, with repeaters in the enclosed bridge and on the upper bridge. The dials were luminous, so that they could be read at night. This apparatus has the advantage that it is independent of immediate outside influences. It is usually supposed that at 65° north or south it ceases to be effective, but we found that the directive force was still sufficient at 69° south. It is interesting to note that this compass was designed by a German scientist to enable a submarine to reach the North Pole. It has been of the greatest use to ships in a general way, but for the one specific purpose for which it was designed it proved to be useless owing to the loss of directive power at the Poles. We found that bumping the ship through ice caused derangement, and as the compass took several hours to settle down again to normal, it proved ineffective while we were navigating through the pack.

Fitted into the enclosed bridge and looking forward were two Kent clear-view screens. They were electrically driven. They proved, when running, to be absolutely effective against rain, snow or spray.

The ship was fitted throughout with electric lighting, including the navigating lights. While in the South, however, the necessity for economy of fuel forbade the use of electricity and we had recourse to oil lamps. As we were then completely out of the track of shipping, navigating lights were not used.

Two sounding machines were installed, one an electrically driven Kelvin apparatus for depths up to 300 fathoms. To obtain accurate soundings while the ship was under way, the sinker was fitted to carry sounding tubes, and had also an arrangement for indicating the nature of the bottom, whether rock, shingle or sand. For deep-sea work we had a Lucas steam-driven machine, which was affixed to a special platform on the port bow and supplied by a flexible tube from the steam pipe feeding the forward winch. This apparatus registered depths to 4 miles. Sounding with it was often difficult on account of the swell and the liveliness of the *Quest*, but the machine itself gave every satisfaction. The wire used with the Lucas machine was Brunton wire in coils of 6,000 fathoms, diameter .028, weight 12.3 lbs per 1,000 fathoms, with a breaking strain of 200 lbs.

The meteorological equipment included:

Screens, containing wet and dry bulb thermometers, placed in exposed positions on the upper bridge.

One large screen, containing hair hygrograph, standard thermometer and thermograph. (The heavy seas which broke over the ship and flung sprays over the upper bridge greatly interfered with the efficient working of these instruments by encrusting them with salt, and necessitated constant cleaning.)

Hydrometers, for determining the specific gravity of sea-water, which gives a measure of the total salinity.

Sea-thermometers, for determining the surface temperatures of the sea-water.

Marine pattern mercury barometer.

Aneroid barometers, checked daily from the mercury barometer, in case the latter should be broken.

Barograph, to obtain continuous records of the air pressure.

For upper-air work four cylinders of hydrogen and several hundred pilot balloons were taken. (These latter were sent up on many occasions from the ship, but the *Quest* proved to be so lively that it was impossible to keep them in the field of view of a telescope or even of field-glasses.)

All the instruments were very kindly lent to us by the Meteorological Section of the Air Ministry, and were of standard make and pattern.

We carried a good set of sextants, theodolites, dip circles and other accurate surveying instruments.

Several chronometers of different makes and patterns were placed aboard. Two of them, specially rated for us by Mr Bagge, of the Waltham Watch Company, gave excellent results and, in spite of the violent motion of the ship and the difficulty of keeping a uniform temperature, maintained a remarkably even rating.

The medical equipment was designed for compactness and all-round usefulness.

Sledges, harness, warm clothing, footgear and an amount of scientific equipment were forwarded to Cape Town and warehoused to await the arrival of the *Quest*.

The greatest difficulty was experienced in the housing of the seaplane, but, after dismantling wings and floats, room was eventually found for it in the port alleyway, which it almost filled.

Sir Ernest Shackleton, as has already been said, in choosing his personnel selected first of all a nucleus of well-tried and experienced men who had served with him before, appointing me as second in command of the expedition. They included Worsley, Macklin, Hussey, McIlroy, Kerr, Green and McLeod. Applications for the remaining posts came in thousands, and many women wrote asking if a job could be found for them, offering to mend, sew, nurse or cook.

Two other men with previous experience were obtained: Wilkins, who served with the Canadian Arctic Expedition under Stefansson, and Dell, who had served with Captain Scott in the *Discovery*, and was thus known to Sir Ernest Shackleton and myself. Lt-Com. Jeffrey, an officer of the Royal Naval Reserve, who had served with distinction during the war, was appointed navigating officer for the ship. Major Carr, who had gained much experience of flying as an officer of the RAF, was appointed in charge of the seaplane.

A geologist was required, the selection falling upon G. V. Douglas, a graduate of McGill University, whom Sir Ernest had met in Canada.

Mr Bee Mason was appointed photographer and cinematographer.

Among the remainder there was need of a good boy. Sir Ernest conceived the idea of throwing the post open to a Boy Scout, and the suggestion was taken up with the greatest enthusiasm by the Boy Scout organisation. The post was advertised in the *Daily Mail*, and immediately a flood of applications poured in from every part of the country. These were finally filtered down to the ten most suitable, and the applicants were instructed to assemble in London, the *Daily Mail* making the necessary arrangements and defraying the costs. These ten boys all had excellent records, and Sir Ernest, in finally making his selection, was so embarrassed in his choice that he selected two. They were J. W. S. Marr, an Aberdeen boy, and Norman E. Mooney, a native of the Orkneys.

There remained but three places to fill: C. Smith, an officer of the RMSP Company, was appointed second engineer; PO Telegraphist Watts, wireless operator; and Eriksen, a Norwegian by birth, was taken on as harpoon expert.

Sir Ernest, in order fully to carry out his programme, was anxious to leave England not later than 20 August, but owing to a general strike of ships' joiners, dilatory workmanship and other unavoidable causes, the sailing was postponed well beyond that date.

At length all was ready; food stores and equipment, which included not only the highly technical and specialised Antarctic gear, but also such minute details as pins, needles and pieces of tape, were placed on board, and the ship was ready for sea.

The new expedition had been organised, equipped and got ready for departure all within three months. There are few who will realise what this means. No other man than Sir Ernest would have attempted it, and no other could have accomplished it successfully. It was, as he often said himself, only through the staunch support and active co-operation of Mr Rowett, who aided and encouraged him throughout this period, that he was able to leave England that year. Postponement at such an advanced stage was impossible, and would have meant the total abandonment of the expedition. We left London finally on 17 September 1921.

CHAPTER 2

London to Rio de Janeiro

We dipped our ensign in a last farewell to London as we passed out from St Katherine's Dock, and turned our nose down-river for Gravesend, a tiny vessel even among the small shipping which comes thus far up the river. We were accompanied on this part of our journey by Mr Rowett, who had taken a keen personal interest in everything connected with the expedition. Enthusiastic crowds cheered us at the start, and everybody we met wished us 'Good luck and safe return'. The ensign was kept in a continuous dance answering the bunting which dipped from the staffs of every vessel we met. Ships of many maritime nations were collected in this cosmopolitan river, and these, too, joined in wishing success to our enterprise.

At Gravesend Mr Rowett left us, and Sir Ernest returned with him to London with the object of rejoining at Plymouth. A strong north-easterly wind was blowing, and we lay for the night off Gravesend. In the small hours of the morning we were startled from sleep by the watchman crying, 'The anchor's dragging!' and turned out to find that we were bearing down on a Thames hopper that was moored nearby. The *Quest* would not answer her helm, and before we were able to bring her up she had fouled the stays of the hopper with her bowsprit. Pyjama-clad figures leapt from their bunks, and in the dim light presented a curious spectacle. Two or three of our men jumped on to the deck of the hopper, and by loosening a bolt succeeded in letting go one of her stays, when we swung free.

Kerr rapidly raised a sufficient pressure of steam in the boilers to get the engines going, and we soon regained control.

We brought up with our anchor, which had been acting as a dredge, the most amazing collection of stuff, which gave an interesting sidelight on the composition of the Thames floor.

No damage was received beyond a chafe to the bowsprit. We were anxious, however, to leave with everything in good order, and so proceeded to Sheerness Dockyard, where a new spar was put in for us by the naval authorities with a promptness and dispatch that contrasted strongly with the dilatory methods employed previously in the shipyards.

We had an exceptionally fine trip down Channel under the pilotage of Captain F. Bridgland, who was an old friend of ours, having taken the ship from Southampton to London.

We reached Plymouth on the 23rd, and were joined there by Sir Ernest Shackleton and Mr Gerald Lysaght, a keen yachtsman, who had been invited to accompany us as far as Madeira. The Boss brought with him an Alsatian wolf-hound puppy, a beautiful well-bred animal with a long pedigree, which had been presented to him by a friend as a mascot. 'Query,' as he was named, quickly became a fast favourite with all on board. Mr Rowett also came from London to see us off, and we had with him a last cheery dinner. He was very popular with all of us, for in addition to his support of expedition affairs he had taken a personal interest in every member of the company.

On the 24th we steamed out into the Sound and moored to a buoy, where the ship was swung and the compasses adjusted by Commander Traill-Smith, RN, who kindly undertook this important work. The Admiralty tug used to swing the *Quest* accentuated her smallness, for she was many times our size and towered high above us.

This task completed, we put out to sea, pleased, as Sir Ernest Shackleton said at the time, to be making our final departure from a town that has ever been associated with maritime enterprise.

The following extracts are from Sir Ernest Shackleton's own diary:

Saturday 24 September 1921
At last we are off. The last of the cheering crowded boats have turned, the sirens of shore and sea are still, and in the calm hazy gathering dusk on a glassy sea we move on the long quest. Providence is with us even now. At this time of equinoctial gales

not a catspaw of wind is apparent. I turn from the glooming immensity of the sea and, looking at the decks of the *Quest*, am roused from dreams of what may be in the future to the needs of the moment, for in no way are we shipshape or fitted to ignore even the mildest storm. Deep in the water, decks littered with stores, our very life-boats receptacles for sliced bacon and green vegetables for sea-stock; steel ropes and hempen brothers jostle each other; mysterious gadgets connected with the wireless, on which the Admiralty officials were working up to the sailing hour, are scattered about. But our twenty-one willing hands will soon snug her down.

A more personal and perplexing problem is my cabin – or my temporary cabin, for Gerald Lysaght has mine till we reach Madeira – for hundreds of telegrams of farewell have to be dealt with. Kind thoughts and kind actions, as witness the many parcels, some of dainty food, some of continuous use, which crowd up the bunk. Yet there is no time to answer them now.

We worked late, lashing up and making fast the most vital things on deck. Our wireless was going all the time, receiving messages and sending out answers. Towards midnight a swell from the west made us roll, and the sea lopped in through our wash-ports. About 1 a.m. the glare of the *Aquitania*'s lights became visible as she sped past a little to the southward of us, going west, and I received farewell messages from Sir James Charles and Spedding. [Captain and chief purser respectively of the *Aquitania*.] I wish it had been daylight.

At 2 a.m. I turned in. We are crowded. For in addition to McIlroy and Lysaght, I have old McLeod as stoker.

Sunday 25 September
Fair easterly wind; our topsail and foresail set. All day cleaning up with all hands. We saw the last of England – the Scilly Isles and Bishop Rock, with big seas breaking on them; and now we head out to the west to avoid the Bay of Biscay. With our deep draught we roll along like an old-time ship, our fore-sail bellying to the breeze. The Boy Scouts are sick – frankly so, though Marr has been working in the stokehold until he really had to give in.

Various messages came through. To-day it has been misty and cloudy, little sun. All were tired tonight when watches were set.

Monday 26
47° 53' N., 9° 00' W.

A mixture of sunshine and mist, wind and calm. Passed two steamers homeward bound, and one sailing ship was overhauling us in the afternoon, but the breeze fell light, and she dropped astern in the mist that came up from the eastward. Truly it is good to feel we are starting well, and all hands are happy, though the ship is crowded.

Two hands have to help the cook, and the little food hatchway is a blessing, for otherwise it is a long way round. Green is in his element, though our decks are awash amidship. He just dips up the water for washing his vegetables.

With a view to economy he boiled the cabbage in salt water. The result was not successful.

The *Quest* rolls, and we find her various points and angles, but she grows larger to us each day as we grow more used to her. I asked Green this morning what was for breakfast. 'Bacon and eggs,' he replied. 'What sort of eggs?' 'Scrambled eggs. If I did not scramble them they would have scrambled themselves' – a sidelight on the liveliness of the *Quest*. Query, our wolf-hound puppy, is fast becoming a regular ship's dog, but has a habit of getting into my bunk after getting wet.

We are running the lights from the dynamo, and, when the wireless is working, sparks fly up and down the backstays like fireflies. A calm night is ours.

Tuesday 27 – Wednesday 28
43° 52' N., 11° 51' W. 135 miles.

Another fine day. Not much to record. All hands engaged in general work on the ship. In the afternoon the mist arose and the wind dropped. At night the wind headed us a bit, and we took in the topsail. Marr was at the wheel in the first watch, and did well. Mooney, at present, is useless. A gang of the boys were employed turning the coal into the after-bunkers – a black and dusty job; but they were quite happy. We passed a peaceful night. This morning the wind practically dropped. What little there was came out ahead, so we took in all sail. The *Quest* does not steam very fast, 5½ being our best so far. This rather makes me think, and may lead to alterations in our plans, for we must make our time right for entering the ice at the end of December, and may possibly have to curtail some of our island work or postpone it until we come out of the South. This morning we are in glorious sunshine – the sea sapphire-blue and a cloudless sky; but, alas! noon, in spite of our pushing, gives us only 135 miles. We have allowed a current of 7 miles N. 12° W.

Gerald Lysaght is one of our best workers, and takes long spells at the wheel. Occasionally little land-birds fly on board, and our kittens take an interest in them, as yet unknowing their potential value as food or game (?). How far away already we seem from ordinary life!

I stopped the wireless last night. It is of no importance to us now in a little world of our own.

Wednesday 28 – Thursday 29 September 1921
Lat., 42° 9' N. Long., 13° 10' W. Dist., 116'.
A strong wind, with high seas and SSW swell; strong squalls were our portion. The ship is more than lively and makes but little way. She evidently must be treated as a 5-knot vessel dependent mainly on fair winds, and all this is giving me much food for thought, for I am tied to time for the ice. I was relieved that she made fairly good weather of it, but I can see that our decks must be absolutely clear when we are in the Roaring Forties. Her foremast also gives me anxiety. She is not well stayed, and I think that the topsail yard is a bit too much. The main thing is that I may have to curtail our island programme in order to get to the Cape in time. Everyone is cheerful, which is a blessing, all singing and enjoying themselves, though pretty well wet; several are a bit sick. The only one who has not bucked up is the Scout Mooney. He seems helpless, but I will give him every chance. I can see also that we must be cut down in crew to the absolutely efficient and only needful for the southern voyage.

Douglas is now stoking and doing well. It will, of course, take time to square things up and for everyone to find themselves; she is so small. It is only by constant thought and care that the leader can lead. There is a delightful sense of freedom from responsibility in all others; and it should be so. These are just random thoughts, but borne in on one as all being so different from the long strain of preparation.

It is a blessing that this time I have not the financial worry or strain to add to the care of the active expedition. Lysaght is doing very well, and so is the Scout Marr.

Sir Ernest Shackleton's diary ends at this point, and there are no other entries till 1 January 1922.

We now began to settle down to our new conditions of life.

In the deck-house were five small cabins. The Boss and I had the two after ones, but at this time Mr Lysaght, or the 'General' as he was called by all of us (like most nicknames, for no particular reason), occupied one of them, while the Boss and I shared the other.

Worsley and Jeffrey had a cabin running the full breadth of the house and the roomiest in the ship, but it had also to act as chart-room. Macklin and Hussey occupied a tiny room of 6 feet cubed on the starboard side, which contained the medicine cupboard. Here, in spite of restricted space, they dwelt in perfect harmony, due, as they were wont to say, 'to both of us being non-smokers'. They were known collectively as 'Alphonse and D'Aubrey', but how the names originated it is impossible to say, for though the versatile Londoner might at times have passed as a Frenchman, the same could not be said for the more phlegmatic Scot.

The corresponding room on the port side housed the meteorological instruments and the gyroscopic compass.

Wilkins and Bee Mason had bunks in the converted forecastle, which contained the photographic dark room, a work bench for the naturalist, and numerous cupboards for the storing of specimens. Wilkins, an old campaigner, had used much foresight and ingenuity in fitting it up, and had utilised the limited space to the utmost advantage. Their cabin was indeed a dim recess and at first proved very stuffy, but before we were many days out Wilkins had designed and fitted an air-shoot, which acted very well and enormously improved the ventilation. Green, the cook, had a cabin beside his galley, which was always warm from the heat of the engine-room – too much so to be comfortable in temperate climes, but he looked forward to the advantage he would derive when we entered the cold regions. All the others lived aft and occupied bunks which were situated round the mess-room and opened directly into it, unscreened except by small green curtains, which could be drawn across when the bunks were unoccupied. It was by no means a pleasant or convenient arrangement, but, with the small size of the ship and general lack of space, the only one possible under the circumstances. The mess-room itself was small, boasting the simplest of furniture: two plain deal tables, four forms, a cupboard for crockery, and a small sideboard. At the foot of the companion-way was a rack of ten long Service rifles. Two of the forms were made like boxes with lids, to act as lockers.

The seating accommodation just admitted all hands to sit together, not counting the cook and the cook's mate and four men who were always on watch. They sat down to a second sitting. The food was of good quality, plain, and simply cooked. Three meals a day were served: breakfast, lunch, and supper. The Boss presided, and under his cheery example the new hands soon learned to make light of the strange and rather uncomfortable conditions.

Every day for breakfast we had Quaker oats, with brown sugar or syrup (salt for the Scotsmen) and milk, followed by bacon, with eggs (as long as they lasted), afterwards sausage or some equivalent, bread or ship's biscuit, marmalade, and tea or coffee.

For lunch we usually had a hot soup, followed by cold meat, corned beef, tongue or tinned fish, and bread or biscuit, cheese, jam and tea.

Supper consisted of a hot meat dish, with vegetables, followed by some sort of pudding, bread or biscuit, and tea.

The galley was small, and contained a diminutive range and a number of shelves fitted with battens to prevent things flying off with the roll of the ship. The oven accommodation was small, and admitted of the cooking of one thing only at a time. Here Green reigned over his pots and pans, which, owing to the motion of the ship, proved more often than not to be elusive and refractory.

At meal-times the dishes were passed through a large window port into the mess-room by the cook's mate, and received by the 'Peggy' for the day, who served the food and waited at table. Duty as 'Peggy' was performed by each man in turn (with the exception of the watch-keeping officers), who also washed the dishes, cleaned the tables, and generally tidied up after each meal. Sir Ernest Shackleton had made it plain to all hands that no work was to be considered too humble for any member of the expedition.

Tablecloths were never used, but the tables were well scrubbed daily, so that they soon took on a fine whiteness. Fiddles were a permanent fitting except when we were in port, for the *Quest* never permitted us to do without them at sea, while in the worst weather even they proved useless to prevent table crockery from being thrown about.

In addition to Query there were on the ship two other pets in the form of small black kittens, one presented to us as a mascot by the *Daily Mail*, the other, I believe, the gift of a girl to one of the crew. They suffered a little at first from sea-sickness, but soon developed the most voracious appetites, and showed the greatest persistence in coming about the table for food. They clambered up one's legs with long sharp claws, 'miaowed', and at every opportunity put their noses into jugs and plates. No amount of rebuffs had any effect upon them, and they had a curious preference for food on the table to that which was placed for them in their own dishes. Two more importunate kittens I have never seen. It is to be feared that one or two of the party slyly encouraged them, for we could never cure them of their bad habits.

The companion steps leading from the scuttle to the mess-room were very steep, and at this time Query had not learned the art of going up and down, though he acquired it later. It used to be a common sight to see his handsome head framed in the opening of the window port through which Green passed the food, gazing wistfully at the dainty morsels which were being transferred to other mouths.

These first days with the Boss were very cheery ones, and I like to look back on them. There was little refinement on the ship and more than ordinary discomfort, yet each meal-time was a happy gathering of cheery souls, and conversation crackled with jokes, in the perpetration of which Hussey was by no means the least guilty. The strain of preparation had been a heavy one, and Sir Ernest seemed to be enjoying the quiet, the freedom and the mental peace of our small self-contained little world. I think he liked to find himself surrounded by his own men, and he was always at his best when he had a definite objective to go for.

There is something about life at sea, and the companionship of men who have lived untrammelled lives free from the restraints of convention, that I find hard to describe. I think it must be that it is more primitive. Certainly, one drops into it with a contentment that contrasts strongly with the feeling of effort with which one braces oneself to meet the more conventional circumstances of the return to civilised life. It is, I suppose, a matter of heredity and transmitted instinct which makes falling back to the primitive more easy than progress, meaning by 'progress' the advance of artificiality and the tremendous speeding up of modern existence. Some such instinct must be present, for what else is there to tempt one from a cosy fireside and the morning paper?

We kept three watches, the watch-keeping officers being Worsley, Jeffrey and myself. The Boss kept no particular watch, but was always at hand to give instructions and take charge on special occasions. In my watch were McIlroy, Macklin and Hussey; in Worsley's, Wilkins, Douglas and Watts; in Jeffrey's, Carr, Eriksen and Bee Mason. Dell and McLeod acted as stokers. The two Scouts were at first employed in a generally useful capacity, helping the cook and lending a hand wherever required. In addition to his deck duties, each man had his own particular job to attend to. Before we had been out many days it became clear to all that in this trip we were to have no picnic, and that in life on the *Quest* we would have to adapt ourselves to all sorts of discomforts and inconveniences. However, we were committed to our enterprise, our work lay before us, and we settled down cheerfully to make the best of things.

A few extracts from the official diary will give an indication of conditions about this time.

Tuesday, 27 September

The wind came round to SE and freshened up during the day. The *Quest* is behaving badly in the short head seas. We have had to take in sail and are proceeding under steam, making poor progress. Bee Mason and Mooney are rather off colour.

28 September

The wind has increased, with heavier seas. During the day the engines were stopped for adjustment. Kerr says the crank shaft is out of alignment, and expects further trouble. This happening so early in the voyage does not promise well for the trip, for, as the Boss says, we are already late and cannot afford much time in port.

30 September

A moderate gale blowing from the SW. We made no headway into it, and the Boss decided to heave to with the engines at slow speed. This has given us an idea of the *Quest*'s behaviour in bad weather. The Boss is pleased with her sea-going qualities, for in spite of fairly heavy seas she has remained dry, taking aboard very little water. [The papers at the time made much of this gale. It was, however, little more than a strong blow and a zephyr compared with what we were to experience before our return to these same latitudes on our homeward run.] She has a lively and very unpleasant motion, which has induced qualms of sea-sickness in many of the 'land lubbers'. Bee Mason and young Mooney are *hors de combat*. They are both plucky. The Scout makes no complaint, but it is obvious that life to him just now is a terrible misery. He has tried hard to carry on his work. We wish we could do something for him, but there is little comfort on the ship.

2 October

Head winds have continued to blow, against which we have made little headway. The engines have developed a nasty knock which is appreciable to all on the ship. Kerr insists that an overhaul is necessary, and Sir Ernest has decided to make for Lisbon. We accordingly headed up for 'The Burlings', and picked up the light about 6 p.m.

On 3 October Kerr had to reduce the pressure of steam in the cylinders, as we were now proceeding slowly along the coast of Portugal in the direction of Cape Roca. The coastline is very picturesque, dotted all along with old castles and pretty little windmills. We plugged slowly on, passed by many steamers which signalled us, 'A pleasant voyage,' to which we were kept busy answering, 'Thank you.' One of the beautiful modern P&O liners, coming rapidly up from behind, altered course to pass close to us, and we could not help envying her speed and comfort as, making nothing of the short steep seas in which we were rolling and pitching in the liveliest manner, she rapidly drew out of sight ahead.

Just before nightfall we reached Cascaes, at the mouth of the Tagus, where the pilot came aboard, but decided not to proceed till daybreak. We lay at anchor for some hours, and I rarely remember a more uncomfortable period than we spent here, jerking at the cable with a short steep roll that made one positively giddy. It was more than the Portuguese pilot could stand, for he moved us farther up the river into shelter, enabling us to get the first comfortable sleep since leaving the Scilly Islands.

We were taken by tug up the fast-running Tagus to Lisbon in the early morning, and later the *Quest* went into dock.

The work was entrusted to Messrs Rawes & Co., and put in hand without delay. The source of all the trouble in the engine-room proved to be the crank shaft, which was out of alignment, and thus caused the bearings to run hot. The high-pressure connecting rod was found to be badly bent. The rigging also was altered and reset up.

We did not get away from Lisbon until Tuesday 11 October.

Those whose work did not confine them to the ship made the most of their time ashore, the first move being to a hotel for the luxury of a hot bath and a well-cooked dinner. We were warmly entertained by the British residents, who during the whole of our stay showed us the greatest kindness and hospitality. Mooney was carried off by the Boy Scouts of Lisbon, who showed him the sights of the place. Marr, although an enthusiastic supporter of the Boy Scout movement, did not care to spend his whole time as a 'kilted spectacle for curious Latins', and, doffing his uniform, accompanied the others in their movements. Among other things, we paid a visit en masse to a bull-fight, which we found to be a much more humane undertaking than those carried out under the old Spanish system. The bull is not killed and, though goaded by the darts of the picadors to a fury, does not seem to be subjected to great ill-treatment. The horses, instead of being old screws meant to be gored, are beautiful animals, which the matadors take the greatest care to protect.

We had many visitors on board the ship, including the British and American Ministers, who were shown round by Sir Ernest. All, as in London, expressed their amazement at the size of the *Quest*, imagining her to be far too small for the undertaking.

We set out on 11 October for Madeira, having expended seven days of precious time.

On leaving the Tagus we again encountered strong head winds, which lasted four days, during which the *Quest's* movements were such as to upset the strongest stomachs. Bee Mason and Mooney were once more *hors de combat*, and few except the hardened seamen among us escaped feeling ill, though they managed to carry on their work.

I think there must be very few people in these days of luxurious floating palaces that ever really have to endure the agonies of sea-sickness. If they do feel ill they can retire to their bunks, where attentive stewards minister to their wants. Few, however, have been in such a condition that they dared not take to their bunks, but have spent days and nights on deck, sleepless, sodden and cold, in a vigil of misery unbroken save to turn to when 'eight bells' announces the watch, and struggle through the work until the striking of the bells again announces relief, unable to taste or bear the thought of food, and with a stomach persistently and painfully rebellious in spite of an aching void. Such is the fate of those who go to sea in small vessels, without stewards and without comforts, and where there is work to be done. I have nothing but admiration for the way some of the sea-sick men were sticking to their jobs. Among them was Marr, the Boy Scout, who showed the greatest hardihood and pluck.

Winds continued to blow from ahead till, on 15 October, the weather changed and we had a beautiful clear day, with little wind or sea and bright sunshine. Mooney and Bee Mason continued to suffer from sea-sickness all the way, the latter becoming quite ill with a high temperature. As the conditions we had met were likely to prove mild as compared with those we would encounter in the stormy southern seas, Sir Ernest Shackleton decided to send both of them home from Madeira. Let it be said here that it is probable that, if they had had their own way, each of them would have elected to continue with us, and this decision to send them back carries with it absolutely no stigma, for they showed extraordinary pluck and bore their trials uncomplainingly. To Mooney especially, a young boy gently nurtured, who had never before left his Orkney home, this portion of the trip must have meant untold misery. We greatly regretted losing both these companions.

On leaving Lisbon the Boss had put the other Scout, Marr, to work in the bunkers, where he went through a gruelling test. He came out of the trial very well, showing an amount of hardihood and endurance that was remarkable. He suffered from sea-sickness, but never failed to carry out his allotted task, and thoroughly earned his right to continue as a permanent member of the expedition. I find in his diary the following entry:

> I volunteered to go down the stokehold, and my first duty was that of trimming coal. It is a delightful occupation. It consists of going down to the bunkers and shovelling coal to within easy reach of the fire-men. The bunkers are pitch black, and the air – well, there is no air, but coal dust. This gets into one's ears, eyes, nose, mouth and lungs; one breathes coal dust. After I had trimmed sufficient coal, I commenced stoking. I got on fairly well for a first attempt, but did not like the heat.

Another entry which this boy made during the bad weather shows what he must have gone through, though nothing which he said at the time would have led one to suspect it:

> Indeed, I was feeling more dead than alive … what with the rolling of the ship and the unsteady nature of my limbs – I was sea-sick, and I was much afraid I should fall into the fire or down

the bilges. When I came off (my watch) I immediately made for my bunk, where I remained, without partaking of my breakfast or dinner, until 12.0 noon, when I got up again for my next watch...

Before leaving England the Boss had ordered a brass plate to be made, on which were inscribed two verses of Kipling's immortal *If* – and had it placed in front of the bridge. Hussey, after a heavy day's coaling in bad weather, was inspired to a version specially applicable to the *Quest*, which reads as follows:

If you can stand the *Quest* and all her antics,
If you can go without a drink for weeks,
If you can smile a smile and say, 'How topping!'
When someone splashes paint across your 'breeks';

If you can work like Wild and then, like 'Wuzzles',
Spend a convivial night with some 'old bean',
And then come down and meet the Boss at breakfast
And never breathe a word of where you've been;

If you can keep your feet when all about you
Are turning somersaults upon the deck,
And then go up aloft when no one told you,
And not fall down and break your blooming neck;

If you can fill the port and starboard bunkers
With fourteen tons of coal and call it fun,
Yours is the ship and everything that's on it,
Coz you're a marvel, not a man, old son...

We arrived at Madeira on the 16th. Kerr had again a number of adjustments to make in the engine-room, and, with Smith, toiled hard all the time we were in harbour.

Madeira has been a favourite stopping place for all expeditions to the Antarctic. Here on 4 October 1822, Weddell was received and assisted by Mr John Blandy, whose firm has rendered help to many subsequent expeditions. On this occasion we were welcomed by the present Mr and Mrs Blandy and visited their beautiful estate on the hill.

We left after a two days' stay. 'The General' was due to return from here, but he had made himself so universally popular that Sir Ernest persuaded him to go on as far as the Cape Verde Islands. Neither our discomforts nor the vagaries of the *Quest* had upset him in the slightest, and he had proved himself a useful member of the crew, taking a trick at the wheel and carrying on the work on deck generally. We now entered fine weather, and, running comfortably before the north-easterly trade winds, reached St Vincent on 28 October. The engines had continued to give trouble, and Kerr reported that extensive repairs and readjustments would be necessary before continuing farther. They were carried out quickly and effectively by Messrs Wilson, Sons & Co., who acted as our agents, and most generously supplied us on leaving with 100 tons of coal free of all charge.

We said good-bye to 'General' Lysaght, whom we saw depart with genuine regret. We had a farewell dinner, at which was produced all the best the *Quest* could offer, and when the Boss proposed 'The General!' we drank his health and wished him luck. Although he was returning to home and comforts, he would, I believe, had it been possible, have accompanied us farther on our way. At the conclusion he was presented with an illuminated card, the combined work of all the artists aboard, but chiefly, I think, of Wilkins, which bore the following poem composed by the Boss:

To Gerald Lysaght, AB
After these happy days, spent in the oceanways,
Homeward you turn!
Ere our last rope slipped the quay and we made for the open sea
You became one of us.
You have seen the force of the gale fierce as a thresher's flail
Beat the sea white;
You have watched our reeling spars sweep past the steady stars
In the storm-wracked night.
You saw great liners turn; high bows that seemed to churn
The swell we wallowed in;

They veered from their ordered ways, from the need of their
　　time kept days,
To speed us on.
Did envy possess your soul; that they were sure of their goal
Never a damn cared you,
For you are one with the sea – in its joy and misery
You follow its lure.
In the peace of Chapel Cleeve, surely you must believe,
Though far off from us,
That wherever the *Quest* may go; what winds blow high or low –
Zephyrs or icy gale:
Safe in our hearts you stand; one with our little band.
A seaman, Gerald, are you!

                                                    E. H. S.

On the 28th we set out, making course for St Paul's Rocks. We enjoyed
excellent weather, with smooth seas on which the sun sparkled in a
myriad of variegated points. We felt the heat considerably, which is
natural, considering the confined space and general lack of artificial
means of keeping cool, such as effective fans, refrigerators and iced
water. Most of us slept on deck, under the stars which twinkled
above us, large and luminous, in the tropic nights.

The Boss took Marr out of the stokehold about this time and
placed him to assist Green as cook's mate, a not very romantic job,
but one which he carried out with his usual thoroughness. He had
by now thoroughly found his feet, and took a deep interest in the
sea life of the tropics: flying fish fleeing in shoals before the graceful
bonito, which, leaping in the air to descend with scarcely a splash,
followed in relentless pursuit; dolphins, albacore and the sinister fins
of occasional sharks.

On 4 November a large school of porpoises came about the ship
and played around our bows. Eriksen seized the opportunity to
harpoon one of them, which we hauled aboard. Wilkins found in
its stomach a number of cuttlefish beaks. The meat we sent to the
larder. The porpoise is not a fish, but a mammal, warm blooded and
air breathing. It provides an excellent red meat, against which British
sailors have for many years felt a strong prejudice, but which is eaten

with relish by Scandinavians. We found it a pleasant change from tinned food.

One day we encountered a magnificent five-masted barque becalmed in the doldrums, all sail set and flapping gently with the slight roll. She was flying the French ensign, and on closer approach proved to be the *La France*, of Rouen. She presented such a beautiful sight [on our return to England we learned that this beautiful ship had become a total wreck on the Great Barrier Reef of Australia], with her tall masts and lofty spars reflected in the smooth sea, that we altered course to pass close to her and enable Wilkins to get some photographs. Sir Ernest spoke her captain, who replied in excellent English, asking where we had left the trade winds, voicing what is the uppermost thought in the mind of every master of a sailing ship, the probability and direction of winds, on which depends their motive power.

We were amused to notice that though the Boss sent his voice unaided across the water with the greatest ease, the Frenchman required a megaphone to make audible his replies.

These beautiful vessels are fast being driven off the ocean in the competition with modern steamships, yet it is with a feeling of genuine regret that one sees them go, for with them departs much of the romance of the sea. The apprentice of to-day takes his training in steamers, and the modern seaman is beginning to regard sail as a 'relic of barbarism' (an expression of Jeffrey's). In the days when I first went to sea one might count masts and yards by the hundred in harbours such as Falmouth or Queenstown, but now they are to be found only in ones and twos. They were fine ships, the old clipper ships, and bred a fine type of seaman, yet 'the old order changeth', and in spite of an attempt to bring them into general use again, it is to be feared that they will gradually die out altogether.

Early on the morning of 8 November we sighted St Paul's Rocks, standing solitary and alone in the midst of a wide tropic sea. They were the first objective, and Sir Ernest arranged for a party to land there. We lay to under their lee and dropped a boat. Immediately a countless shoal of sharks came about us, their fins showing above water in dozens on every side. A considerable swell was running, making the approach difficult, but we effected a landing in a little horseshoe-shaped basin lying in the midst of the rocks. Wilkins, assisted by Marr, took ashore camera and cinematograph apparatus, and was able to get some excellent photos of birds.

Douglas, assisted by Dell, carried out an accurate survey and made a geological examination of the rocks. Hussey and Carr carried out meteorological work, taking advantage of a fixed base to send up a number of balloons for measuring the upper air currents. I had charge of the boat, with Macklin, Jeffrey and Eriksen as crew.

We noticed that the cove in which we had made the landing was simply alive with marine life of every kind, and so returned to the ship for fishing tackle. For bait we used crabs, which swarm in large numbers all over the rocks. There were two sorts, a large red variety and a smaller one dark green in colour. They were evil-looking things, and seemed always to be watching us intently, moving stealthily sideways, now in this direction, now in that. At the least sign of approach they darted with amazing rapidity into crevices in the rocks. Occasionally we saw them gather their legs under them and give the most extraordinary leaps of from 2 to 3 feet. Their jaws worked continually and water sizzled and bubbled at their mouths. Some of them had found flying fish which had flown ashore or been brought by the birds. It was a horrible sight – they tore the flesh into fragments with their powerful claws and crammed it into their mouths. The ownership was often disputed, the bigger crab always winning. Occasionally a small crab, hoping for some of the crumbs which might fall from the rich man's table, would creep cautiously up behind. The bigger crab, however, permitted no depredations, but, waiting till the smaller one reached within a certain limit, would kick out suddenly with an unoccupied leg, causing the smaller one to hop hastily out of reach.

We spiked what we required with a boat-hook, and they made excellent bait, for it was necessary only to lower the hook to get an immediate bite. The landing of the catch, however, proved not so easy. The little cove swarmed with sharks, which were attracted by the boat, and came about us in scores. Looking down through the clear water, we could see fish in plenty flitting hither and thither with leisurely whisks of their tails, obviously quite at ease and not at all perturbed by the proximity of the marauders. The moment, however, we hooked one and started to pull it up, the sharks turned like a streak and went for it with such voracity that we had the greatest difficulty in getting it to the surface. What was worse, they frequently bit through the lines and took the hook also. Finally, we were compelled to reinforce the lines with wire. On one occasion I succeeded in getting a fish clear of the water, and, thinking that for once I had eluded the sharks, was in the act of swinging it aboard when there was a flash of something white, an ugly snout broke water, and I was left gazing stupidly at half a head which still dangled from my line. The shark had got the rest. Indeed, it was not safe to put a hand over the gunwale, for immediately a head rose towards it.

We had with us in the boat a harpoon and trident, and getting tired of losing our fish, waged war upon the sharks. We harpooned several, which we killed and threw back to their brethren, who voraciously set upon them and tore them to bits. While they were thus distracted we secured a number of fish. There is something sinister and evil-looking about sharks. Some of them grow to large size, attaining a length of 13 or 14 feet; there are records of larger ones than that, the largest I know of being 25 feet, but this is exceptional. Their mouths, which are composed of a curved slit, are situated on the under surface of the head some distance from the snout. Their teeth, which are sharp and set backwards, are not true teeth, but modified scales. The eyes are small and poorly developed, but they have a phenomenal sense of smell which attracts them from long distances to potential sources of food. Macklin and Hussey dissected the brain of one of them, which showed that the olfactory bulbs – the portion devoted to the sense of smell – is larger than all the rest of the brain.

These rapacious beasts are the most dreaded and most generally hated of all animals in the seas, and have accounted for many sailors who have fallen overboard. They are very suspicious of bait on a line, but have often been caught and hauled on board. It was at one time the custom on sailing ships to perpetrate in revenge all sorts of mutilating atrocities upon them, such as gouging out the eyes and filling the sockets with gunpowder, removing the heart and entrails, afterwards throwing the animal back into the sea to be torn to pieces by others of the species.

In addition to the sharks, we caught with the trident a number of large, round, black-coloured fish of a kind commonly regarded as poisonous. Their flesh looked so firm and white and excellent that we decided to try them. When cooked, they proved to be of good flavour, and no one suffered from the experiment of eating them.

We caught a number of smaller 'black fish' but I took them for specimens only, for I have seen them in other waters and know them as garbage eaters of the worst kind, though it is possible that those we caught here, living far from the filth and sewage of towns, might prove edible enough. The kind, however, of which we obtained the greatest number were yellow and blue.

Merely to sit in the boat and gaze down through these pellucid waters was a pleasure, for the bottom showed clearly, covered with countless seaweeds, while over it passed fish of all sizes and of the brightest and most varied colourings in endless panorama.

We enjoyed the day immensely, providing as it did a pleasant change from the routine of ship's life.

The recall flag was hoisted by the Boss at 4 p.m., when we gathered up our lines and took off the shore parties.

Before finally leaving the rocks we encircled them slowly to enable Worsley to get a series of soundings. There is very little shoaling in the approach to these rocks, which rise sheer and straight from the sea bottom. The soundings of the depth of water round about them, which were verified and amplified by those taken by Worsley on this occasion, show that the 'hundred fathom line' is nowhere distant more than four cables from the rocks, and in places is within 900 feet.

As we set off on our course we were surrounded by a number of bonito, which followed us in graceful leaps and dives. They can be caught sometimes from the jib-boom by dangling a strong line, baited with a piece of white rag, in the foam of the bow wave. When pulled out of the water they are difficult to hold on account of a strong vibration which is set up by rapid movement of the tail. It is customary to have a sack handy into which the fish is dropped, when it can be safely passed on board.

For a while after leaving St Vincent the engines had run smoothly, but now they started to give more trouble, requiring the most careful nursing by Kerr and his staff. The rigging also was not proving satisfactory, and the scarfed topmast yielded in a most alarming manner to the strain of the gaff. Sir Ernest Shackleton began to worry tremendously about her condition, and confided to me that he had trusted too much to others in the preparation of the engine-room. The work had been placed in the hands of a consulting engineer in whom he had reason to feel that he could place the most implicit trust.

Sir Ernest decided, however, before continuing the southern part of the expedition, to put into harbour at Rio de Janeiro and make a complete overhaul of every part of the ship under his own direct supervision, though he was possessed of no special engineering knowledge. We had intended calling first at South Trinidad Island, but, conditions becoming worse, we made direct for Rio.

Before entering harbour we repainted the ship, changing the white deck-house and superstructure and the yellow funnel to a uniform naval grey. This was done at the suggestion of Jeffrey, who also entered energetically into the carrying of it out, and there is no doubt that the grey was a much more serviceable colour. The ports, skirtings and boats were painted black, which relieved the monotony of the grey and gave the whole a pleasing effect.

On the night of 21 November we sighted the lights of Rio de Janeiro stretching in a row along the sea shore. It was a lovely still night, and the Boss was in good spirits. We gathered outside the surgeon's cabin while Hussey strummed tunes on his banjo. The Boss loved these little musical gatherings, and though he himself was unable to produce a tune of any sort, he liked listening to music.

The next day dawned with a wonderful sunrise which lit up the mountains round the harbour, tinting them with crimson, rose and pink. A slight mist on the surface of the water was turned into a wonderful red haze, through which appeared the masts and spars of sailing ships at anchor. The harbour is magnificent, dividing with Sydney the claim to be the finest in the world.

We steamed slowly in, past the Sugar Loaf Mountain which guards the entrance to the harbour, and came to anchor opposite the town.

CHAPTER 3

Rio to South Georgia

Sir Ernest Shackleton lost no time in going ashore to make arrangements for the necessary work, and set it going with the least possible delay. Messrs Wilson, Sons & Co. were appointed agents, and their engineer, Mr Howard, came aboard the same day. In addition, a consulting engineer was employed to make a report on the condition of the engines. The crank-shaft was badly out of alignment, and from this had resulted all the other disabilities which had so continuously cropped up during the voyage. It was considered also that the heavy four-bladed propeller was too great a strain for the small engines, and that a lighter two-bladed propeller, giving of a greater number of revolutions, would prove more satisfactory. The scarfed topmast, which had been badly strained, required renewing, for which purpose it would be necessary to take out the foremast.

It was decided also, while this work was in process, to recaulk and tar the hull.

On the second day we moved across the harbour to Wilson's Island, where the ship was emptied of all stores and equipment, which were placed for the time being in a large covered lighter. A large floating crane, of which we were allowed the use by courtesy of the Brazilian Government, was placed alongside, and the foremast taken out and placed in the sheds. This completed, the ship was placed on the slips and the work proceeded rapidly, the firm concentrating their resources to get us ready for sea in the shortest possible time. Mr Howard worked unceasingly on our behalf, and we received at all times the greatest help from all responsible members of the firm.

Sir Ernest Shackleton decided during the early part of the voyage that the living accommodation, which had been adequate for his original scheme, was insufficient for a programme which entailed prolonged periods aboard ship, and planned an addition to the deck-house. The existing structure was carried forward to within a few feet of the foremast and the new portion made 2 feet broader on each side. This meant enclosing the main hatch, but the difficulty was overcome by building another hatch in the roof of the deck-house and cutting the coamings of the original hatch flush with the deck. Although an uncomfortable arrangement in many ways, it had the advantage that Macklin could open it up at any time he wished to go below independent of weather conditions, for under the old arrangement the getting up of stores was limited to fine weather, there being no other access to the hold than through the hatch, rendering the work in other conditions very dangerous.

While this work was in progress it was impossible to live aboard, and a number of the British residents offered to billet the different members of the expedition in their houses. To Mr and Mrs Causer, Mr and Mrs Lloyd, the Secretary of the British Club, and the members of the Leopoldina Chacara I must take this opportunity of offering my most sincere thanks for their kindness and hospitality. Thanks are due, not only to these 'god-parents' (as we called them), but to others too numerous to mention, from the British Minister downwards, from all of whom we received the greatest hospitality and who took a keen interest in our project.

In spite of all the energy employed in getting the *Quest* ready for sea, it became apparent that it would take fully four weeks to complete the work. The delays caused through repairs since leaving England had now amounted to six weeks. It would be quite impossible to carry out the programme and reach Cape Town in time to enter the ice this season. It was this factor which caused Sir Ernest to decide to abandon, or postpone, the first part of the programme and make direct for South Georgia. Unfortunately, much of our scientific apparatus, stores and nearly all the special winter equipment, clothing, sledges, etc., had been sent to Cape Town, which was to have been our base of operations. Sir Ernest decided, however, that much of the foodstuff necessary to make up the deficiencies could be obtained locally, and hoped to get sledges, dogs and winter clothing at South Georgia. The German *Deutschland* expedition, under Filchner, had been abandoned there, and when we visited the island in 1914 we found that the whole of the equipment had been carefully stored and was in excellent condition. Sir Ernest hoped that much of this would still be available. Previous to this, in the belief that we should still be carrying on the full programme, the aeroplane had been sent on to the Cape by mail steamer, and we should therefore be compelled to do without it at the time when it would be of the greatest value. At the end of the month most of the essential work had been completed, but there was still much that required doing. Mr Howard was anxious that we should delay another week to enable him to put in the necessary finishing touches, but already we were late, and the Boss decided that further delay was impossible.

The new addition to the deck-house, intended as a forward mess-room, was a mere unfinished shell. Four bunks were hastily and roughly knocked up, and we left with no other furniture than a plain deal table, which was built round a central stanchion, and two benches. I may say here of the work put in for us at Rio by Messrs Wilson & Sons that it was all good and reliable, and withstood all the usage to which it was subjected, and Kerr never again had any trouble with the engines beyond minor adjustments. Mr Howard had done all that was possible short of building new engines, which he maintained was what we required, making no secret of his opinion that the present ones were unsuitable for the work to be undertaken. There was nothing for it, however, but to go forward, and Sir Ernest, though fully alive to the *Quest*'s disabilities, determined to do the best possible under the circumstances. He had that peculiar nature which shows at its best under difficulties. He was the most undefeated and unconquerable man I have ever known. His whole life had been spent in forcing his way against what to most people must have seemed unsurmountable obstacles. Yet he had always triumphed, and I, who knew him, felt no doubt that he would carry this expedition through to a successful conclusion. Yet, if the reader will but cast his mind over the part of this book which he has read and think of how, since the inception of the expedition, one difficulty after another had risen to baulk the enterprise, and how on board the ship one thing after another had gone wrong and required repair, he will agree that the Boss might well have thrown in his hand and retired from the unequal struggle. But nothing could have been more foreign to his mind – each obstacle but strengthened his resolve to carry on, and we who served with him never for one moment felt distrust or doubt that under his leadership all would go well.

While at Rio a change was made in the personnel. Eriksen returned home, and three new men were taken on: Young and Argles as stokers, and Naisbitt as cook's mate.

We left Wilson's wharf on 17 December, and lay at anchor for the night in a small bay on the Nictheroy side, close to the entrance to the harbour. In the morning we made a final complete stowage, lashing securely all the loose articles on deck and getting the ship trimmed ready for sea. While we were engaged in this an urgent message was sent by motor boat for Dr Macklin to go to Sir Ernest, who had slept ashore as the guest of the Leopoldina Chacara, and who had been taken suddenly ill. Macklin went off at once, but on arrival found him fully recovered, saying that he had merely felt a slight faintness and had really sent for him to know whether the stores were complete. That this attack had a greater significance than was appreciated at the time later events showed.

We set off on 18 December. Sir Ernest, who had naturally worried a good deal over the continual troubles which cropped up, became once more his old cheery self, looking forward to a respite from further alarms regarding the welfare of the ship.

On the day of sailing Jeffrey suffered an injury to his leg which Macklin pronounced serious, and ordered three weeks' complete rest in bed, to which Jeffrey, being an active man, none too willingly assented. As a matter of fact, as a result of this injury he was incapacitated for nearly six weeks. Sir Ernest kept his watch.

The first few days at sea were fine and pleasantly cool. The old system of watches was altered, the men taking their turns at the wheel in rotation, following alphabetical order. For the day's work they were called at 7.00 a.m. and knocked off at 5.00 p.m. The messes were divided. Sir Ernest, myself, Hussey, McIlroy, Worsley, Macklin, Kerr, Jeffrey, Carr and Douglas messed in the new wardroom forward, and Smith took charge of the after mess-room, with Dell, McLeod, Marr, Young, Argles and Watts. Green and Naisbitt messed in the galley.

Three of the bunks in the forward mess-room were occupied by McIlroy, Kerr and Carr, the fourth being used as a locker for their personal gear.

Although we had increased the accommodation, it was still far from being commodious, and the bare, unfinished condition of the new quarters offered little comfort. 'Roddy' Carr was appointed to make some cupboards and shelves, and his work, though a bit rough and ready, answered its purpose well, which was the main thing. Hussey congratulated him on his new appointment as joiner, calling him thereafter 'Roddy Carr-penter', which I can assure my readers is the least of the atrocious puns which we endured from him. Always a cheery soul, his very presence was worth much to us on the trip, for it is the small jest which goes farthest and still sparkles when the more subtle wit has fallen flat.

On 22 December we saw our first albatross, a fine 'Wanderer' which attached itself to the ship and followed us on our way South. We saw also a 'Portuguese man-o'-war'. The two form a combination rarely seen in the same latitude (30° 47' S.).

The albatross has a wonderful flight, and our flying experts, Carr and Wilkins, watched the bird as it soared and dipped and 'banked' and 'stalled' and performed numerous evolutions, for each of which they had a technical or a slang expression.

I had the 4.00–8.00 a.m. watch on 24 December, during which the wind blew up wet and misty and came ahead. The Boss gave instructions to call the hands to take in sail. While the square sail was being taken in a corner carrying a heavy block and shackle was whipped across the deck, catching Carr a violent blow in the face. He was badly stunned, but picked himself up, with hand to face, blood flowing freely from between his fingers. When examined, it was found that his nose was broken. After some trouble the surgeons replaced the bones in position, but Carr, standing in front of a looking-glass, attempted to improve the work, with the result that the operation had to be carried out a second time, with pertinent remarks from Hussey as to the effects upon his personal appearance if further interfered with.

Later in the day the mist cleared and the sun came out. In the evening we were able to set sail again.

This being Christmas Eve, we sat after supper and talked of the various Christmases we had spent. Each man pictured the Christmas he would like to spend to-morrow if he got the chance.

It is funny how we cling, in spite of long years of disillusionment, to the mind-pictures of our childhood, and conjure up visions of a snow-covered countryside, with robins, holly trees, waits, and all the things that go into the Christmas card. We forget the warm, wet, miserable Christmas days; and perhaps it is just as well.

Our position, situated as we were in the midst of a waste of stormy waters, was not an ideal one, but we looked forward to celebrating Christmas in a cheery way. Mr and Mrs Rowett had sent us as a parting gift a big box of Christmas fare, which included such delicacies as turkeys, hams, plum puddings, and muscatels and raisins. The evening was fine, and in spite of sundry croakings from Hussey, our weather prophet, we anticipated a cheery Christmas dinner.

During the night it became apparent that a gale was brewing, and Hussey's prediction seemed to be only too correct, for by Christmas morning the *Quest* was heaving and pitching and behaving in such a lively manner that we saw that any attempt at festivity on this day would be futile. At breakfast-time it was almost impossible to keep anything on the table; cups, plates and crockery generally were thrown about, and the fiddles proved useless to keep them in position. We therefore put away Mrs Rowett's delicacies for a more favourable occasion. Green had a hard and trying time in his galley. The Boss told him not to bother about serving a decent lunch, but to serve out each man with a good thick bully-beef sandwich. This we ate in the shelter of the alleyways, well braced against the roll of the ship. It was a pleasant surprise when Green was able to produce some hot cocoa, which from its taste I suspected to have been made from engine-room water. It was, however, hot and wet and comforting to our chilled bodies.

For our Christmas dinner we had a thick stew, which was not bad. Two bottles also materialised, one of rum and one of whisky. Each man was allowed a tot of whichever he preferred. Rum, being the stronger, was generally selected. The Boss gave us the toast of 'our good friends, John and Ellie Rowett', which we drank enthusiastically. Afterwards the Boss asked each man where he had spent the last Christmas, and it was interesting to find how much scattered over the globe we had been. The Boss was in

London, McIlroy and myself were in Central Africa, Worsley in Iceland, Macklin in Singapore, Jeffrey in New York, Kerr in Hamburg, Carr in Lithuania, McLeod in Mauritius, Naisbitt in Rio, and Young in Cape Town. Green was wandering somewhere round the East as steward of a tramp steamer, and of all of us only the Boss, Hussey and Marr, the Boy Scout, seemed to have spent theirs at home.

During the day we were visited by numbers of seabirds which seemed to be in no way perturbed by the high winds: albatross, whale birds, Mother Carey's chickens, Cape pigeons and a Cape hen. It was cheering to see them again, these old friends of ours, and to watch their flight as they sailed cleverly from the shelter of one wave to another, rarely meeting the full force of the gale.

On the 26th the weather had abated somewhat, though a strong wind continued to blow from the west. The temperature dropped to 60° F, making the air quite chilly, and we were glad to don heavier clothing.

Kerr came to me with a report that the forward water tank was empty. He had sounded several times, and had gone below to tap the sides, the tank yielding a hollow note, so that there was no doubt about it. The small after tank, which had been freely used since leaving Rio de Janeiro, was also nearly empty, so that there was very little fresh water left on the ship. It was necessary to report this to Sir Ernest, though I did not like doing so, for I knew that the former troubles had caused him much worry, and he was now in hopes that he had heard the last of them. Though he took the news, which was serious enough, in all calmness, I could see that it caused him some uneasiness. We had to economise rigidly in the use of what water was left, using it for cooking and drinking purposes only, and making the best use we could of sea water for washing and cleaning. There was a small exhaust tank in the engine-room, which collected the steam after it had passed through the cylinders. The amount of water from this source was small, and tasted somewhat oily, but it helped to eke out the supply. Kerr removed the tank lid and made a search from inside for the site of the leak, which proved fortunately to be not in the walls of the tank itself but at the junction with the feed pipe.

During the night of the 27th/28th the wind again freshened. I had the middle watch. By 2.00 a.m. a furious gale was blowing from the WNW. Rapidly rising seas came along in quick succession with big curling tops, and breaking with a roar ran along our rails with a venomous hiss. The wind was on our starboard quarter, and under topsail and square sail we made good speed before it. The ship's log registered 9 knots. With each drive forward of the big seas the ship overran her engines, ultimately compelling us to shut off steam. We were making such good headway that I was loath to heave to, and we continued to rush along in a smother of foam and spray, veering and twisting to such an extent that the man at the wheel had all his work cut out to maintain a course and prevent her from broaching-to. I was afraid that some of the gear might carry away, and strained continuously into the darkness ahead. There was, however, something about the leap and swing of the ship as she tore along that caused our spirits to rise and created a tremendous feeling of uplift.

I was relieved at 4.00 a.m. by Worsley, who carried on for another two hours. At 6.00 a.m. the seas had risen to such an extent that Sir Ernest decided to heave to, and all hands were called to take in sail. Putting the ship straight before the wind we let go the square sail with a run, all hands rushing forward to gather up the canvas and stow it securely. Dell, jumping to assist another man, got his foot caught in a coil of rope, which, running out at high speed, threw him violently off his feet, causing an injury from which he took months to recover. We let go the topsail sheets and started to clew up, the wind causing the sail to flap with loud reports and bending the yard like a bow. Worsley and Macklin clambered aloft to take it in and pass the gaskets which secure it to the yard.

The gale increased in violence. I was agreeably surprised with the *Quest*'s behaviour, for she lay-to much more comfortably than I had expected, and took comparatively little water over her sides. There was enough, however, to make things uncomfortable, for it filled the waist of the ship, flooded the cabins, and sweeping along the alleyways entered the galley and extinguished the fires. Green stuck valiantly to his post and managed at each meal-time to serve us out some good solid sandwiches and, what was of especial value under the circumstances, a good hot drink, which sent a warm glow through our arteries and put new life into us. We considerably reduced the amount of water coming on board by placing a series of oil bags over the bow, which subdued the seas in a manner scarcely credible except to those who watched its effect upon them, as with breaking tops they rushed angrily upon us, suddenly to lose all their sting and slip harmless under our keel. With regard to the use of oil bags, if they are to be used at all, it is necessary to let the oil run freely, though not necessarily wastefully. Small driblets are valueless and not worth the trouble of putting over the side.

The next day there was still a strong sea running, but it was merely the aftermath of the gale, which lost its sting about midnight. In the morning the sun came out and brightened things up considerably. Later in the day we were able to set sail and proceed on our way. Our friendly seabirds, which had disappeared during the worst of the storm, returned and followed in our wake.

We had not long been under way when Sir Ernest approached, saying quietly: 'Wild, you came to me with bad news the other day; I have some news for you.'

'Good or bad?' I asked.

'Bad,' he replied; 'worse than yours; bad enough perhaps to stop the expedition.'

He then told me that Kerr, who had been the harbinger of so much evil tidings, had again to report the discovery of a most serious condition. While cleaning fires he had discovered a leak in the furnace from which the water bubbled out and ran in a thin stream down the sides. He was unable to state definitely the exact condition, which could not be examined until our arrival in South Georgia, as it required that the fires should be drawn to enable him to creep bodily into the furnace. He explained that it might be a small matter which could be repaired, or it might prove to be so serious that the boiler could not be used further. In spite of the quiet way in which Sir Ernest took this news, and the calm which he outwardly exhibited, I think it proved to be a pretty severe blow and the cause of a good deal of worry.

Indeed, all this recurrence of trouble from below decks, in departments which he personally had not been able to supervise, must have proved very trying. From the very first inception of the expedition he had had difficulties innumerable which might well have broken the spirit of a lesser man.

For the present Kerr was instructed to keep a watchful eye on the condition and, unless it appeared to be getting worse, to carry on under reduced pressure.

The wind again blew up to a moderate gale from the westward on 30 December, much less severe, however, than the last one, though with very violent squalls. We ran off before it, making good speed, and though the rising seas rushed down upon our stern as if to poop us, the *Quest* rose to let them pass frothing and sizzling, but harmless, under our counter.

Towards evening, however, both wind and sea had increased, and Sir Ernest decided to take in sail and heave to. Much water came on board and found its way into Sir Ernest's cabin and my own, the doors of which opened on to the waist of the ship. The bunks were sodden, so much so that Sir Ernest left his and made up a bed on one of the benches in the wardroom, refusing to deprive any other man of his bunk. During the long spell of bad weather he had spent nearly the whole time on the bridge, and though I repeatedly suggested to him that he should lie down and rest, he would not do so. On this particular night he took Worsley's watch as well as his own, so that Worsley's rest might not be disturbed. He was always doing little things like this for other people.

About this time I began to feel a little bit uneasy, for it seemed to me that he was doing too much and subjecting himself to too great a strain.

Macklin's diary shows that he had the wheel during the second dog-watch, and was relieved at 8.00 p.m. by Sir Ernest, who told him to lash the wheel and go to bed.

Macklin noticed, however, that the Boss was looking tired and ill, and urged him to call Worsley (whose real watch it was) and turn in himself. The Boss would not hear of it, saying: 'You boys are tired and need all the sleep you can get.'

The diary says:

He was looking so tired that I offered with some diffidence, for I am not a trained seaman, to stay on myself, saying that on the least sign of anything untoward happening I would blow a whistle. Somehow or other a long conversation ensued, in which he told me many things. He said: 'If this crack in the furnace proves serious I may have to abandon the expedition – my reputation will stand it – but I am not beaten; John Rowett understands me, and will trust me to make the best of things, even if I have to get a new ship.'

He reverted to his original northern scheme, saying: 'The *Quest* would have been suitable for that; in the Davis Strait, even if we lost her, we should have had no difficulty in reaching land, where we could subsist on game and carry on without her.'

So ended the Old Year. New Year's Day brought us a calm sea with long oily swell, and over all a drenching mist. Being a Sunday little work was done, and all hands were allowed a rest after the somewhat trying days we had just experienced.

With the new year Sir Ernest Shackleton again commenced to write in his journal, which I insert verbatim.

1 January 1922
Rest and calm after the storm. The year has begun kindly for us; it is curious how a certain date becomes a factor and a milestone in one's life. Christmas Day in a raging gale seemed out of place. I dared not venture to hope that to-day would be as it was. Anxiety has been probing deeply into me, for until the very end of the year things have gone awry. Engines unreliable; furnace cracked; water short; heavy gales; all that physically can go wrong, but the spirit of all on board is sound and good.

There are two points in the adventures of a diver,
One when a beggar he prepares to plunge,
One when a prince he rises with his pearl.

2 January 1922
Another wonderful day, fine, clear, a slight head wind, but cheerful for us after these last days of stress and strain. At 1 p.m. we passed our first berg. The old familiar sight aroused in me memories that

the strenuous years had deadened. Blue caverns shone with sky-glow snatched from heaven itself, green spurs showed beneath the water.

> And bergs mast high
> Came sailing by,
> As green as emerald.

Ah me! the years that have gone since in the pride of young manhood I first went forth to the fight. I grow old and tired, but must always lead on.

3 January 1922

Another beautiful day; fortune seems to attend us this New Year, but so anxious have I been, when things are going well, I wonder what internal difficulty will be sprung upon me. All day long a light wind and clear sky was our happy portion. I find a difficulty in settling down to write – I am so much on the *qui vive*; I pray that the furnace will hold out.

> Thankful that I can
> Be crossed and thwarted as a man.

4 January 1922

At last, after sixteen days of turmoil and anxiety, on a peaceful sunshiny day, we came to anchor in Gritviken. How familiar the coast seemed as we passed down: we saw with full interest the places we struggled over after the boat journey. Now we must speed all we can, but the prospect is not too bright, for labour is scarce. The old familiar smell of dead whale permeates everything. It is a strange and curious place.

Douglas and Wilkins are at different ends of the island. A wonderful evening.

> In the darkening twilight I saw a lone star hover
> Gem-like above the bay.

These were the last words written by Sir Ernest Shackleton.

I continue my own narrative.

Early in the morning of Wednesday 4 January, we sighted Wallis Island, and soon after the main island of South Georgia opened into view, with its snow-clad rocky slopes and big glaciers running to the sea. With fair wind and in smooth water we passed along the coast. Sir Ernest at sight of the island had completely thrown off his despondency, became once more his active self, and stood with Worsley and myself on the bridge, picking out through binoculars, with almost boyish excitement, the old familiar features, and recognising places with such words as, 'Look, there's the glacier we descended!' or, 'There, do you see, coming into view, the slope where we lit the Primus and cooked our meal?' He kept his spirits throughout the day, and it was with the greatest pleasure that I recognised once more the old buoyant, optimistic Boss.

The day cleared beautifully, and we entered Cumberland Bay in bright sunshine, with not a ripple on the surface of the water. How familiar it all seemed as we rounded the point and entered Grytviken harbour, with the little station nestling at the foot of the three big peaks, the spars of the *Tijuca*, the small whalers along the pier; all exactly as we had left them seven years before. The Boss, looking across at the slopes above our 'dog-lines', remarked, 'The Cross has gone from the hillside!' [Referring to a conspicuously placed cross set up by the crew of the *Deutschland* to one of their members who had died there.]

The poles which had been set up by us to mark the north and south direction were still standing; we were informed that they were used regularly by the whalers in adjusting their compasses.

We passed the spit with the little Argentine meteorological station, behind which lay the house of the Government officials, and dropped anchor in the *Endurance*'s old anchorage.

One familiar landmark was missing – the little hospital hut in which I had lived with McIlroy, Macklin, Hussey, Crean and Marston, the dog-drivers of the last expedition. We found later that it had been moved from its old site close to the 'dog-lines' to a more central position among the huts of the station.

Mr Jacobsen, the manager, an old friend of ours, came aboard, and shortly afterwards returned to the shore with Sir Ernest, who was full of vigour and energy.

I had the boat lowered and went ashore with McIlroy, Hussey, Carr, Macklin and some others to look about our old quarters.

The season was now midsummer, the snow had disappeared from the lower slopes, and with the bright sunshine and warmth the place had a very different aspect from what it had when we were here in 1914, much earlier in the season. In other respects there was little change, and we recognised among the workers at the station a number with whom we had been familiar; in particular, one of the flensers, a hard-bitten individual who was standing with spiked sea boots on a huge whale carcass, assisting the stripping process by deft cuts here and there with his long-handled knife.

We visited our old hut in its new situation. It was now being used as a hospital again, and a young Danish doctor was in charge. We passed along to its old site beside the stream, which runs clear and icy cold straight from the snows. There was much less volume of water than when we were here before, but the little basin we had cut out as a bathing place was still there. Here, with the others, I used to take a morning dip. That was in the days of my hardihood. Macklin used to lie down in it, and stand in the snow to dry himself.

We went on to the 'dog-lines', passing *en route* the little cemetery, which we glanced at casually enough. The stakes to which we had secured the tethering lines were still standing as we had left them, as were also the boards with which we had made a flooring for the tent. We climbed the hill to a lake, on the frozen surface of which we used to exercise the dogs – it was now a sheet of open water. We sat down on the banks, enjoying the lovely sunshine, and watched the countless skua gulls and terns which, attracted by the unwonted visitors, flew close down over our heads. The younger spirits, full of exuberance, and revelling in the change from the confinement of the ship, threw stones at them, and tempted Query, who had accompanied us, to retrieve pieces of wood from the lake.

On our way back we were accosted by an incongruous figure – a coal-black nigger, on whose head was perched a bowler hat many sizes too small. He addressed us with a marked American twang: 'Say, you boys from the *Quest*, you goin' to the South Pole, ain't you? Wal, guess I'm comin' along with ya!'

We guessed he wasn't, and passed on. We learned from Mr Jacobsen that he was a stowaway from St Vincent, who was a perfect nuisance to them, and who was being sent away at the earliest opportunity.

This being the first time we had been on an even keel since leaving Rio de Janeiro, we had dinner in comfort and spent a cheery evening, the Boss being full of jokes. At the finish he rose, saying, 'Tomorrow we'll keep Christmas.' I went on deck with him, and we discussed a few details of work. He went to his cabin to turn in. I arranged for an 'anchor watch' to be kept, and also turned in early for a good sound sleep.

CHAPTER 4

Death of Sir Ernest Shackleton

On Thursday 5 January, I was awakened about 3.00 a.m. to find both of the doctors in my cabin – Macklin was lighting my oil lamp. McIlroy said: 'We want you to wake up thoroughly, for we have some bad news to give you – the worst possible.'

I sat up, saying: 'Go on with it, let me have it straight out!'

He replied: 'The Boss is dead!'

It was a staggering blow.

Roused thus in the middle of the night to receive this news, it was some minutes before I felt its full significance. I remember saying mechanically: 'The Boss dead! *Dead*, do you mean? He can't be dead!'

On asking for particulars, I learned from Macklin that he was taking the 2.00–4.00 a.m. anchor watch. He was patrolling the ship, when he was attracted by a whistle from the Boss's cabin, and on going in, found him sitting up in his bunk. His own account, written almost immediately after, is as follows:

Was called at 2.00 a.m. for my watch. A cold night but clear and beautiful, with every star showing. I was slowly walking up and down the deck, when I heard a whistle from the Boss's cabin. I went in, and he said: 'Hullo, Mack, boy, is that you? I thought it was.' He continued: 'I can't sleep to-night, can you get me a sleeping draught?' He explained that he was suffering from severe facial neuralgia, and had taken fifteen grains of aspirin. 'That stuff is no good; will you get me something which will act?'

I noticed that although it was a cold night he had only one blanket, and asked him if he had no others. He replied that they were in his bottom drawer and he could not be bothered getting them out. I started to do so, but he said, 'Never mind to-night, I can stand the cold.' However, I went back to my cabin and got a heavy Jaeger blanket from my bunk, which I tucked round him. He was unusually quiet in the way he let me do things for him ... He talked of many things quite rationally, and finding him in such a complacent mood, I thought it a good opportunity to emphasise the necessity of his taking things very much more quietly than he had been doing ... 'You are always wanting me to give up something. What do you want me to give up now?' This was the last thing he said.

He died quite suddenly.

I remained with him during the worst of the attack, but as soon as I could leave him I ran to McIlroy and, shaking him very roughly I am afraid, said: 'Wake up, Mick, come at once to the Boss. He is dying!' On my way back I woke Hussey, and told him to get me certain medicines. It must have been rather a shocking awakening for both of them, but they leapt up at once. Nothing could be done, however. I noted the time – it was about 2.50 a.m.

I had Worsley called and informed him of what had occurred. To the rest I said nothing till the morning.

At 8.00 a.m. I mustered all hands on the poop, and told them the bad news. Naturally it was a great shock to them all, especially to those who had served with him before and thus knew him more intimately. I added briefly that I now commanded the expedition, which would carry on.

On that day, and on the several that followed, rain fell heavily, fitting in with our low spirits.

I immediately set about making arrangements for sending home the sad news to Lady Shackleton, and for notifying Mr Rowett.

I sent for Watts, our wireless operator, and asked him if he could establish communication. He said he would try. From his log:

My ambition was to get the type 15 set working, so as to pass the news as quickly as possible. The whole set I stripped and tested thoroughly, and 'made good' minor defects, but luck was still against me. The dynamo was run at 5.45 p.m., and whilst testing the installation the machine suddenly raced, and fuses were blown out, so further working of the set had to be abandoned.

I went ashore to see Mr Jacobsen, who was deeply shocked at the news. I learned from him that there was no wireless apparatus on the island other than those carried by the oil transport steamers, none of which, however, had a sending range sufficient to get into touch with a receiving station from here. He told me that the *Albuera*, a steamer lying at Leith harbour farther round the coast, was due to sail in about ten days. He said that if I cared to go to Leith and make arrangements with her captain for sending the news, he would put at my disposal the *Little Karl*, a small steam whaler used by him for visiting different parts of the island.

I accepted his offer, and while the vessel was being got ready went with McIlroy and Macklin to notify the resident magistrate. He was away at another station, but I saw Mr Barlas, the assistant magistrate. It is curious how one notices small things at a time like this. One incident stands out vividly in my memory. At the moment of my telling him he was lighting a cigarette, which he dropped on the tablecloth, where it continued to burn. I remember picking it up for him and placing it where it could do no harm. This done I left for Leith with McIlroy, who during the whole of this time was of the greatest help and assistance. Everyone at Leith showed the greatest kindness and sympathy, and Captain Manson, of the *Albuera*, readily undertook to send off the message as soon as he got within range of any wireless station.

Arrangements for the disposal of the body I left to Macklin, and to Hussey I entrusted the care of papers and personal effects.

At first I decided to bury Sir Ernest in South Georgia. I had no idea, however, of what Lady Shackleton's wishes might be, and so ultimately decided to send him home to England. The doctors embalmed the body, which was placed in a lined coffin kindly made for us by Mr Hansen, of Leith. There was a steamer named *Professor Gruvel* lying in Grytviken harbour, which was due to sail in about ten days, and her captain, Captain Jacobsen, offered to carry the body as far as Montevideo, from where it could be sent on by mail boat.

As soon as the necessary arrangements had been made we carried him ashore. All hands mustered quietly and stood bareheaded as we lifted the coffin, covered by our silk white ensign, to the side of the *Quest*, and passed it over into a motor launch. All the time the rain soaked heavily down. From the pier we carried him to the little hospital and placed him in the room in which we had lived together seven years before.

The next day we carried him to the little church, which is situated so romantically at the foot of towering snow-covered mountains, over ground which he had so often trod with firm, eager steps in making the final preparations for the start of the *Endurance* expedition.

Here I said good-bye to the Boss, a great explorer, a great leader and a good comrade.

I had served with him in all his expeditions, twice as his second-in-command. I accompanied him on his great journey which so nearly attained the Pole, shared with him every one of his trials and vicissitudes in the South, and rejoiced with him in his triumphs. No one knew the explorer side of his nature better than I, and many are the tales I could tell of his thoughtfulness and his sacrifices on behalf of others, of which he himself never spoke.

Of his hardihood and extraordinary powers of endurance, his buoyant optimism when things seemed hopeless and his unflinching courage in the face of danger I have no need to speak. He always did more than his share of work. Medical evidence shows that the condition which caused his death was an old standing one and was due to throwing too great a strain upon a system weakened by shortage of food. I have known personally and served with all the British leaders of exploration in the Antarctic since my first voyage in the *Discovery*. For qualities of leadership and ability to organise Shackleton stands foremost and must be ranked as the first explorer of his day.

I felt his loss, coming as it did, most keenly.

In order to ensure safe disposal of the body, and to arrange for its transference at Montevideo, I detailed Hussey to accompany it home. I could ill spare him, but I considered him the most suitable man I could select for the purpose. Naturally it was a disappointment to him to give up the expedition, but he accepted the responsibility without demur, and I am grateful to him for the spirit in which he complied with my arrangements.

As subsequent events turned out, Hussey received a message at Montevideo from Lady Shackleton expressing her wish that Sir Ernest should be buried in South Georgia, which was the scene of one of his greatest exploits, and which might well be described as the 'Gateway of the Antarctic'. The coffin was returned to Grytviken by the *Woodville*, through the courtesy of Captain Least, and Sir Ernest was ultimately buried in the little cemetery beside our old 'dog-lines'. Of his comrades, only Hussey was present at the funeral, for the rest of us had already sailed into the South, but there were many among the hardy whalers of South Georgia who attended, men who knew him and could, better than most people, appreciate his work. Nor was the sympathetic presence of a woman lacking, for at the funeral was Mrs Aarberg, wife of the Norwegian doctor at Leith, who with kindly thought had placed upon his grave a wreath made from the only flowers on the island, those which she had cultivated with much care and patience inside her own house. She was the only woman on South Georgia.

I have not the least doubt that had Sir Ernest been able to decide upon his last resting-place, it is just here that he would have chosen to lie, and would have preferred this simple funeral to any procedure carried out with greater pomp and ceremony.

Not here! the white *South* has thy bones; and thou,
Heroic sailor-soul,
Art passing on thine happier voyage now
Toward no earthly Pole.

[Adaptation from Tennyson's lines on Franklin.]

CHAPTER 5

Preparations in South Georgia

We can make good all loss except
The loss of turning back.

Kipling

Though we all felt very keenly the loss we had suffered in the death of the Boss, we could not allow our depression of spirits to take too strong a hold on us, for there was much work to be done.

The season was now well advanced, and I had to make up my mind at once as to what we were going to do. Sir Ernest Shackleton's death, occurring at this critical juncture, left me with no knowledge of his plans, for he had withheld any definite decision as to future movements until he should be able to arrange for another complete overhaul of the engines. Since hearing of the crack in the furnace he had outlined several alternative propositions without, however, showing any definite leaning to any one of them.

The entry in his diary of 1 January shows how fully he realised the condition of the engines. Yet he added: 'But the spirit of all on board is sound and good;' and later, 'I must always lead on'! There is not the slightest doubt that he intended to go on with the work, and I knew that had he lived he would have found some way to carry on.

My position, when summed up, was as follows:

I was out of communication with the rest of the world, and there was no possibility of my receiving any message from Mr Rowett. I had therefore to act for myself.

The Antarctic open season was well advanced, and thus limited the time available for manoeuvring in the ice. I had therefore to act without delay.

With regard to the ship, the recent heavy storms had shown her to be a fine sea-boat, capable of standing any weather at sea. Rigging and hull were sound. The troubles which had so continuously cropped up since our leaving England had shown, however, that the engines could not be regarded as reliable.

We were short of both food stores and equipment, for our depot for the South was to have been Cape Town, and as a result of all the delays involved since our start we had not been able to go there and take them up. The food stores included those things most suitable for cold regions. The general equipment included warm clothing, footgear, sledging gear and harness; special ice equipment in the way of ice picks, ice-anchors and hand harpoons; oil and paraffin for the engines and dynamos; and a quantity of scientific gear.

As to personnel, I knew that I had with me men who would staunchly stand by me and support me in whatever decision I should come to.

Sir Ernest had spoken on one occasion, just before arrival at South Georgia, of proceeding down Bransfield Strait, finding a suitable spot somewhere on the western side of Graham Land, and freezing the ship in for the winter. When summer appeared he would cross Graham Land to the Weddell Sea and explore the coastline on that side as far as time and conditions should permit.

Of his different plans, this and his published programme of proceeding eastwards and making an attempt to penetrate the pack ice as near to Enderby Land as possible, and from there to push south, were the only two which I could consider.

As to the first, for the carrying out of this I should require a large quantity of stores, sledging equipment and good winter clothing. As before stated, these were at Cape Town, and unless I could obtain them in South Georgia this scheme must fall through.

Sir Ernest's last message home had been that all was well with the ship and the expedition, and he had never had a chance to announce publicly the final situation. Mr Rowett might therefore wonder at any change of plan occurring after his death. On this score, however, I was not greatly concerned, for I felt that in anything I should undertake I would have his support and carry his trust.

With regard to the original published programme, I realised that to enter an area which had hitherto proved impenetrable to every ship which had made the attempt would with the *Quest* be a hazardous undertaking even under the most favourable circumstances. Any ship entering heavy pack ice runs a risk of being beset and frozen in, and when that has occurred her fate lies absolutely with the gods. Should the ship be crushed, the chances of escape from the area in which we should be working could only be regarded as remote, for even if we succeeded in escaping from the pack with our boats, the nearest point we could make for would be Cape Town, a distance of over 2,000 miles, through stormy seas, dependent for water supply upon what we could collect in the way of rain.

Any fool can push a ship into the ice and lose her – my job was to bring her back again.

On careful weighing of the two alternatives the Graham Land proposition appealed to me more strongly, for it offered the prospect of good work; and in case of accident we should be within measurable reach of whalers, which in their search for whales penetrate deeply among the islands of the Palmer Archipelago.

Though I was faced with an innumerable number of smaller considerations, the above represents roughly the situation at the time.

Therefore with these points of view in mind before coming to any decision at all, I gave instructions to Kerr to examine thoroughly and overhaul the engines and boilers and report to me his considered opinion. This he did. The work done at Rio had been good and sound, and he considered the condition of the engines to be fit for proceeding. The boiler presented a difficult problem. On looking up the record of the *Quest* (or the *Foca I* as she was previously named) in the Norwegian *Veritas*, I discovered that though the ship was comparatively new, the boiler had been built in 1890, and was thus thirty-one years old.

Kerr made an examination from inside, and I had also the second opinion, by courtesy of Captain Jacobsen, of the chief engineer of the *Professor Gruvel*.

The report showed that the condition was not reparable, but at the same time was not likely to develop further and become serious.

I threw upon Kerr the onus of deciding as to whether the engines and boiler were fit to continue with into the ice or not. With true native caution (he comes of Aberdeen stock) he replied that there was always a risk of breakdown, but not an unreasonable one; he was willing to take it himself.

So far as that was concerned I decided to go ahead.

My next step was to see about the special winter equipment which Sir Ernest had hoped would be available here.

I learned to my dismay from Mr Jacobsen that Filchner's store had been opened up and the contents scattered. There were no dogs on the island. They had proved so voracious and such a nuisance to the station that they had been shot. Food could be obtained, and a certain amount of clothing from the slop chests [clothing stores] of the different stations, but this was considered of doubtful quality and not recommended for our purpose. I thought bitterly of the good stuff lying in a Cape Town warehouse.

These considerations caused me reluctantly to rule out the Graham Land proposition.

There remained now only to carry on as the Boss had intended or to go back. As a matter of fact, I hardly gave the latter a thought. To go back was intolerable and quite incompatible with British prestige. To carry out against all difficulties the work the Boss had set out to do appealed to me strongly. I made my decision, and let it be known to all hands, giving each one a chance to back out before it was too late. I believe there was not one who ever so much as thought of it, and none seemed to doubt but that we would go on. Such is the onus of leadership. Where you must concern yourself for the safety and welfare of those under your charge, they place in you their trust and do not worry at all. This is as it should be.

I told Macklin, who was in charge of stores and equipment, to take a complete and accurate tally of everything we had aboard and then work out and make a list of requirements for the period to be spent in the ice.

When this was done I sent him to visit the different stations and pick out from their slop chests anything that he might consider necessary in the way of clothing.

Nothing was available at Grytviken, and so on 16 January we left for Leith harbour, where we received the greatest kindness from Mr Hansen, the manager of the whaling station. His keen interest and practical assistance meant a great deal to me at this critical time, and his genial qualities and kindly hospitality did much to dissipate the gloom which had fallen upon us. We obtained from him all the food stores we required and a general outfit of clothing and blankets, which, though by no means the equivalent of our own specially prepared stuff, was at least adequate to meet the demands of a single season. Among other things, each man was provided with a fur-lined leather cap, an abundance of socks and mitts, a pair of stout ankle boots, a pair of sea boots, a quantity of warm underclothing, heavy pea-jacket, light windproof jacket, a stout pair of trousers, three good blankets and a warm coverlet.

It was necessary before starting to fill the bunkers with coal. Mr Hansen had none to spare, but he took me round in a whaler to Husvik harbour, where Mr Andersen, the manager, promised to supply me with what we required.

On 14 January I told Worsley to take the *Quest* to Husvik, where she was placed alongside the *Orwell*, the station oil carrier, from which we took aboard 105 tons of best Welsh coal. In the meantime work had been going on busily on board, for Worsley and Jeffrey had much to do in their preparations for the ice. The forward water tank had been made sound and a hand pump fitted. Dell, McLeod and Marr tested all running gear and rigging, which was set up in good order and any defective material replaced. Marr, since leaving Rio, had been replaced in the galley by Naisbitt, and now assisted Dell about the deck, a job very much more to his taste. He was also appointed 'Lampy', having charge of all the non-electrical lighting of the ship.

Wilkins and Douglas, who had preceded us here from Rio de Janeiro in order to have more time for their scientific work, rejoined us, and were much shocked at the news we had to give them.

We were now ready for sea, but returned first to Leith harbour to pick up two ice anchors and a number of hand harpoons, ice picks and ice axes which Mr Hansen had turned out for us in his workshop.

We received from the Norwegian people in South Georgia during the whole of our stay nothing but the greatest kindness and sympathy and the most valuable practical assistance in our somewhat extensive preparations. This is the more remarkable in that they are not of our nationality and Norway has ever been our keenest rival in Polar exploration. They were, however, as Sir Ernest would have said, 'of the Brotherhood of the Sea', and that explains much.

We were about to embark upon what would most certainly prove to be the most arduous part of our programme, which I had briefly outlined in a last letter to Mr Rowett as follows:

As I am at present out of communication with you, and in view of the lateness of the season, which necessitates that any attempt to enter the ice must be carried out without delay, I have decided to carry on the work of the expedition, adhering as nearly as circumstances permit to the plans as most recently expressed by Sir Ernest Shackleton.

Consequently ... I intend pushing to the eastward to a position dependent upon the date as marking the advancement of the season, striking south through the pack ice, and making an attempt to reach the Great Ice Barrier. If I am successful in this, I will turn westwards and map out, as far as possible, the coastline in the direction of Coats Land, but taking steps to escape before the ship gets frozen in.

There are, however, certain factors which may compel me to use my discretion in altering the programme, as follows:

1. In addition to the defects of the ship already notified to you by Sir Ernest Shackleton, compelling alterations at Lisbon, St Vincent and Rio de Janeiro, during this last stage of the voyage two other grave defects were discovered: a crack and a leak in the boiler furnace, and a leak in the forward water tank which almost emptied it. On arrival here the boiler was examined by Mr Kerr, the chief engineer of the *Quest*, and by engineers from the whaling station. After careful consideration they have decided that it is possible to go forward, and Mr Kerr states that it is quite reasonable to enter the ice under the conditions.

Whilst ashore, I took the opportunity of looking up the record in the Norwegian Record of Ships, and found that the boiler was built in 1890, and is consequently 31 years old, a fact of which I feel quite sure Sir Ernest was ignorant ... From the time the expedition started various defects of the engines have appeared, and any further developments in this respect may entail change of plan.

2. The capability of the *Quest* to deal with pack ice. It has been shown during the voyage that she is of lower engine power than was originally expected, and much will depend upon what speed and driving power she can maintain in the ice.

3. The lateness of the season limits the amount of time in which it is possible to operate in the pack ice.

4. Progress will depend upon conditions which cannot altogether be foreseen, viz. weather conditions, and the depth and density of the pack ice when we encounter it, varying greatly as it does from year to year … I expect to leave the ice towards the end of March, and will probably return to this island (South Georgia) or the Falkland Islands for coal and water…

This briefly indicates my plan and the outlook at the time we left South Georgia. In working to the eastward I intended to make for the charted position of 'Pagoda Rock', and verify or wash out its existence; also, if possible, I wished to visit Bouvet Island.

It will be seen that throughout this projected route we should have the winds to the best advantage, for while working east we should be in the westerly belt, which extends approximately from lat. 35° S. to lat. 60° S., while above these latitudes, on our return, we should enter the belt of prevailing easterly winds.

CHAPTER 6

Into the South

We left Leith harbour on 17 January, and proceeded along the coast to Cooper Bay. Douglas and Carr had gone there some days before to carry on their geological examination of the island.

On arrival we found that they had set up a tent on the beach and had built outside it a fireplace of stones. For fuel they used driftwood, which lined the beach in large quantities. Douglas came to meet us in the kayak, a small skin-boat which had been presented to us by Mr Jacobsen. I lowered the surf-boat and went ashore. Both Carr and he looked well, being very sunburnt and fatter than when they left us. A meal was in process of preparation in the fireplace, and when I saw the quantity of food they were about to dispose of I felt satisfied as to their health and the state of their appetites.

I wanted a supply of fresh meat to take with us on the ship, for although we had no refrigerator on board, there was no fear of the meat going bad in the low temperatures of these regions. I sent Macklin and Marr to catch and kill a dozen penguins, and went myself, with McIlroy, to shoot some skua gulls. I intended taking a seal also, but found that Douglas, with considerable forethought, had already killed and cut one up.

The day was bright, with warm sunshine, turning Cooper Bay, which I had previously visited under less favourable circumstances, into a beautiful spot. Seabirds of all sorts covered the rocks and flew overhead, filling the air with raucous cries, which sounded, however, not unpleasant, fitting the wild environment. Seals and sea-elephants were ashore in hundreds, lying lazily on the shingle of the beach or in the hollows of the tussock grass behind. Ringed and gentoo penguins strutted solemnly about like leisurely old gentlemen taking the sea air. On the hills behind were large rookeries where these quaint birds were gathered together in thousands.

I had no difficulty in obtaining the necessary number of skua gulls, and I saw that Macklin and Marr had made a little heap of penguins close to the boat, Macklin rejecting, with the discriminating care of one whose staple diet they have formed for months, the old tough birds and picking out the young and tender. Marr was delighted with his new experiences, being particularly fascinated with these almost human-looking little creatures.

So pleasant was the day that I was loath to tear myself away.

We returned to the ship, where we prepared the birds for the larder, and hung them, together with the meat, from the mizen boom, the poop at the finish resembling a butcher's shop.

Green, who had been before into the Antarctic and had wintered with me on Elephant Island, came out of his galley to regard with a professional eye this new addition to his larder. I asked him if he had forgotten how to cook seal and penguin meat, to which he replied, 'Not likely! If I was to live to be a hundred, I would not forget that.'

We weighed anchor and proceeded to Larsen harbour, which is approached through Drygalski Fjord, a long, narrow channel situated at the extreme south-eastern end of South Georgia. The entrance, which is very picturesque, lies between steep and high mountains. As one nears the end it appears as if one is about to charge a steep wall of snow-covered rock, but suddenly the little opening of Larsen harbour comes into view, and one enters a wonderful little basin shut in on all sides by steeply rising mountains and offering a secure anchorage for small vessels. Across the entrance lies a ledge of rocks from which grows a belt of kelp, where the soundings gave a depth of 38 fathoms.

Douglas went ashore in his kayak to make a geological examination of the place and bring away some specimens of rock.

At daybreak on 18 January we made our final departure from South Georgia, setting course to pass close to Clerk Rocks. Douglas and Carr had reported that while ascending the slopes behind Cooper Bay they had seen what appeared to be a volcano in eruption. They had taken a rough bearing of its direction, and from their description generally we concluded that the site of the phenomenon could only have been Clerk Rocks. I was anxious, therefore, to visit them; but the day unfortunately turned out to be thick and misty, and we were unable to get a good view of them. As every day was now a matter of importance to us in our attempt to push South, I did not delay in the hope that we might effect a landing. From observations made by Worsley and Jeffrey, their position as charted seems to be incorrect, but as the thick weather prevented accurate sight, their exact position cannot be definitely given.

We were now about to undertake the most difficult part of our enterprise, the plans of which I have indicated in the preceding chapter.

I divided up the hands into three watches: in my own – McIlroy, Macklin and Carr; in Worsley's – Wilkins, Douglas and Watts; in Jeffrey's – Dell, McLeod and Marr. The Boy Scout had become a fine, handy seaman, and developed an all-round usefulness which made him a valuable member of the expedition. The engineers, Kerr and Smith, kept watch and watch about in spells of six hours. I had added, in the person of Ross, to their staff in South Georgia, where a number of Shetlanders are employed at the flensing. Young and he acted as firemen, and Argles as trimmer. Green and Naisbitt, who formed the galley staff, were, of course, exempt from watch keeping.

At first we had misty weather, and soon encountered a heavy swell in which the *Quest* rolled heavily. We met numerous icebergs travelling in a north-easterly direction – beautiful works of Nature passing slowly to their doom.

Hundreds of seabirds tailed in our wake, including numbers of every species known to this part of the world: albatross, cape pigeons, whale birds and every kind of petrel, from the giant 'Stinker' to the dainty, ubiquitous Mother Carey's Chickens.

Thursday 19 January broke bright and clear. We were surrounded on all sides by bergs, those in sight numbering more than a hundred. Many of them were flat topped, evidently pieces which had recently calved from the Great Ice Barrier and floated out to sea. Others were more irregular in shape, with pinnacles, buttresses, and caves and tunnels through which the water rushed with a roar. The imaginative could see in them a resemblance to all sorts of things; churches with spires, castles with heavy ramparts, steamships, human profiles, and the figures of every conceivable kind of beast. Some were stained with red-coloured mineral deposits, blue bottom-mud and yellow and brown diatomaceous material. A few sloped towards the sea at such an angle as to enable penguins, all of them of the ringed variety, to clamber up. Some of the groups of penguins thus formed numbered as many as 200 or 300.

There was a high following sea, and the deeply laden *Quest* wallowed in it heavily, dipping both gunwales and filling the waist with water, which rushed to and fro with every roll. Smith was thrown off his feet and swept violently across the deck, fetching up with considerable force against the lee rail. He was much bruised and shaken.

During the day a number of soundings were taken with the Kelvin apparatus, but no bottom was found with 300 fathoms of wire.

In the evening Worsley altered course to look at what appeared to be a small half-submerged rock, but on approach it proved to be a heavily stained piece of ice.

20 January was another fine day. I saw Marr come on deck wearing a fur cap, heavy sea boots, and a belt from which hung a ferocious-looking sheath knife. The scrubby promise of a thick beard adorned his chin, and I had the greatest difficulty in associating the kilted boy who joined us in London with this tough-looking sailor man. If Hussey had been there he would have sung, 'If only my mother could see me now!' Indeed, I would have liked to have had for a short while the use of a magic carpet and been able to transfer him exactly as he stood to the bosom of his family.

Jeffrey, who had been confined to his cabin since leaving Rio de Janeiro, returned to duty on this day.

We continued to pass through a sea filled with icebergs, which in the sunshine stood out white and glistening against the blue-black of the sea. Worsley saw what looked like a new island with high summit, but even as he pointed it out a breeze flattened off its top, proving it to be only a cloud. These little rebuffs on the part of Nature have no influence upon Worsley, whose enthusiasm is unconquerable.

In the afternoon we sighted a number of icebergs in line, and a few minutes later Zavodovski Island showed up. The bergs were evidently aground, most of them having a distinct tide-mark and showing considerable wear along the water-line. As we drew nearer we saw that all those which were accessible were thickly covered with ringed penguins, which showed the most marked astonishment at our approach. There were many also in the sea, and they came swimming towards us, uttering their familiar 'Cl-a-a-k!' Some of the bergs were so steep that we wondered how the penguins ever managed to get a footing on them. We passed one with a side which sloped gradually to an edge some 20 or 30 feet above water, against which the sea broke heavily. A number of penguins were attempting a landing, and we watched their efforts with interest. They took advantage of the swell to leap out while the sea was at its highest, often to fail and fall back with a splash into the wash below; but they sometimes succeeded in getting a footing in a crack in the ice. They showed the greatest agility and skill in clambering from one little foothold to another, and their attitude of triumph when at last they gained the gentler slope and waddled off to join their companions in the group was most amusing. These little creatures are so absurdly human in every one of their aspects that one could watch them for hours without tiring. Those of the party who had not been previously in Antarctic regions were greatly fascinated by them and laughed outright at their quaint antics.

The island takes its name from Lt Zavodovski, chief officer of the *Vostok*, of Bellingshausen's expedition, who landed in 1820. It is barren and snow covered, except on the western side, which presents an unattractive bare surface of rock. Bellingshausen described this bare surface as being warm from volcanic action, and says that the penguins found it an attractive nesting-place. On that occasion the island presented the appearance of an active volcano, with thick clouds of steam belching from the summit. Owing to the low-lying mist we could not see the top of the island, and so were unable to gauge accurately the height, but from general contour it seemed to be not more than 3,500 feet.

The coastline presents a rugged face of rock broken here and there by glaciers which descend from the slopes behind to finish abruptly above narrow beaches of black sand. A red line of volcanic staining surrounds the island. Generally speaking it is inaccessible, and there are no good bays or anchorages for a ship. There are places where a landing could be effected by boat, but at no time would it be easy, for the rock faces rise sheer from the sea and the beaches are shut off from the island by the glaciers behind and laterally by steep cliffs. Nevertheless, penguins are able to get ashore. On the beaches were a number of the large and beautifully marked king penguins, while covering the slopes behind were whole battalions of the ringed variety, forming very large rookeries. I have seen larger rookeries than these in one place only – Macquarie Island, which I visited during the Mawson Expedition. There one can look over square miles and never see a piece of ground for the number of penguins of all varieties which collect there.

On the southern side of Zavodovski Island are a number of caves, from the mouths of which sulphurous fumes were issuing in a thin reddish cloud. We could feel their effects in a smarting sensation of the eyes, nose and throat. It was noticed that the penguins did not collect round the caves, but gave them a pretty wide berth. Larsen, who explored this group in the *Undine* in 1908, was overcome by these fumes while attempting to land on this island, and became seriously ill.

We made a running survey of the island and obtained a number of soundings. Before leaving I took the ship close to a berg which was thickly covered with ringed penguins to enable Wilkins to get some cinematograph pictures. To stimulate them into movement I told Jeffrey to fire two or three detonators. The loud reports caused the utmost consternation among them, and, stretching their flippers, they rushed en masse for the lower edge of the berg. Those in front were loath to take to the water, which is not surprising, seeing the difficulty they have in climbing back again, but those behind pressed them so hard that they were forced over into the sea, and, as Kerr facetiously remarked, 'It was just as well that they could swim.' Their attitude of surprise and indignation was very amusing.

We continued (Saturday 21 January) to pass innumerable bergs. The sea was literally filled with them. It is fortunate that in these latitudes there is comparatively little darkness at this time of the year, for at night these bergs form the most unpleasant of companions and necessitate a continuous and unremitting look out. The long swell rushes against them with a heavy surge, and a collision with any one of them would prove a nasty accident from which we would not be likely to escape scot free, while the dislodgement of a heavy portion on to our decks could have nothing but the most disastrous results.

The *Quest* rolled like a log and the seas in the waist rushed like a swollen flood from side to side, so that one rarely passed about the ship without a wetting. The water foamed over the tops of our sea boots and filled them up. This was particularly annoying when going to take over the watch, for one had then to endure the discomfort of four hours on the bridge with wet feet, which in this temperature is extremely unpleasant.

Before leaving England Sir Ernest Shackleton had designed a weather-proof bridge, completely enclosed, but with windows which could be opened up on all sides. Owing to the strikes which occurred before our start, skilled labour was not available, and the work done in the building of it was so bad, and the windows and doors were so ill-fitting, that it was quite impossible to exclude draughts. Except that it was to some extent rain- and snow-proof, we would have been much better off with an open bridge protected with a canvas dodger. There was always a strong draught along the floor, which made it very hard to keep the feet warm, no matter how well clothed and shod we might be. When the footgear became wetted the difficulty was increased, and in the long night watches we often endured agonies from this cause.

Macklin reported to me on the 21st that there were 15 inches of water in the hold. The ship had always leaked, but hitherto the engine-room pumps had been sufficient to keep down the water. I instituted a daily pumping, which, as the hand pump was situated in the waist amid a rush of water, was no pleasant task for those engaged in it.

I began to feel my responsibilities now, for each day made it more abundantly clear to me that this trip was to be anything but a picnic and demonstrated the fact that the *Quest* was by no means an ideal ship for the work. Often I was made to doubt the wisdom of the undertaking, but, having put my hand to the plough, there was to be no turning back.

This being Saturday night, we drank the time-honoured toast of 'Sweethearts and Wives', to which some wag always added, 'May they never meet!' On such occasions as these I issued to each man who wanted it a tot of whisky or rum. Rum was generally selected, as being the stronger drink.

On Monday 23 January, we passed close to two large and beautiful bergs, full of cracks and chasms, with a number of caves of the deepest blue colour. This appearance of blue in cavities surrounded by colourless ice is a phenomenon for which physicists have not yet offered a satisfactory explanation.

There is something about these huge bergs, bucking and swaying in the long heavy swell, which always attracts. One wonders at their age and where they have come from. It is a pity that there is no way of marking them. Worsley, ever inventive, and never at a loss for a suggestion, proposes firing into them bombs filled with permanganate of potash, or, better still, to have rifles firing small projectiles, by which one could mark the date. 'Why not?' says he.

There is much difference of opinion regarding the length of life of these bergs, some saying two or three years, while others suggest that they last forty or more. Much undoubtedly depends upon their movements. A grounded berg is likely to exist for a long time, and I have seen many, marked by the rise and fall of tide and washed by the action of the sea, which had obviously endured for many years. Those which do not go aground drift about for varying periods till carried eventually to the north; they meet their fate among warm currents, which leave not a vestige of their original selves. A berg floats with about seven-eighths of its bulk below water, and is consequently more susceptible to deep than to surface currents. I have often seen them moving through pack at a rate of 2 or 3 miles an hour, brushing aside the lighter ice in their undeviating progress. In open water, too, I have seen them moving up against strong winds at a similar speed.

During our boat journey from the breaking-up pack on the *Endurance* expedition we nearly came to grief from this cause, a large berg of several hundred yards in length almost jamming us against a line of floe ice, and requiring all our efforts to pull free.

Worsley met with a slight accident on the 23rd. While passing round the front of the deck-house he was struck by the forestay-sail sheet block, and was hurled across the deck. He picked himself up, with blood running freely down his face, but the intensity of his imprecations relieved me from fear of a bad injury, and, indeed, on examination it proved to be slight. He felt a little hurt when someone asked him if he could not do it again because there were several who had missed the incident. I omit his reply.

Our daily mileage had proved disappointing up to this point, and it became clear to me that we could not hope to reach Bouvet Island and still be in time to enter the ice this year. The coal consumption also proved higher than I had anticipated. I decided, therefore, to make a more southerly course to meet and enter the ice in a position somewhere about 20° E. long. On my westward run I intended to cross the mouth of the Weddell Sea, and attempt to examine and sound the charted position of 'Ross's Appearance of Land', probably call at Elephant Island to obtain sand for ballast and blubber for fuel, and proceed to Deception Island for coal for the return to South Georgia.

After a long spell of bad weather, on 25 January we at last experienced a change for the better, the day breaking bright and clear, the water a deep blue and the icebergs a dazzling white. The sea was comparatively smooth, and the *Quest* behaved moderately well.

I seized the chance to get on with an amount of work which had been difficult during the bad weather. Worsley, Dell and Carr overhauled the Lucas sounding machine and fixed a roll of wire all ready for a running out. When this was done, I set Carr to blocking some of the scupper holes, in the hope of keeping a drier deck. Macklin, assisted by Marr and Green, spent a busy morning in squaring up the hold, and there was work for everyone in one way or another. McIlroy and I baled out our cabins and put the wet gear out to dry. [On leaving South Georgia, I had moved into Sir Ernest's cabin, and McIlroy took my old one. Both cabins opened on to the waist of the ship, and were consequently frequently flooded with the heavy seas which rushed to and fro there.]

The ship was found to be taking more water, Macklin reporting that it had reached the level of the kelson, and I had to institute longer spells at the pumps, each taking from one and a half to two hours to pump her dry.

I got McIlroy to cut my hair, after which I acted as barber for him, and for Kerr and Worsley also. They were no half cuts, but good convict crops! Wilkins, with a view to stimulating the laggard hairs on his crown to more active growth, shaved the top of his head, and looked like a monk. He was growing a beard, as were a number of the men. McLeod's was the most flourishing; Dell and Macklin each showed a respectable growth; and Kerr, Smith, Young, Argles and Watts gave a promise of better things. Marr, not to be outdone, was also making the attempt, but so far could show only a stubble, which gave him rather a ferocious appearance.

In the afternoon Worsley took a sounding, with the unsought assistance of all the men on board, who crowded round with a great willingness to help, but who, like the cooks at the broth, only impeded things. Four miles of wire were reeled out without finding bottom, but, this being the first time we had used the Lucas machine on this trip, it was probably incorrect. When it came to winding up, the machine ran well, but when only about half the reel had been taken in the wire broke, and we lost the sinkers and the snapper (which is used to bring up specimens from the sea bottom). From this time forward Dell took charge of the sounding machine, and under his management it ran without a hitch. It was often a cold and tedious job, but he took the greatest interest in the work, and enabled Worsley to get some excellent results.

While the sounding was in process a mass of pultaceous material floated past the ship, some of which we collected. Macklin examined a small portion of it under a microscope, and reported that it was composed of feathers in a state of decomposition. Its occurrence was hard to explain, but Wilkins thought it may have come from one of the carnivorous mammals of these seas: a sea leopard or a killer, which had swallowed a number of penguins or other birds, and afterwards vomited the indigestible portions of them, just as our sledge-dogs used to vomit bones which they had eaten.

Naisbitt asked me if he might start a ship's magazine, to which I assented.

I saw an Antarctic petrel, the first I had seen this trip. The presence of these birds usually indicates proximity of ice.

The fine weather did not last long, for the next day the wind and seas increased, and the *Quest* took full advantage of the excuse to behave as badly as ever. We encountered fewer bergs, but were never out of sight of them altogether. One which lay 2 or 3 miles to starboard had a very peculiar appearance, closely resembling a sailing ship under canvas. Worsley examined it long and attentively through binoculars, and exclaimed, 'A sailing vessel!' I cast some doubt on the probability, but after a second look he cried excitedly, 'It is a sailing vessel; I can see her topsail yard! Let us go and talk to her!' A gleam of sunshine lighting upon the 'topsail yard' dispelled the illusion. I wonder what ship he expected to see down there!

An extract from Marr's diary on this date gives an interesting sidelight:

> A fairly strong sea was running when we came on deck for 'the middle', but this did not deter us from our usual occupation in the night watches, i.e. the consumption of food and drink. Indeed, it must appear that our watch is very hungry, but it is not so. This is merely our very effective method of passing the four long hours on the bridge.

It was customary for the engine-room staff to make a hot drink once a watch. The galley fire was always allowed to go out at night because of the necessity for economy in coal consumption, and the stokers used to boil the water in a tin on the furnace fires. The result was that there was often some difficulty in diagnosing the nature of the concoction, but under circumstances like this one could not be over particular. We used to turn to each other, saying: 'Well, at any rate it is hot and wet.'

We had two casualties on 30 January. Douglas, while skipping to keep himself warm, sprained his ankle, and had to take to his bunk. Worsley also came to grief in a much more serious way. Shortly after leaving South Georgia I had instructed Macklin to provision each of our three boats for thirty days. As the surf-boat was likely to be in frequent use, I had the provisions moved from her and divided equally among the port and starboard life-boats, the total in each weighing not less than a quarter of a ton. I decided to swing the port life-boat outboard on her davits, both in order to have her the more ready to lower away and to give us a little more sorely needed space on the bridge deck. The sea was smooth, but there was a long swell running which caused the *Quest* to give an occasional heavy roll. We were in the midst of proceedings, and I had got into the boat the better to direct operations, when suddenly a guy fixing the forward davit carried away; the heavily laden boat took charge, swinging inboard and out and in a fore and aft direction with the swing of the unsecured davits. It was all I could do to hold on, for I had been steadying myself with the after davit head, which now swung in a semicircle. Many times I felt as if I must be flung headlong into the sea. All hands gathered round to regain control, but with the strain the after davit guy also parted. The boat swung aft, sweeping Wilkins and Macklin off the bridge deck on to the poop, where they met with no damage, and, surging forward again, caught Worsley and drove him with tremendous force against the after wall of the bridge house. The impact was heavy. I heard a cry and a crash of splintering wood as the wall gave way. I felt sure Worsley was killed. McIlroy immediately went to his assistance, while the rest of us, after an effort, secured the boat and lowered her on to the skids again.

Worsley appeared at first to be terribly damaged. His face turned a deathly grey and was covered with perspiration, and he could scarcely breathe. We carried him to his cabin, where the surgeons made a careful examination. He had sustained severe damage to his chest and broken a number of ribs. His whole body was covered with bruises and abrasions, and he was suffering severely from shock. The doctors reported his condition as serious, but thought that the outlook was favourable unless signs of internal haemorrhage appeared. It was a great relief to feel that I had with me as surgeons two reliable and experienced men. Worsley had undoubtedly to thank the workmen who had this particular job in hand for his life, for had the bridge house been of more solid workmanship and shown greater resistance to the impact, he must infallibly have been crushed to death.

On this same day we reached the charted position of Pagoda Rock. It was first reported by Lt T. E. L. Moore, in the *Pagoda*, in 1845, in the following words:

In the afternoon of the same day (Thursday), January 30th, 1845, we fell in with a most singular rock, or rock on an iceberg. It appeared to be a mass of rock about 1,600 tons, and the top was covered with ice, and did not appear to have any visible motion, with a heavy sea beating over it. It had a tide mark round it. We tried for soundings with 200 fathoms, and the first time we fancied we had struck the ground, but before we could try again we had drifted some distance off. We could not send a boat or beat the ship up against the breeze that was then blowing.

In our position, lat. 60° 11' S. and 4° 47' E. long., however, there was no sign of it, though we made a traversing cruise, and a sounding which showed a depth of 2,980 fathoms gave no indication of shoaling in the vicinity.

It is rather remarkable, however, that towards evening we saw a very curious-looking berg, very dark green in colour and heavily stained with some earthy material. We altered course to pass close to it, and examined it carefully. It was an old, weather-beaten berg which had evidently capsized. Our meeting with it in this particular spot was a curious coincidence.

On the first day of February the maiden number of *Expedition Topics* appeared under the editorship of Naisbitt. It was got up simply, consisting of a number of sheets of typewritten matter, chiefly on the humorous side, and containing a sly hit at most of the company. There were also some clever drawings. Like everything else that created an interest it was of value just then when the daily life in those cold grey stormy seas was necessarily very monotonous.

On 2 February we had a strong gale from the south-east, during which I was compelled to take in sail and heave to – very disappointing, as we needed every mile we could make to the eastward. The *Quest* behaved in the liveliest possible manner, and everything that was not tightly lashed took charge. A bookcase in my cabin had battens 3 inches wide placed along the shelves, but they proved useless to keep in place the books, which hurled themselves to the floor, where they were much damaged by the seas which found their way in and swished up and down with every roll.

On deck everything had been lashed up and tightly secured, but in the galley pots and pans took charge and defied all Green's efforts to make them remain on the stove. All kinds of utensils escaped into 'Gubbins Alley', where they were carried up and down by the wash of water, while Green splashed knee-deep in pursuit. As he recovered one lot so another leapt away, regardless of his imprecations, till, some helpers coming along, order was once more restored.

Naisbitt, whose work compelled him to pass frequently between the wardroom and the galley, often with both hands full, had a very trying time. At meals we had the greatest difficulty in keeping things on the table, and we had to hold plates, cups, etc., in our hands, balancing them against the roll of the ship. We had to abandon all idea of comfort and wait patiently till the rage of the elements should abate.

During this time of bad weather Worsley suffered very much, for, with the violent rolling, he could get no rest in his bunk. He improved, however; the doctors pronounced him out of danger, and he spoke of soon getting up.

Macklin reported another 15 inches of water in the hold – it was obvious that it would be necessary to increase the daily spells of pumping. All hands took to this unpleasant and monotonous job very cheerfully, saying that it was good exercise! Indeed, there is not much else that can be said for it.

In lat. 65° 7' S. and 15° 21' E. long, we entered, on 4 February, what appeared to be the edge of very open pack, which lay in several strips and bands of light, loosely packed ice, with large open spaces of water between. I made my course due south and pushed into it. For some time I had doubts as to whether it was the real pack or streamers carried north by the late south-easterly gale. The sky to the south was very indefinite, and from the crow's nest the same conditions of loose ice and open water extended as far as the eye could reach. The two 'signs' which one looks for in the sky are 'ice-blink' and 'water sky'. A sky with ice-blink presents near the horizon a hard white appearance which indicates the proximity of close pack, ice barrier, or snow-covered land. A 'water sky' is a dark patch in a lighter sky, which indicates open water below the horizon. In each case when these skies are well marked they are definitely of value, but it requires much experience to gauge accurately the meaning of some of the more indefinite appearances, and conclusions too hastily drawn often prove erroneous.

While we were at sea I had watched the petrels which followed in our wake attempting to come to rest on the water, but breaking seas always drove them up again. I was interested to note that as soon as we reached the pack they flew forward and came to rest on a piece of ice, where they preened their feathers and settled down on their breasts.

The ice had a wonderfully settling effect upon the sea, deadening all but the heavier swells. The *Quest* became more comfortable than she had been for a long time, and at lunch we dispensed with the fiddles. This she would not tolerate, and a sudden roll swept everything to the floor. Later in the day the belts of ice became broader and the pools of water much smaller. There could be no doubt that this was the real pack ice and that the most strenuous part of our work was now to begin. Quoting from a diary:

> Now the little *Quest* can really try her mettle. What is in store for us? Will the pack, as variable in its moods as the open sea, prove friendly or will it rise in its wrath to punish man's temerity in thus bringing to the attack so small a craft? Before this effort the smallest ship to make a serious attempt to penetrate the heavy Antarctic pack was the *Endurance*, and she lies crushed and broken many fathoms deep in the Weddell Sea. We are but half her size! Shall we escape, or will the *Quest* go to join the ships in Davy Jones's Locker, and the queer deep-sea fish nose about among her broken spars? We are not in the least pessimistic, but the man who blinds himself to the possibility is a fool.

My sense of responsibility was growing daily, for though I always welcomed the suggestions of my senior officers I realised that on me alone must devolve the final decision in every plan and in every movement. This was my fifth expedition – nearly half my life has been spent in Antarctic exploration – and every accumulated year of experience has taught me more and more how much in this work we are the playthings of chance. Experience counts a great deal, of course, but no amount of experience, care or skill can be of much avail against prolonged and overwhelming pressure. Yet in those first days in the ice, as I stood on the bridge and looked down on the decks I saw among my men nothing but elation. Carr, Douglas and others who saw the ice for the first time were fascinated by it, and among the old hands there was obvious pleasure at again meeting the pack. Old McLeod, veteran of many expeditions, said to McIlroy: 'Here we are home again! Doesn't it do you good to get back!' Even Query was affected with the general air of uplift, and with paws on gunwale gazed with twitching nostrils at this new phenomenon. Nor could I long resist a similar feeling, for as I gazed south over the ice, with the cold, keen air in my nostrils, I, too, felt pleased and elated, glad of a tough problem to tackle and rejoicing in the long odds.

We soon began to meet old acquaintances in the form of crab-eater seals which, wakened from sleep on the floe, turned a curious eye in our direction and, scratching themselves the while with their queer hand-like flippers, pondered drowsily on the strange phenomenon which had come among them. Most of them seemed satisfied with their scrutiny, treating us as of no particular importance, and rolled over to sleep again. With their light silvery coats these are the most elegant of the southern seals and also the most active. They are characteristic of the pack, being found in large numbers about its free edge, where they obtain their living from the small crustacea of these regions, *euphausiæ* and amphipods. These small creatures live on the diatoms of which the Antarctic seas are so rich, and which often become embedded in the floe ice, which is stained brown or greenish-brown by their presence. *Euphausiæ* resemble small shrimps, and the amphipods are very like the sandhoppers of home beaches, but redder in colour. Whalers speak of them collectively as whale food, for they form the staple diet not only of the crab-eaters but of most of the Antarctic whales. It is an extraordinary thing that so large an animal as the whale should depend for its existence upon so small a creature, especially when one considers the millions necessary to make one meal. The side of natural history which interests me most is the consideration of animal habits, mode of life and source of food. There is something intensely fascinating about this study, but I confess to a lack of enthusiasm when it comes to a question of minute differences in structure and classification of species.

The ordinary whale has a gullet so small that one can scarcely pass one's fist into it, and no whale could certainly ever have swallowed Jonah. The animal referred to in the Bible story is no doubt the *Orca gladiator*, which, though commonly known as the killer whale, differs considerably in many features from the true whale. It is much better referred to by the name killer only. It is smaller than the larger varieties of true whale, but it has immense jaws and a wide gullet, and lives not on whale food but on seals and penguins, and it is conceivable that it has on occasions accommodated a man; though whether it ever let one go again is a different matter. The killer is certainly an evil-looking monster. Before we had entered deeply into the pack we saw numbers of them gliding about us, driven smoothly forward by almost imperceptible movements of their powerful flukes, the downward strokes of which produce small whirlpools on the surface of the water. One could mark their progress by watching these whirlpools. Every now and then they rise to breathe, for they are not fish but mammals, and exhale a spout of fine vapour which in the distance looks like water. It is dangerous to cross leads of young ice while killers are about, for they are able by charging upwards from below to break through considerable thicknesses with their heads. The round holes produced in this way are quite common, and one frequently sees their evil heads and wicked little eyes appear suddenly above the surface, scattering fragments of ice in a wide circle. When sledging along newly frozen leads, it is customary to keep close in to solid ice, and when a crossing is necessary it is made as rapidly as possible.

By 5 February there was a certain amount of daylight all night, and we were not held up on account of darkness. The ice had increased all the time in density and thickness, and at times it was all we could do to push ahead. Already I began to feel the need of greater engine power, though the small size of the ship made her very handy to manoeuvre, and we were able to dodge and squeeze past where a bigger ship would require to push and ram. For the man at the wheel the spell was no longer two hours of monotony, but a period of hard work for which he shed his bulky garments, finding all the warmth he required in the exercise entailed. It was only when we entered the leads that we could keep a steady course, and usually the commands, 'Port! Steady! Starboard!' etc., followed each other in rapid succession as we turned and twisted and wriggled our way ahead.

Worsley appeared again to-day. This evergreen youth of fifty years certainly made a rapid recovery, for I did not think when I saw him after his accident that he would be up so soon. Although a very good patient, he chafed so much at his confinement to bed that Macklin thought it better to let him out of his bunk, taking, however, the precaution to strap and bandage his injured parts in such a way that he could not do himself much harm, and was unable to make any attempt to climb aloft – which is the first thing he would have wished to do! He was keenly anxious to take his watch, and I must confess I was looking forward to his return to duty, for Jeffrey and I had been doing 'watch and watch' alternately, and I had to be frequently on deck during my watch below, which under the arduous circumstances was a heavy strain.

I kept a keen look out for a convenient floe with seals on it, for I was anxious to obtain fresh meat. Our food stores included an ample and varied supply of all foods, with the exception of meat, for which we were prepared 'to live on the country'. Seal meat is quite palatable when one is used to it, and has the advantage over tinned stuff of being fresh. It is also a valuable antiscorbutic, and I was relying on its regular consumption to prevent the onset of scurvy.

Sighting a good solid floe with three seals on it, I put the ship alongside and shot them all with my heavy rifle. I went over on to the floe with Macklin to bleed them, which done, they were hoisted aboard, and McIlroy, Dell and Macklin flensed and cut them up. The blubber went to the bunkers to eke out our supply of coal. Practically the whole of the meat of the seal can be used for eating; while the liver, kidneys and heart make very dainty fare. Fried seal's brain is a dish that can hardly be excelled anywhere in the world. The seal's brain is large and well developed, and when shooting these animals I always make a point of aiming at the neck just behind the skull so as not to spoil the brain for cooking. There is quite an art in removing the brain, and the heads were usually handed over to Macklin and McIlroy, who took them out complete and unbroken. While the flensing was going forward Worsley seized the opportunity to take a sounding, finding it lat. 66° 12' S. and 16° 21' E. long., 2,330 fathoms of water.

On 6 February we continued pushing on through fairly heavy pack. Often the *Quest* was brought to a stop by heavy pieces of ice across her bows, which she was powerless to move or break up. When this occurred we backed down the lane formed in our wake, where her short length usually enabled her to turn, and getting her nose inserted between two floes, we pushed ahead with all the power the engines could give us till she finally worried through. So far we had not been held up for any considerable time.

Macklin reported another 15 inches of water in the hold, requiring an extra spell at the pumps to clear. There can be no doubt that the continual bumping and jarring of the ship against the ice caused a starting of the timbers which had then no chance to settle and swell.

Everybody was in wonderful health and spirits, and appetites were keen. For lunch on that day we had the seal brains taken the day before; they were delicious. All hands took to the seal meat, with the exception of Jeffrey and Carr. Carr tasted it and said that it produced a sickly feeling, but with the former it was a case of pure prejudice, for he would not even taste it, and preferred to live on what else might be going. Stefansson, in his books, dilates upon the theory that men who in their normal lives have been used to all sorts and varieties of food take more readily to kinds which they are experiencing for the first time than those whose dietary has been more monotonous and composed of much the same thing day after day and week after week. That this is very true there can be no doubt, but it does not hold in the case of Jeffrey and Carr, for out of the whole party I doubt if there was anyone more used to the highly faked and varied dishes which the modern chef succeeds in producing. Hunger is a wonderful sauce and will break down most prejudices. Those of us who accompanied Sir Ernest Shackleton on his previous expedition lived entirely on seal and penguin meat for eleven months, and except that we were thin at the time of rescue as a result of not having enough of it, we were otherwise healthy and fit and had no sign of scurvy.

Stefansson, in speaking of scurvy, attributes his freedom from it to eating his meat raw or 'rare done', and states definitely that this is the secret of preventing and curing scurvy, whatever the food may be. On the occasion to which I have referred we always cooked our meat, except when circumstances or the exigencies of the moment did not permit of it and when we were short of fuel.

Nature has providentially arranged that most of the animals of south Polar regions, for example the seals, provide in addition to meat the fuel necessary to cook it in the form of blubber. It is true that the use of heat in cooking meat does *very slightly* destroy the antiscorbutic principle, but when the consumption is sufficiently large this factor can be neglected. Much depends upon the method of cooking, for a more thorough investigation of the subject shows that the detrimental influence is not *heat* but *oxidisation*. It is also stated that scurvy may be cured by eating meat which has gone bad. It is possible that a few isolated cases may have recovered in spite of the additional intoxication, but this teaching must be regarded as a most dangerous one. The subject is one of the greatest importance to explorers, for scurvy has caused the failure of many well-found expeditions. I cannot enter more fully into it here. The investigation of scurvy and other food deficiency diseases is at present occupying the minds of the medical profession, much new knowledge is being brought to light, and it is probable that the next few years will show great advances. I am greatly opposed to the making of generalisations based upon one or two isolated observations by writers with little or no knowledge of the fundamental facts; they are of little value for guidance and are apt to prove misleading.

Query was in great spirits at this time, never having been in better condition since we left England; his coat was thick and bushy, and his tail made a fine brush. He was really a most handsome dog. He became a thorough ship's dog, and climbed all over the place. Wilkins fixed a camera case to the front of the deck-house, and Query discovered via it a way to the top. So delighted was he with his new discovery that he ran up and down just for the joy of doing it. All day long he pestered one to play with him, bringing in his mouth a stick or tin or a lump of coal, or even a potato looted from the galley, which he wished thrown for him to fetch. Of this game he never tired, and no matter where one threw the object, he searched until it was found, when he brought it back, calling one's attention to the fact by a short bark or a dig in the calves with his nose.

Another game which he was very fond of was to drop things from the deck-house on to the head of someone standing below, whose share in the game was to return the thing dropped so that he could do it again. He was greatly excited by a seal which followed the ship and whenever we were stopped by floes rose high out of the water alongside us as though trying to come aboard. Possibly it regarded us as a strangely elusive and inaccessible piece of land. Up to now we had not seen any penguins in the pack.

On coming on deck at 4.00 a.m. on 7 February I discovered that during Jeffrey's watch the ship had entered a cul-de-sac and that further progress was impossible. From the crow's nest I could see nothing but dense pack stretching away to the southward as far as the eye could reach, with no sign of a water sky beyond it. To the east and west the same conditions prevailed, and there was no hope of working the ship in any direction except that in which we had come. I therefore decided to stay where we were for a day (lat. 67° 40' S. and 17° 6' E. long.), and if there was no sign of opening of the ice at the end of that time to retrace my steps and look for open leads farther to the west.

There were a number of seals within reach which I determined to collect, and so putting the ship alongside a suitable floe I sent off some of the men to kill and bring them aboard. They secured nine altogether, far more than we required for meat, but I wanted the blubber to help out the coal supply. We took for the larder, therefore, only the dainties, such as the brains, kidneys, livers and hearts, and the choicest pieces of flesh, which are the undercuts from the inside of the ribs.

We saw that day the first emperor penguin of the trip standing solitary, as is the wont of this species, upon a floe. Wilkins secured it as a specimen. The emperors are the most stately of all the penguins and have the finest markings. The king penguin is more brightly coloured, but the emperor has the more delicate shades which merge gradually into one another. Seen on the floe in bright sunshine they have a really beautiful appearance.

If approached slowly they make no attempt to run away, but may even take a few sedate steps forward to meet the stranger. When within a few paces they stop and commonly make a profound bow, just as if they were greeting one's arrival. If approached quickly and suddenly they take alarm and retire, first of all upon their feet; but if hustled they drop upon their bellies and using both feet and flippers, sledge themselves along at a considerable speed. Seen from behind they look like gigantic beetles, and there is something about this mode of progression which is provocative of laughter. I have noticed this when I have been showing pictures upon the cinema screen, the audience invariably breaking into laughter when it occurs.

This species is found only in the far south, and has the peculiarity of nesting during the winter. The term 'nesting' may be misleading, for they do not make any nests but lay their egg (only one egg is laid by each bird) upon the snow surface. Both male and female birds take turns in hatching out. They have a small depression on the foot into which the egg is wriggled by means of the beak. They are able to move about carrying the egg, and as Sir Ernest Shackleton used to say, 'They act both as a cradle and a perambulator.' When they wish to transfer the egg from one to another they stand belly to belly and indulge in a vast amount of wriggling; but in the process the egg is often dropped on to the ice and has to be wriggled on again from there. Two of the most marked characteristics of penguins are their patience and tenacity of purpose, both of which are extraordinary.

A few days before we entered the cul-de-sac Dell killed the South Georgia pig which was presented to us by Mr Hansen, of Leith harbour. It proved excellent eating and a pleasant change from seal meat. The head remained, and as it would make a meal for only one of the messes, we agreed to gamble to decide which should have it. Kerr was deputed to represent us, but lost to the after-mess. Even such small incidents as this attracted an interest just then.

A sounding taken on this day (7 February) showed 2,356 fathoms in position lat. 67° 40' S. and 17° 6' E. long.

At 5.00 a.m. on the following day the ice had shown no signs of opening, so I decided to turn back and look for a more open route to the east or west. We steamed north until noon, when, not caring to expend coal in going away from our objective, I gave orders to reduce steam, and proceeded under sail. The wind was southerly and of moderate strength. I gathered in this way some idea of what ice navigation meant in the days before the introduction of the steam engine. Progress, in spite of favourable winds, was slow, but I was surprised at the effect of a long-continued steady pressure against floes, some of them of quite considerable weight. They gave way slowly before our bows, and the *Quest* slipped of her own will (for she would not answer her helm) into the cracks between them and slowly wedged her way through.

We were now so deep in the pack that there was no appreciable swell, and the *Quest* was consequently steady. I continued the operation which we had been compelled to give up before, and swung out the port life-boat, Worsley being a spectator only. This time there was no accident.

Worsley now started to go on the bridge and keep a watch, though of course he was compelled to take things very quietly, at any rate in so far as his movements were concerned. Quiet in other respects his watch certainly was not, for members of it carried on long-continued, and often argumentative, dialogues, usually at the top of their voices. This was especially the case with one of them, and many times I have leapt on deck with a sense of impending danger, wakened by shouting that proved to be the most trivial of remarks.

The weather was fair during the day, with a moderate southerly wind, no sunshine, and occasional snow squalls. At 7.30 p.m. we had made 35 miles to the northward. This was all to the bad and a bit disappointing. However, we hoped for a change before long. Seals appeared on the floe in quantity during the day and also a number of emperor penguins standing, as usual, stately and alone.

Killers were about and a large number of birds – Antarctic petrels, Wilson's petrels, and a few pretty pure white snow petrels.

During the night (9 February) our luck changed and we were able to make southerly again. Throughout the morning we met loose pack and a number of leads of open water, so that by 12.00 noon we were only 11 miles north of the previous position. We had the same conditions till 4.00 p.m., when we met with dense pack. From the crow's nest, however, I saw 'water sky' to the southward and determined to push on to the utmost ability of the ship. We progressed very slowly and only with the greatest difficulty. It took much hard steaming and consumption of valuable coal for the *Quest* to make any impression on this heavy floe.

The evening of this day was fine, beautiful and still, the sort that takes hold of one and sends mind and memory wandering far afield. There was not a ripple on the small pools between the floes, in which were numbers of small *euphausiæ* swimming about. Four or five seals came about the ship and accompanied us, rubbing themselves against the sides and popping their heads out to regard us with large eyes of a beautiful soft brown colour. They were evidently in a playful mood. On the ice seals are sluggish and very helpless, but in the water they are wonderful, and their swimming movements are most graceful as they dart about twisting and turning and occasionally rising to look round.

Killers were about earlier in the day, but no penguins. An ugly-looking sea leopard put his head out of the water and gazed malignantly over the edge of the floe. In a pool at some distance from the ship I caught sight of a black mass rising and falling, and through my binoculars witnessed what appeared to be a fight between two sea leopards. One of them leapt continually from the water to a height of some 6 feet, and the water was churned to a mass of foam. Suddenly it all ceased. What tragedy was enacted on that perfect evening? On such a night, amid the pure whiteness of one's surroundings, it was hard to realise that in the struggle for existence the unrelenting laws of Nature must hold.

We passed close alongside a floe with a seal on it. I shot it; Macklin jumped off on to the floe and made fast a line; scarcely taking time to stop we hauled it aboard and proceeded on our way. Looking back I saw the surface of the snow smirched with its blood. So Man passed leaving a red stain; and yet but a few moments before I had been moralising on 'Nature red in tooth and claw'.

Very few birds were about, with the exception of snow petrels, a few Antarctic petrels and a single young Dominican gull.

We were pushing on, but the prospect at the moment was not promising. From aloft there was nothing to be seen but ice closely packed and stretching as far as the eye could reach in all directions. I distrust fine weather in the pack; it usually means lowered temperature, close ice and little open water.

10 February opened as a beautiful morning, with bright sunshine. The ice was white and sparkling and the water a deep blue. The air was keen and crisp, and all hands revelled in the improved weather conditions. Less so myself, however, for I feared what was portended. I prefer damp misty weather in the pack, for that means the presence of a considerable amount of open water among the ice and better conditions for navigating, in spite of poor visibility.

The number of seals that accompanied us increased to twenty or more. They refused to leave us, though they occasionally took fright and dashed off with a swirl of water. Seen from aloft a school of seals is a wonderful sight. There was evidently something on the ship's side which had an attraction for them, for they seized the chance of every stop to rise out of the water and nibble at frozen pieces of ice which had formed just above the water-line. The ice on the patent anchors which projected from the hawse holes 2 or 3 feet above the surface especially attracted them, and they collected in clusters of five or six to nibble at it.

In the early morning the pack was composed of dense, heavy old floes, much broken up and bearing the remains of pressure ridges through which progress was very slow. At 7.30 a.m. we entered a lead with surface just freezing over, which offered little resistance to the ship. It was literally full of killers, which crossed and recrossed our bows and 'blew' all about us. Our seal friends did not accompany us into the lead, for which the presence of the killers was no doubt a good and sufficient reason. The crab-eaters seem to have no fear of them while in closely set pack with only small pools of water between the floes, but one rarely sees crab-eaters in larger stretches of water. Occasionally they have been seen in large numbers travelling at high speed. Hurley, the photographer of the last expedition, was able to get a photographic record of them passing close to the ship, the number being so great that the surface of the water was lashed to foam. That they are hunted by the killers is beyond doubt, for one frequently sees them shoot out of water and land with a heavy wallop on a piece of ice, look all round and bump themselves violently along, finally disappearing with a dive into the water again. This differs largely from their ordinary method of landing when they wish to rest. In this case they may be seen first of all rising high out of the water and looking over the edge of the floe, obviously noting its nature, and searching for a shelter from the wind. They land with the same heavy flop, but show none of the excitement when up.

On one occasion at my base in Queen Mary's Land during the Mawson expedition I was standing on an ice foot with Mr Harrison, my biologist, when I saw a killer actually attack a seal which, however, escaped and effected a landing on the ice foot. It was bleeding profusely and was in a very exhausted condition. On close examination we found six large wounds, all of which had penetrated the blubber to the flesh, none of them less than 3 inches deep. At first I was inclined to put the animal out of its misery, but my biologist asked me to let it remain so that we might see whether or not it would recover. It lost an amazing amount of blood, which melted its way into the ice beneath, but on the fourth day it had recovered sufficiently to enter the sea again. Nearly all seals bear the scars of old wounds in vertical strokes down their sides. Wilkins collected a number of skins in which these scars were more extensive than usual, and prepared them for sending back as specimens to the British Museum.

The water in the hold had increased so much by now that it required 4 hours of hard pumping to reduce. It was hard, monotonous work.

In the afternoon we encountered the first Adélie penguin which we had seen on this expedition. It was standing alone on a flat piece of floe, and at sight of us evinced the most marked surprise, looking at us first with one eye and then the other, and finally started towards us at a run. Its waddling gait resembled that of a fat old white-waistcoated gentleman in a desperate hurry. Many times it fell forward, but, picking itself up, hurried on till, reaching the edge of the floe, it tumbled rather than dived into the water. In a few seconds it shot out, to alight upright upon another floe where it continued the chase, but by this time we were drawing away and he gave it up, uttering a last 'Cl-a-a-k,' as much as to say, 'Well, I'm jiggered!' Later we saw many more who showed the same interest, some of them taking to the water and coming about the ship or following in our wake.

We entered a broad belt of large flat pieces of one-year-old floe interspersed with thinner new ice which the *Quest* was able to crack, although it usually required several blows to split it widely enough to let her through.

Following on this we entered a broad lead of open water, but about 10 p.m. encountered very thick and solid floe. Owing to the dim light it was impossible to distinguish rotten mushy ice which we could safely ram from solid pieces which badly jarred the ship. About midnight I lay to till more light should give me a chance to get a better view from the mast-head.

We obtained a sounding of 2,163 fathoms in position lat. 68° 3' S. and 16° 12' E. long., and as soon as the light improved we set off again and spent the whole of 11 February energetically pushing south. The temperature fell rapidly, reaching 18° F at midnight. All the open water started freezing over and was covered with a skin of ice which offered little resistance to the ship when she was well under way, but impeded her considerably when in the dense pack she was forced to be continually stopping and restarting again.

As far as the actual weather was concerned the Antarctic can offer nothing better than that which we were experiencing, fine and clear, the air crisp and cold, yet not sufficiently so to be unpleasant. As the sun sloped down to the horizon with the gentle decline it takes in these latitudes, in contrast to the suddenness with which it disappears in the tropics, we had a beautiful long sunset, the sky taking the most wonderful colours, crimson, amber and gold. The snow surface was a lovely pale pink except where each hummock threw a long black shadow. The surface of the newly freezing parts, still and polished, reflected a pale green. Across the vault of the sky were little fleecy rolls of pink cloud, while nearer the horizon were heavier banks of a deep crimson. Stretching away behind in an ever-narrowing ribbon one saw the lane cut by the passage of the ship disturbed only in the foreground by the ripple of the screw. In contrast to the vivid colouring ahead that astern had the black-and-white effect of a pencil sketch. A perfectly wonderful evening and yet – *timeo Danaos* – I do not like the pack when it smiles. The prospect was not good. I knew that unless we got a rise of temperature things might be bad for us, for it would be quite impossible to forge through the thickening ice, which had the effect of cementing together the heavier floes so that a much more powerful ship than the *Quest* would have been quite unable to make any impression upon them.

There was one thing I knew I must avoid. The *Quest* was not suitable for 'freezing in'. Her shape was not such as would cause her to rise with lateral pressure, and it was almost certain that should she become involved in any of the heavy disturbances which frequently occur she was not likely to survive. The hazard of a boat journey was not likely to meet with the same fortunate ending that we experienced in the *Endurance* expedition, where our escape was indeed a miraculous one. Nearly all our special winter equipment was at Cape Town, which was to have been our base of operations. But weighing even more than these factors was another on which one can only briefly touch: in spite of a solid nucleus of old, tried Antarctic men, and others of proved worth in different fields, there was a discordant element in the personnel which I was anxious to adjust before I exposed the party to the trials and vicissitudes of a Polar winter.

During the afternoon Worsley took a sounding, finding in lat. 68° 52' S. and 16° 55' E. long., a depth of 1,555 fathoms, which showed a shoaling of 608 fathoms in 49 miles of southing. The snapper contained a specimen of grey mud which was handed to the geologist.

I had no rest during the night, for I realised that on the next few hours hung the fate of this effort. Unless the temperature rose and the ice showed signs of loosening it would be necessary to turn back, little though I liked the prospect. I was in the crow's nest the moment that the dim midnight light began to improve, searching all round the horizon with binoculars. Everywhere the ice lay tightly packed and solid. McIlroy reported a further drop of 2° F. The filmy, freezing surface of the leads had become definitely frozen over, so that there was not a drop of water to be seen anywhere. Even to the northward the outlook was bad, and I began to fear that after all we might be beset. That we could push no farther into the heavy ice was certain. I decided to remain where I was for the day, but longer than that would be fatal unless a change occurred in the meantime. I manoeuvred the ship to a large solid floe to enable the scientists to take their instruments over the side, and give all hands a chance of exercise after the cramping spell of shipboard. Nearby a fat Weddell seal lay asleep. I shot it, and McIlroy and Macklin skinned it and took the blubber to the bunkers. Carr, with the assistance of Marr, Naisbitt and Argles, brought in some ice for use as drinking water.

Sea ice, although salt, has the peculiar property that if piled up for two or three days, either naturally as pressure ridges or artificially by heaping up a number of frozen slabs, the salt leaves the upper pieces, which can be melted down and freely used as drinking water. Physicists have not been able to explain fully the phenomenon. It is, however, an easily demonstrable fact, and it is by this property of the ice alone that ships have been able to winter in the pack. In the height of summer, when the sun beats down strongly upon the ice, pools of water form on the surface of the floes. They are fresh and can be used for drinking. It is necessary, however, if water is being taken from this source, to see that the floe is a good solid one, not 'rotted' underneath, in which case it may be brackish. During some of our marches over the ice of the Weddell Sea after the loss of the *Endurance* the going was very bad and the work tremendously hard on account of soft snow, which let the men down to the hips and the dogs to their bellies, and we suffered severely from thirst. When we encountered any of these pools they were freely used by men and dogs for drinking, and we never noticed any salty flavour.

The eating of snow is bad; of this there can be no doubt, though I have seen it stated in the writings of some explorers that it is quite suitable for quenching thirst, and all that is necessary is to overcome the prejudice against its use. The eating of a little snow is harmless, but if one indulges in the practice for a long time the mouth becomes very dry due to the paralysing effect of cold on the salivary glands. The result is that more and more of it is required and the dryness of the mouth is intensified. Any weak spots which may have developed in the teeth are at once discovered, with consequent severe facial neuralgia. The swallowing of the scarcely melted water tends to upset digestion, as is well seen in the United States of America, where the frequent taking of iced drinks is a national practice and dyspepsia is the national complaint. This is not a theoretical observation, for as an enthusiastic young man in my early days of exploration I made the experiment to my sorrow, and I have noted the effects upon other members of the different expeditions which have entered these regions.

Worsley, with the assistance of Dell and Watts, took a sounding, finding bottom at 1,089 fathoms in lat. 69° 17' S. and 17° 9' E. long. This showed a shoaling of 466 fathoms in 29 miles, and certainly indicated the approach to the continental shelf. Once again I climbed to the crow's nest and scanned the horizon to the south. The sky in that direction had a hard white look such as one would get over snow-covered land, but is also seen over densely packed ice. I felt sure that if we could only work our way for another 50 miles to the south we should sight or find indications of land, but no ship ever built could possibly have pushed through the ice to the south of us, not even the most powerful ice-breakers.

Of animal and bird life there was very little, but though if present they would have been additional evidence in favour of the proximity of land, their absence did not necessarily negative it.

Looking backwards to the north I saw that the ice in that direction, though less dense than that to the south, was settling firm and hard, and I decided that as soon as the scientific staff had completed their observations I must beat a hasty and energetic retreat.

Few people can realise what an effort it had been to force the little *Quest* to this position. It was hard to have to turn back. It was necessary, however, to make every effort to escape this freeze up, but once in loose pack I was determined to seize the first chance to push south again.

CHAPTER 7

The Ice

At about 4.00 p.m. on 12 February, having come to my decision, I blew the steam whistle for the recall of all hands, who had thoroughly enjoyed their day on the ice. Query had had a splendid time in spite of having once or twice fallen through mushy holes into freezing water, and he came back to the ship thoroughly tired from the unwonted exercise.

We had some difficulty in getting under way, but once the ship had gathered momentum she was able to push on through the new ice. Navigation required the utmost watchfulness and care; we could not afford to delay, for minutes totalled up, and the ice was increasing hourly in thickness. Every stop added to the difficulties of getting under way again. I must pay a high tribute to the unremitting energy and unfailing resource of Worsley and Jeffrey at this critical period as we forced our way from the closing grip of the pack. Macklin writes in his diary:

The way in which the *Quest* is made to push ahead and to dodge and wriggle past the most awkward places is wonderful. Kerr is excelling himself below – I hope he does not bust her up, for these engines have given at one time and another a lot of trouble. It is interesting to compare the different watches at work. Commander Wild goes about the job quietly and steadily, without fuss or shouting, and undoubtedly makes the best headway. Old Wuzzles (Worsley) also goes ahead energetically, but to an accompaniment of noise that might waken the dead, for which, perhaps, he is less responsible than some members of his watch. Jeffrey also makes surprisingly good headway, with a running commentary usually the reverse of complimentary on all things frozen.

I was wakened at 4.00 on the following morning by McLeod, who shouted in at my door, 'One bell and the ship's afire!' In a moment I was out of bed and on deck, to find dense smoke and flame ascending from what appeared to be the engine-room skylight. Rushing to the engine-room door, I was met by Smith, who said that everything was all right below. The flames were leaping up alongside the funnel. I went up on to the bridge and shouted to the other members of my watch who had turned out to get Pyrene extinguishers, of which we kept a number always on hand. We squirted their contents vigorously into the midst of the flames, and soon had them subdued, when I discovered that the cause of the trouble lay in some cork fenders and coils of tarry rope which had been placed against the funnel on the previous day. The flames had spread to two large wooden sidelight boards and to some canvas gear. Our portable hand-sounding machine was also involved, and was, unfortunately, rendered almost useless. The fire, while it lasted, was a brisk one, and had we been compelled to rely on the old hose system for its extinction there is no doubt that it would have proved serious. The rapidity with which we were able to control it speaks much for the efficacy of the extinguishers in use, which were of the carbon-dioxide-producing type.

Having leapt straight from our bunks, we were exceedingly lightly clothed, and, now that the excitement was over, we noticed the cold atmosphere and scampered off to garb ourselves more warmly.

We continued vigorously pushing north all day. Numerous crab-eater seals were seen, many of them on our direct route; but although I was anxious to lay in a store of their blubber I did not stop. We saw also a number of emperor penguins. Bird life, as I have said, had been very scarce, and represented only by snow petrels, a number of which, outlined in silvery whiteness against the blue of the sky as they passed overhead on their way south, presented a very beautiful picture.

In the evening we passed by a floe on which five large seals lay asleep, and I determined to stop for a short time and take them up. There is no difficulty in killing and obtaining any number of Antarctic seals, no matter how small the floe they are on, provided one approaches them quietly and gets within a range at which they can be picked off rapidly and with certainty one after the other. On this occasion I gave the word to withhold fire till we were close alongside, but Douglas, apparently unable to restrain his impetuosity, fired too soon and succeeded in wounding one, which heaved itself about frantically and startled the others to sudden wakefulness. To make matters worse, Douglas continued firing, and some of them dived into the sea. It is a characteristic of these seals that if wounded they prefer to be on a floe, and all but one came back again, when they were properly dispatched and hoisted aboard for removal of their blubber. The moment they were aboard I set off again, scarcely waiting for the men on the floe, who scrambled up as the ship was moving away.

There is a great difference between Arctic and Antarctic seals. In the North the seal has always to be on the look out for the polar bear, and when it comes ashore to sleep does so fitfully, frequently raising its head to look about, and slipping back to the water on the least alarm. Its enemies are above and not below water. The contrary holds in the Antarctic, where the seals are vigorously preyed upon by the killers and sea leopards. On the surface, however, they have no enemies, and although they take fright if approached quickly or noisily, one can, by moving quietly, get so close to them that they can, if so desired, be clubbed instead of shot. This clubbing should be done with a heavy instrument, such as the loom of an oar, and the point to be aimed at is the nose. If the blow is delivered accurately and with sufficient weight, the seal is immediately rendered unconscious, after which the jugular veins and the main arteries of the neck are severed with a knife, without one of which at his belt no good sailor or explorer goes anywhere. In any case the carcass of the seal should always be thoroughly bled. Another useful instrument by which the animal can be instantaneously killed is an Alpine ice pick, the point being driven by a smart downward tap through the vault of the skull. This has the disadvantage of destroying the brain, which we always used for cooking, and is, indeed, the greatest dainty provided by these animals. The method of killing seals which we always adopted when we had plenty of ammunition was to shoot them. I always aim at the neck, just behind the skull, where many vital structures are brought into close relationship. Death is instantaneous, bleeding takes place freely, and the brain is not destroyed.

Macklin sustained a nasty cut during the flensing, running his hand off the haft of the knife on to the blade. He rather prided himself on his knives, on which he kept a razor edge, and on his flensing, and I think he felt annoyed at his clumsiness, for it was with an almost shamefaced air that he went to McIlroy to get his hand bound up.

The art of keeping a hunting-knife in really good order is one which few people understand. A keen edge is essential for neat and rapid work, yet I have seen many people hacking laboriously away with a blade which would scarcely penetrate butter. I always carry a pocket carborundum stone, and I carefully clean and sharpen my knife every time I use it. Before using the stone it is important to see that there is no blood or blubber remaining on the blade. After a heavy day's flensing it may take from half an hour to an hour to bring the edge to perfection again, and I am always amused at the man who brings something resembling a butcher's steel and says: 'You might just sharpen that for me, will you?'

Another art is the making of a good leather sheath, for that is a thing one cannot buy. It is careful and continued attention to small things that makes for efficiency at this kind of work.

It did not get completely dark at midnight. The increasing light in the early morning produced a wonderful sunrise. Owing to the gradual upward curve of the sun in these latitudes, the effects last for hours and change slowly, contrasting strongly with the evanescent tropical skies, where the sun rises abruptly above the horizon and in the evening falls back so suddenly that there is no twilight. The sky to the eastward was lit up with the most delicate and beautiful colours, which were reflected on the surface of the floe. The old floes passed slowly from pale pink to crimson and, as the sun came over the rim, to the palest and most delicate heliotrope. The darker newly frozen ice changed from bronze to light apple-green. To the westward a large golden moon was poised in a cloudless sky, turning the floes to the palest of gold. No words of mine can adequately convey the beauty of such a morning.

These days impressed themselves vividly in one's memory, which has the knack of picking out the brighter spots in the greyness of these regions. I think it is impressions like these which, working perhaps subconsciously, produce that haunting restlessness which makes one feel suddenly, and without apparent cause, dissatisfied with civilisation, its veneer and artificiality, its restrictions and its ugliness. Certain it is that few people who have travelled away from the beaten track and spent long, unbroken periods face to face with Nature can hope to escape the sudden feelings of restlessness and disquietude which come upon one without warning and drive one to pacing up and down, to face the rain on a gusty night, or do anything so long as one can be alone for a while. I think that every living being has at one time or another experienced that curious feeling – it is hard to say of what exactly – a sort of wondering lostness that comes over one in certain circumstances. In our own country one feels it on fine nights in the gloaming, when everything is stilled and the silence unbroken save by the full-throated song of some bird, which seems only to accentuate it. One feels something of it even in the cities in the quiet of a summer evening, with the smoke of countless chimneys winding lazily upwards, but it is in the great untouched areas of the earth that it makes its deepest impression and grips one with the greatest intensity.

It has been my fortune to visit many parts of the world, and I can recall wonderful evenings in many places which have created a deep impression on me, but there particularly stand out in my mind's eye some of the long Antarctic autumn twilights too beautiful to describe. I have seen the most materialistic and unimpressionable of men strung to an absolute silence, scarcely daring to breathe, filled with something intangible and inexplicable. The very sledge dogs stand stock still, gazing intently into the farness, ears cocked, listening – for what? Suddenly the spell is broken and with a deep breath one turns again to work.

We pushed on and on throughout the 14th and made on the whole pretty good headway. I stopped just long enough to let Worsley take a sounding, depth 1,925 fathoms (lat. 68° 21' S. and 16° 0' E. long.). With every hour the ice increased in thickness and the *Quest* had all she could do to push forward. Work at the wheel was strenuous, for in the new ice the ship did not make a straight track, but swerved all the time from side to side, and the helm had to be swung repeatedly in either direction to check the deviation.

About midday we encountered heavy floe against which we made poor headway, and I began to realise that it would be touch and go as to whether we would get out or not. I sent for Kerr and told him to give his engines all they would stand. He increased the pressure of steam, and the ship began to make headway slowly but surely.

In the early afternoon the weather changed. McIlroy reported a rise of temperature to 22° F, and there was a swell, very faint but quite noticeable. A skua gull and a giant petrel appeared. All these signs were good, indicating a more open pack ahead of us and open water within reasonable distance.

By 8.00 p.m. we were once more making good headway, and I went below, to fall soundly asleep after my days of anxiety and broken rest.

Owing to the darkness we were compelled to heave to for two hours at midnight, for with the northing we had made there was less daylight, and one cannot distinguish in the dim light between rotten floes and solid ones, which if rammed would fetch up the ship all standing and possibly start the timbers and carry away a certain amount of gear.

The temperature had risen to 24° F, but when I came on deck in the early morning of the 15th the outlook was not good. The air was not warm enough to prevent freezing of the ice, and from the mast-head I saw heavy pack to the northward. There was one good sign, however, and that was an increased northerly swell coming along in slow leisurely rolls. It is a fine sight to see a huge field of ice rising and falling in this manner.

We pushed energetically on and later in the day we entered loose open pack. I had no doubt now that we were out of danger of being beset. It was a relief to be able to relax a little after the constant effort of the last fortnight.

Although we were now free from danger of being beset we had entered a new set of conditions which were by no means a sinecure. The ice had the effect of deadening swell, but the pieces of floe about the pack edge were often thrown into violent motion and made to bump and grind together by the action of the sea. By coming north also we were losing daylight, and we had now from two to three hours of darkness to contend with each day. Navigation under these circumstances required constant care and watchfulness, so that I had still to maintain a pretty active vigilance. For much of our journey about the northern limits of the pack I was compelled for the sake of economy to shut off steam and proceed under sail only, which gave me some idea of the difficulties which Bellingshausen and Biscoe had to contend with, and enabled me to appreciate their reticence to push deeply into the ice. To both of these predecessors I must pay a tribute of the highest praise for their determined and persevering work about this segment. In the whole of my experience as a seaman I have never encountered a part of the world where weather and sea conditions generally are so uncomfortable. Periods of gale, with heavy swell and grinding floe, when the outlook is obscured by driving wind and blinding snow squalls, alternate with periods of calm, when fog settles in a dense pall of fine mist which forms heavy rime on all spars and running gear, and freezing solid interferes greatly with their working. It takes days for the huge rollers to subside, and the floes grind and groan incessantly. I had always the feeling that I could raise steam at short notice, but these early explorers were dependent entirely on winds, which blow either too hard or not hard enough, and never seem to strike the happy medium. To John Biscoe, British seaman, the trip must have been one of long continued struggle, for he was ill equipped, scurvy set in and he lost the greater part of the crews of both his vessels. On his own ship, the *Tula*, there were only three men able to stand when the ship reached Hobart, and on the *Lively* only three were alive when she reached Port Philip. His story, told baldly, makes enthralling reading for those who can appreciate it.

We made good progress to the northward, the day's run at noon on the 16th being estimated by Worsley at 77 miles. We passed through much open water with a strong easterly swell, but encountered also several belts of heavy, closely packed ice consisting of old floe which had undergone heavy pressure. Owing to the swell it was impossible to avoid some severe bumps. Birds were about in large numbers, including Antarctic petrels, giant petrels and terns. We saw numerous killers, and witnessed a most interesting display by two of them which were playing and disporting themselves on the surface, flinging their huge bulks high into the air, and creating a tremendous turmoil in the water. Crab-eaters were seen in numbers on the floes, sometimes singly, often in bunches of five or six. We saw no penguins or snow petrels. Worsley reported a single Mother Carey's Chicken as having been about. They all pointed to the proximity of open ocean, and I expected that we should be clear of ice by next day.

A sounding taken in lat. 67° 07' S. and 14° 29' E. long. gave a depth of 2,341 fathoms.

In the evening we again entered an area of heavy old floes, which moved about and pressed together in the swell. Snow squalls and dim light made the navigation of them a difficult matter, but by noon of the following day we had got clear of pack and were in open water with a clear sky to the northward. Numerous solitary pieces of floe and heavy growlers were still dotted about. Growlers are heavy, solid pieces of ice, grey or greenish-grey in colour, which float with their tops just awash. They are consequently difficult to see, especially in poor light, and a close watch has always to be kept for them.

Some of the floes carried passengers in the shape of crab-eater seals. We saw a number of huge blue whales, which are recognised by their large size, high vertical spout which opens out into a dense cloud of spray, and the presence of a fin. Killers also were about in large numbers.

In the early morning of the 18th we turned south again in another attempt to push through to land or ice barrier. From the lateness of the season we knew this must necessarily be the last attempt for this year.

We had not proceeded many miles when we again encountered pack, which compelled us to take a south-westerly direction, passing through a good deal of brash, but keeping clear of heavy ice. The weather was thick and snowy. Later we encountered some very old floes full of small caves, and with well-defined necks where the sea had worn them away by the continual wash, so that they resembled gigantic mushrooms growing from the surface of the water.

Marr was taken ill at this time with sore throat and high temperature. He said nothing of the condition himself and would have struggled on had not Dell informed Macklin that he looked a bit sick. He is a hardy youngster and showed his contempt for the cold by walking about inadequately clothed. He had a vivid maroon-coloured muffler, beautifully soft and warm. I once asked him if it was a present from his best girl.

'Yes,' he replied, 'from my mother.' I threatened him that if he appeared without this round his neck in future I would pack him off to bed and keep him there. The doctors reported that his condition was not serious, and a day or two in bed would put him right again.

We continued in a southerly direction till the night of the 20th, when we met heavy pack which compelled us to turn west. At noon on the 21st we were forced to come back in a north-westerly direction. In the evening we skirted a line of ice running west-south-west, and on the morning of the 22nd again entered open sea.

The 22nd was Worsley's birthday. He had reached his fiftieth milestone, but could easily have passed for ten years less. We celebrated the occasion by an extra special spread at which, to the surprise and (needless to say) delight, of nearly everyone, some bottles of beer materialised. The *pièce de résistance* was a large pink cake bearing in sugar the inscription 'Wuzzles' 21st'. He was called upon to cut it himself, and was given a large steel chopper with which to do it. Having performed a Maori war dance, he proceeded to cut it into slices. It proved to be a bit hard, so he attempted to lift it to a better position, to find, to his amazement, that he could scarcely budge it. The cake turned out to be a 56-lb sinker, which Green had covered with sugar. However, a proper cake was forthcoming, and the evening was spent merrily.

The *Quest* was not a comfortable ship, and there was little to take the mind from general routine and the business in hand. The continuous struggle with the pack became after a time very exhausting, and there was a chance also of its becoming something of an obsession. Consequently, occasions such as birthdays, which provided a diversion and helped to lift the men out of themselves, were of the greatest value.

23 February was a dull grey day. We hoisted the square sail at daybreak and continued to run off before a strong easterly wind.

With sails set there was great difficulty in getting the wardroom stove to burn, for both topsail and square sail created a powerful and baffling down draught for which we designed and made all sorts and shapes of cowls, but without much success. The wardroom became filled with dense acrid smoke, and the fire was generally allowed to go out when the temperature fell so much that no one could use it to sit about, and those taking their watch below were driven to their bunks. Wilkins and Douglas in the forecastle had the same difficulty. Wilkins, ever resourceful, built a cowl, but it fouled the sheet of the forestay sail and was swept away. Nothing daunted, he built another, which met the same fate. With exemplary patience he built a new one each time the other was lost! We did our best to protect the cowls when setting or taking in sail, but in heavy winds, when the square sail was let go at the run, it was almost impossible to do so.

Since the evening of the 21st we had made in a west to west-south-westerly direction, but, seeing what appeared to be open seas with sky to the horizon a deep black, I now turned south again. Within an hour, however, we met with small pieces of ice, which became more numerous as we proceeded. We then entered an area of sea full of small round pieces, like snowballs, covered with a fine powdery ice. Snow settling on this area gave it the appearance of a 'sea of milk'. The swell continued, but the surface was like oil, unbroken by a single ripple. We passed from this into a belt where the surface was just beginning to freeze, forming the thinnest possible film of ice. The snow on this gave the impression of a grey sea. Visibility, owing to the snow which fell quietly and continuously, was poor. The whole outlook gave a curious impression of greyness, grey sea, grey sky, and everything grey wherever one looked.

As we progressed still farther the filmy surface was replaced by definite pancake formation. Among the pancakes were numerous heavy old lumps, much water-worn at sea level, but heavy underneath with long projecting tongues.

The night was cold and snowy and the decks became covered with a very slippery slush on which, with the rolling of the ship, it was not easy to keep a footing. We took in sail, a cold and unpleasant job because all spars, sails and running gear had become coated with a thick covering of ice.

Dinner that night was a cold business, and the dullness of the day and general outlook had rather damped our spirits. Macklin writes on this date:

> Owing to the stove refusing to burn, the wardroom was cold, and we gathered round the dinner-table feeling pretty miserable. Green had prepared a big dish of hot potatoes in their jackets. I placed the biggest I could find under my jersey and it warmed me up finely. I kept moving it round so as to warm as much of my body as possible, and finally ate it, warming also my inside. One has to be economical these hard times.

As the light failed the ice began to thicken, and as the swell was causing the floes to grind heavily together I lay to till daybreak. All night long we heard the moaning and complaining of the grinding floes, a number of which, with long underwater tongues, drifted down upon us, causing the ship to take some very bad bumps. To economise our now much-depleted coal I had given Kerr instructions to let the steam fall off, and we had to be constantly sheeting home the topsail and pointing the yards to get her to fall away from our unpleasant neighbours, contact with which might prove dangerous.

The floes looked very weird in the darkness as they surged up on the swell and fell back again into the trough of the sea, the water sucking and gurgling among the cracks and chasms and making the most uncanny noises.

At daybreak on the 24th steam was raised and we continued south, pushing through pancake ice which contained many heavy floes. Seen from aloft the pancake formation makes a most beautiful mosaic. Much of our finest art is surpassed by Nature, and in these southern regions there is much to attract those who have an artistic temperament.

The ice rapidly increased in thickness, and by noon we were again held up by dense impenetrable pack in position lat. 68° 32' S. and 0° 5' E. long. To the south the outlook was hopeless. I climbed to the crow's nest to scan the horizon to the southward, but saw only closely packed and heavy ice stretching away to the horizon, while in the sky was a strongly marked ice-blink. It was bitterly disappointing. There was no alternative but to retrace our steps and work to the westward. I went below, where once more I pulled out all the charts and examined again the records of old explorers in these regions. I had a long talk with Worsley and Kerr. The season was well advanced; the *Quest* had neither the driving power nor the amount of coal to enable me to batter hard at heavy floe. As a matter of fact, I do not think that any ship, however powerful, could have made any impression on the stuff to the south of us. As far as finding land in this segment was concerned I felt that we had shot our bolt. I was, however, determined to have another try, and to make Cape Town my base, where I could overhaul and refit my ship, where there was a big supply of good winter stores and equipment, and where I could readjust the personnel. I intended to make the start early in the season, and I felt confident that with the time to spare to enable us to wait for the ice to move we should reach new land.

My intention was now to make as directly as possible for the charted position of 'Ross's Appearance of Land', the accuracy of which I hoped either to verify or to disprove, and to take a series of soundings on the spot. We should by that time be very short of coal and consequently also in need of ballast. I determined, therefore, to call at Elephant Island, where I felt sure we would find sea-elephants in sufficient numbers to supply us with blubber as fuel. Blubber is by no means an ideal form of fuel for the furnace, for it burns with a fierce, hot flame and is very messy. Mixed judiciously with coal, however, I knew it would materially help to spin out the supply. I hoped, also, to be able to take aboard a quantity of sand or shingle as ballast. From there I proposed proceeding to Deception Island to coal, and thence return to South Georgia.

At this point I must mention that which is not a pleasant subject, but one which should not be glossed over, because it indicates what is a most important feature in the preparation for a Polar expedition: the choice of personnel. It is a matter which requires the greatest possible care, for one discordant or unadaptable spirit can do a vast amount of harm in infecting others.

There can be no doubt that since leaving South Georgia we had had a very wearing time and one which tried the temper and patience of all hands. It must be admitted that before leaving England the arrangements for the comfort of the personnel had in some directions been overlooked, and long-continued discomfort is bound sooner or later to have an effect upon the temper. Life on board ship entails a certain amount of dull routine, providing at times an amount of exhausting work but very little active exercise. We had experienced long spells of bad weather, with a large proportion of dull, grey days and little sunshine. I therefore expected and was prepared to find that individuals would experience periods of irritability, and that things would not always run as smoothly as might be desired. The personnel had been selected from men of marked individual character, and in order that a body of men of this type shall be able to live in absolute harmony over a long period of time it is necessary that an outstanding quality of each shall be a good 'give and take' sporting spirit. The effect of one or two selfish and discordant natures can easily be understood. There was surprisingly little friction among the various members of the expedition, which is due largely to the sound qualities of the nucleus of old, tried men.

I began to be aware, however, about this time of an amount of dissatisfaction and grumbling occurring in both the forward and after-messes that I did not like. Men who sat at table with me and to a certain extent enjoyed my confidence discussed and freely criticised expedition affairs with members of the after-mess. Of this I had ample confirmation. Some of those thus employed were officers who from their position on the ship should have been my most loyal supporters. In the after-mess also I was surprised to find that the men affected were those in whom I had placed the most implicit trust. It was a condition of things that required prompt measures. I assembled each mess in turn, and going straight to the point told them that further continuance would be met with the most drastic treatment. I pointed out that although I would at all times welcome suggestions from the officers and scientific staff, and would consider any reasonable complaints, I could consider no selfish or individual interests, and my own decision must be final and end discussion of the matter.

I was glad to notice an immediate improvement.

Above: Ernest Shackleton. (Library of Congress)

Below: Grytviken harbour, South Georgia, in 1914. (Frank Hurley)

Above: A whale on the flensing pan at Grytviken whaling station, South Georgia, 1916. (Edward Binnie)

Below: The memorial cross set up for Shackleton by the crew of the *Quest*, seen in 1988/89. (NOAA)

Above: The midnight sun on the Antarctic ice. (Library of Congress)

Below: Seals on pancake ice, Antarctica. (Library of Congress)

Above: The approach to Elephant Island, as seen in 1962. (NOAA)

Below: Cape Wild, Elephant Island. (Library of Congress)

Above: Another view of Cape Wild, Elephant Island. (Library of Congress)

Below: Groote Schuur, Cape Town, where Wild and his companions were entertained by General Smuts, the Prime Minister of South Africa, and his wife. (Library of Congress)

On 25 February we passed through a lot of loose ice, and in the evening entered a patch of heavy, old, deeply stained diatomaceous floes. Scores of crab-eater seals lay asleep on them in batches of five or six. Passing close to one piece on which six were lying in a clump, I laid the ship alongside and with my heavy rifle shot them all. I sent Macklin, with Douglas and Argles, on to the floe to secure them, which is best done by passing a strop round the body and tightening it close up under the flippers. Having fixed up a block and tackle we hauled them aboard – an awkward job on account of the swell in which the *Quest* rolled heavily. In the subsequent flensing Douglas jabbed his knee, the knife penetrating the joint. The wound itself was small, but Macklin insisted on absolute rest until he could be sure that there was no infection. Carr also cut his finger. These accidents were largely due to the movement of the ship, which rendered the operation a difficult one. Two inexperienced men wielding their knives on the same seal are a source of danger to each other, for with the sweeping strokes employed there is the chance of a mutilating cut. I always insisted in cases like this that only one man at a time should have a knife in his hand.

Watts succeeded in getting Greenwich time by wireless from Rio de Janeiro, which enabled us to check our chronometers. Long-distance messages were not easily obtained owing to bad atmospheric conditions, which produce loud noises in the ear-pieces.

By 28 February, as a result of our depleted bunkers, the ship was very light and ill-ballasted. I told Worsley to remove from the decks all heavy gear and place it below, for which purpose I arranged to clear the coal from the forward part of the bunkers and put it aft into the side pockets. I divided the men into two working parties, one to go down in the morning, consisting of McIlroy, Marr, Macklin and Dell, and one to work in the afternoon, of Wilkins, Carr, McLeod and Watts. So much vigour did the morning party put into this work, however, that at lunch-time there was little for the others to do beyond stow the gear from above.

1 March was another fine day, and we took full advantage of it to hang up the spare sails to dry prior to placing them below. All hands seized the opportunity to put out blankets and bedding for an airing.

The deck clearance made a wonderful improvement to the ship. Unfortunately, it made it necessary that we should have the gear up again when we coaled at Deception Island.

Worsley obtained a sounding of 2,762 fathoms in position lat. 65° 22' S. and 10° 17' W. long.

In the late afternoon we passed a very curious berg composed of a solid mass with a long, upright tooth-like portion separated from it on the surface by 10 or 20 yards of water. Perched on it were several Antarctic petrels and one solitary ringed penguin. How the latter ever attained its position is a mystery, for the sides of the berg were steep and precipitous.

On Saturday 4 March, there was a strong north-east to easterly wind, with heavy swell, and the motion of the *Quest* was simply awful, so bad, indeed, that in spite of our long time at sea several of the party were sea-sick. Macklin writes under this date:

It has been impossible to stand without holding firmly to some support, and movement about the ship can only be accomplished by sudden jerks and starts, with hurried gropings for something to catch hold of. A wet, snowy slush on the deck does not help matters. Argles was thrown off his feet and, crashing across the deck, fetched up on the other side against a bucket, severely bruising face, chest and hands. Meals are a screaming comedy or a tragedy, as you like to take them; everything placed on the table promptly charges for the scuppers, and fiddles are almost useless. McIlroy, 'Kraskie', Kerr and myself were sitting on a wooden bench, secured to the floor, holding on to plates and spoons, and endeavouring to guide some food into our mouths. Suddenly, during a particularly violent roll, the bench was torn from its fastenings, and we were thrown backwards into the lee of the wardroom, intimately mixed with knives, forks, plates and treacle dough. During the evening watch Commander Wild was talking to Mick and myself on the bridge when suddenly he shot away into the darkness, and a few moments later sounds the reverse of complimentary were heard issuing from the end of the bridge-house. Ross brought some tea a few minutes later, apologising for having spilled much of it *en route*. He, too, suddenly disappeared in darkness, and when he next materialised there was less tea than ever, but it was a good effort his getting it there at all. When I went below I saw Wuzzles trying to work out his calculations on the wardroom table, with first a book, then a pencil or a ruler shooting suddenly to the floor. The *Quest* is a little 'she-devil', lively as they are made. She has many uncomplimentary things said of her, and deserves all of them.

On 5 March we passed within sight of several large and beautiful bergs emerging from the Weddell Sea, the mouth of which we were now crossing, and met with heavier floes than we had hitherto encountered. On the 9th we ran into broad belts of heavy ice. I took this chance of 'watering' ship, placing her alongside a floe with some solid pieces of blue ice. Owing to the swell the ship would not lie comfortably, and so, taking with me Macklin, Carr and Douglas, I went off to secure her fore and aft. We broke up and passed aboard a considerable quantity of fresh ice. The men thoroughly enjoy a job of this nature and make a great joke of it. On this occasion they broke the ice into fragments of convenient weight and threw them at Jeffrey, who had undertaken to catch them all, subjecting him to a regular fusillade from which it was all he could do to defend himself. On the floe there was a seal which had come up to sleep, and we took this also. While this work was going on, Worsley took a sounding, finding in position lat. 66° 5' S. and 38° 16' W. long., 2,521 fathoms.

Query came on to the floe, where he took a tremendous interest in a killer which was swimming about. The killer rose close to the floe and 'blew' with such a blast that Query tucked in his tail and ran for dear life – much to our amusement.

On Friday 10 March, we encountered still heavier belts, and were compelled to take a north-easterly direction. In the evening it turned much colder, the temperature dropping to 17° F.

A number of Adélie penguins were seen on the floe. Seals were scarce, only one being seen. Snow and Antarctic petrels flew about the ship in considerable numbers.

During the night we continued to push in a north-easterly direction, meeting very heavy broken-up old Weddell Sea floe. The temperature rose again to 24° F. A strong easterly wind was blowing, with snow, which made it difficult to see far in any direction.

Water was again reported in the hold to the level of the kelson, and required three hours' additional pumping to reduce.

At 6.00 p.m. the snow thickened so much that we could see nothing, and so lay to for the night. All about we heard the cries of Adélie penguins. The wind and snow continued all night, but at 4.30 a.m. on the 12th we started off again, pushing through thick pack composed of heavy old Weddell Sea floe with the water in between freezing solidly, making headway difficult. Often during this period I bemoaned to myself the low driving power of the *Quest*. With the onset of darkness we again lay to. During the night Marr, who was now a trustworthy seaman, was on the look out. He makes the following entry in his diary: 'There was no one to talk to and all round lay that vast cold wilderness of ice. Never in my life have I felt so lonely…' This is indeed a feeling which one gets frequently in these regions, especially at night – a great sense of loneliness such as I have never felt elsewhere. On Monday 13 March, the temperature dropped during the night to 8° F, and the sea froze solidly about the ship. In the strong wind, with jib and mizen set, there was just enough way to keep the ship from being beset. About 4.00 a.m., however, she did become fast, but as soon as daylight came in we got up steam and proceeded as rapidly as possible. The skies cleared beautifully, but the sea continued to freeze so swiftly and solidly that we had the greatest difficulty in getting ahead, and many times we had to back off into our own water to get up sufficient impetus to break through. How we got the *Quest* along at all I cannot understand.

The outlook was very bad. Worsley and I spent long hours aloft searching for signs of land in the direction of 'Ross's Appearance', but though it was a beautifully clear day, we could see no indication of it. Ahead of us the ice stretched thick and solid as far as we could see. Headway became more and more difficult, and soon I saw that it would be useless to attempt to push on. A sounding showed 2,331 fathoms of water in lat. 64° 11' S. and 46° 4' W. long., which did not indicate the proximity of land. Owing to the low driving power of the ship I could make no impression through the ice ahead, nor could I afford the coal for prolonged ramming. It seemed to me that we were in imminent danger of being beset, and I decided that we must push north in the hope of meeting more open pack. I had to give up all thought of attempting to return to 'Ross's Appearance', because I was now desperately short of fuel, and unless we could get blubber at Elephant Island we should be in a bad way.

About us during the day were numerous Adélie penguins, occurring in twos and threes, and in a few larger clusters of forty or more. None of the floes bearing the large clusters were accessible to the ship, or I would have taken them up, for their skins burn well. Crab-eaters were scarce. Seeing two on a floe, with about a dozen penguins, we lay alongside. Argles jumped off to try and catch one, but in the soft snow the penguin had the advantage, and Argles' efforts were very amusing to the rest of us. He is an active fellow, however, and was at last successful, bringing a squawking young Adélie in his arms to the ship, where Query paid it marked attention. We killed the rest of them, also the seals, and put them aboard the ship. Owing to the darkness, we lay to at night in rapidly freezing ice with the outlook as regards escape not at all promising, and at 4.30 the next morning we raised full pressure of steam and attempted to get away. After two hours of hard ramming we had made so little headway that I gave up the attempt and lay to alongside a floe. By breakfast it had become apparent that we were fast, hard frozen in. The temperature had dropped to 6.5° F.

It blew hard all day. Birds with the exception of a few snow petrels disappeared early. Macklin says of these birds:

I always regard the snow petrel as symbolic of the Spirit of the Pack, for they are never entirely absent, in fair weather or foul. Even in winter when all is dark one can hear the gentle 'whisp-whisp' of their wings as they fly close. Their pure white bodies with jet black beak and legs give them a beautiful appearance when seen at a distance, but when gathered about a piece of offal at closer range, there is something unpleasant and almost evil in their appearance, with their sinister curved beaks, hard bright eyes and pock-toed waddling gait. They are seen at their best on a bright clear day with a background of blue sky. Like the pack they can give an attractive impression or a most unpleasant one.

Killers were about during the day.

We were still solidly frozen in on the 15th. A fairly strong westerly wind blew with a temperature of 8.5° F. The day was bright and clear, and Jeffrey and Douglas took theodolite and dip circle on to the floe for observations, which were impossible on a moving deck. In the morning I put all hands to cleaning up the ship and pumping her dry, a process which took two hours daily. While engaged in this a killer appeared in a small lead which had formed on the port bow, and continued to swim slowly backwards and forwards, affording us an excellent close view. His motion through the water was a marvel of graceful movement, but in other respects he was an ugly looking monster, with slightly underhung jaw and a small wicked eye which gave him a very evil appearance. His back and flanks were covered with large brown-coloured patches, probably parasitic. I called Marr's attention to him; he remarked that it did not make him feel inclined to fall overboard.

At noon Worsley got an observation of the sun and worked out a position which showed a drift of 18 miles in direction N. 43° E. This was very encouraging, for I knew that if it continued we should not be long in reaching a point at which the floe would begin to open up and give us a chance to get away. A sounding gave 2,321 fathoms in lat. 63° 51' S. and 45° 13' W. long. The steam pipe of the sounding machine froze, so that Dell was unable to get in the wire, which was left all night in the hope of getting it in next morning. By daylight, however, the ship had altered her position relative to the hole in the ice by about 50 yards and the wire was as taut as a harp string. I made an effort to clear it with an ice-axe, but did not succeed in doing so. This single sounding wire held the weight of the ship, maintaining it and the floe in the same relative positions for forty-eight hours before finally parting. It was not subjected to any jerking strain, but this test says much for its strength.

We remained frozen in till 21 March. At times I felt very anxious, for with the lateness of the season, failing light and shortage of coal, I realised that our position might turn out to be a very awkward one. Indeed things looked so bad on the sixth day that I made up my mind that we might remain a long time before breaking free, and told Macklin, in dealing with the issue of stores and equipment, to have in mind the possibility of wintering. I had taken care to provision the ship with a view to this eventuality, but it would have necessitated the most rigid economy and a much more monotonous dietary than we had hitherto enjoyed, for it must be remembered that the bulk of our equipment was awaiting us in Cape Town. I did not, however, mention the possibility to the men, for they seemed quite to enjoy the break from routine, and I did not wish their minds to be occupied with any sort of gloomy forebodings. I encouraged them to amuse themselves in any way they could by taking walks out over the floes and by playing football. They were not slow to avail themselves of the opportunity. On one occasion I watched Douglas, Argles, Carr and Macklin earnestly engaged in a strange pastime, which more resembled a free fight than anything, and consisted of flinging themselves at one another and grappling and wrestling fiercely in the snow. At the finish they all bore marks of the contest, Douglas with an eye that threatened closure within a few days. They informed me that they had been playing *American* football, and said they enjoyed it!

'Soccer' was the favourite game. I frequently joined in, as did Worsley, whose fiftieth birthday we had celebrated a short while before, but who was by no means the least active. The games were marked by many amusing incidents. On one occasion Naisbitt while chasing the ball sank suddenly from view through a hole in the ice, from which he was promptly rescued, soon to be covered with a coating of icicles. On another day we were visited by a small Adélie penguin which spotted us from a floe some distance away, and came running as fast as his short legs would carry him to join in the game. What he thought of it all I do not know, but he insisted on taking an active part, neglecting the ball and fiercely attacking with beak and flippers any man who came near. Query took a great interest in the visitor, but was fiercely repulsed when he showed too marked an inquisitiveness. In the ordinary way too inquisitive penguins pay for their temerity with their lives and go to swell the larder, but this little fellow showed such pluck and sportiveness that we let him go free. He waddled off to join his companions, to whom, no doubt, he would spin the most marvellous yarn.

In honour of our two Irishmen, Jeffrey and McIlroy, we celebrated St Patrick's Day with a specially good dinner, for which Green had produced some shamrock-shaped scones tied up with green ribbon. I was also able to produce some cigars and a bottle which we cracked for the occasion.

On the 18th Worsley and Wilkins put down a dredge with reversing thermometer attached. At first steam was used for heaving up, but this proving very slow we fell back on man power. It was hard work, but the men, as they always do on these occasions, threw themselves into it with a will, and we soon brought it to the surface. We obtained fifty-seven specimens of quartzite, tuffs, etc. There was no living matter, but the rocks were filled with worm cells.

The next day we were closely invested by dense pack, composed of heavy old pressure floes. On one was a huge sea-leopard which I shot with my heavy rifle. With the assistance of Worsley, Douglas and Watts I brought it in to the ship, where Wilkins claimed head and skin as specimens.

Later in the day I went with a party composed of Worsley, McIlroy, Kerr, Carr and Macklin to look at a berg, distant 4 or 5 miles from the ship. It was a bright morning and we much enjoyed the walk. The ice was very treacherous, and we had to proceed carefully from floe to floe, making many wide detours.

On the morning of the 20th the outlook was bad, for we were closely beset on all sides, and the clouds to the north showed no signs of 'water sky'. The temperature was 10° F, and the new ice was freezing more thickly than ever. Macklin, Carr and Marr set off to visit a large berg which appeared on the horizon. They thought they were making wonderfully good progress till it became evident that the berg was moving rapidly towards them, charging heavily through the floe, throwing aside fragments which lay in its path and leaving a wide lane of open water behind it. I watched it anxiously as, travelling at from 2 to 3 miles an hour, it approached the ship, and I feared that we might be involved in pressure as a result of the displacement of floes about it. To my relief, however, it passed about three-quarters of a mile astern of us and finally disappeared over the horizon to the northward. There was something awe-inspiring about this huge structure as it moved inexorable and undeviating on its path, relentlessly crushing and pushing aside the smaller structures which sought to impede its progress.

In the evening there was a marked change in the weather. The temperature rose to 14.5° F, and the day became more dull and grey. From the crow's nest I could see a distinct water sky to the northward.

I was up at daybreak on 21 March and climbed to the mast-head to scan carefully the horizon to the northward for signs of opening up of the ice. There was a heavy black water sky, and as daylight increased I could distinguish fairly open and easily navigable pack. Unfortunately, between us and it were 3 miles of dense heavy floe solidly cemented by a foot of new ice. An irregular line of weakness ran through the heavy floe towards the now open pack, about half a mile distant from the ship. I thought that if I could cut my way into this a hard and determined effort might succeed in getting us free or at any rate into a more favourable position for escape should the ice about us begin to open up. I had to consider very carefully whether to make the effort or not, for the coal supply was such that we could not afford a day's hard steaming with no tangible result.

Accompanied by Macklin I walked across the ice to examine this line of weakness more closely. It did not look promising and I cogitated for some time as to what to do. While we were walking back a crack opened in the new ice ahead of the ship. It presented a chance and I determined to take it. I gave orders for all hands to stand to, and told Kerr to get up full pressure of steam so that at any minute he could give the engines every ounce they would stand. He accomplished this very quickly, but before I had time to get under way a large, solid, heavy floe had turned across our bows and was completely blocking the lead. The full pressure of the engines could make no impression. I sent Macklin over the side with an ice anchor, and put all hands to warping her ahead. After a long effort we effected a turning movement of the floe, and the *Quest*, being able to insert her bow as a wedge, slowly but surely forced her way into the lead.

After some hard ramming and pushing at the floes we reached the line of weakness, to find that the most difficult part of our work lay before us. For a long time, in spite of tremendous efforts, we made little headway.

We persisted, however, and after several hours of hard ramming and squeezing our way between heavy floes we won at last into loose pack, and soon after into comparatively open water. It was a great relief to me to get away. Had we remained frozen in till mid-winter and the ship been involved in heavy pressure our position would have been a precarious one, for there would have been little daylight to enable us to see what was happening, and there would have been long hours of darkness in which to contend with the heaving pack.

Throughout the whole period that we were navigating about the pack edge, I was constantly made to feel how extremely fortunate we were to have escaped unscathed from the ice after the loss of the *Endurance*. That we got away at all is truly marvellous, for not once in a dozen times could a frail ship's boat win free under similar circumstances where the floes, coming together, must have cracked her like an eggshell.

For a while I continued north, entering all the time a more and more open sea dotted all about with bergs and large solitary pieces of floe.

The day after leaving the pack we encountered heavy swell, which caused the *Quest*, with her empty bunkers, to pitch and roll in the most uncomfortable manner. Decks, rails and running gear became iced up with sprays which broke over her gunwale and froze solidly, necessitating the greatest care in moving about.

At night I could not distinguish white horses from growlers, and so took in sail and lay to. I sent McLeod and Macklin aloft to take in the topsail, which they found an unpleasant job on account of the treacherous condition of the rigging, which was ice-covered and slippery, and the jerky movement of the ship.

We continued on at daybreak encountering a few bergs but no floe ice. There was a heavy swell from the east-south-east, and though the wind seemed to have dropped a little squalls of great violence continued to pass over us. On this day we reached the maximum of discomfort, and though the men maintained their cheerfulness I see now from some of the diaries that it must have cost an effort:

> It has been another unpleasant day with all the discomforts of yesterday accentuated, the ship rolling just as heavily and all gear more thickly coated with ice, which is hanging in festoons and stalactites from every possible place. Sprays have been flying over all day and everything in the ship is damp. There is no comfort anywhere except in one's bunk, and even there it is all one can do to prevent being thrown out. On the bridge to-day Commander Wild remarked: 'The man who comes down here for the sake of experience is mad; the man who comes twice is beyond all hope; while as for the man who comes five times (himself)…' Words failed him.
>
> Poor Query is utterly miserable; he cannot get a minute's rest anywhere. Nor can any of us. Yesterday I caught my thumb in the jackstay, and it is so swollen and tender that to touch anything gives me agony. This beastly motion makes me sea-sick – I am full of sorrows to-day. We are getting near to Elephant Island, the home of all foul winds that blow – what crazy impulse sent me again to these abandoned regions? [writes Macklin]

Indeed at this stage of the voyage it took all our fortitude to keep up our spirits. We again hove to for the night, and the gale increasing in violence we lay to all next day.

It moderated about midnight of the 24th, and we set off under topsail only in the direction of Elephant and Clarence Islands.

CHAPTER 8

Elephant Island

The wind hauling ahead about 6.30 a.m. on 25 March, we took in sail and under steam proceeded south-west by south in the direction of Clarence Island. We got a sight of it at 7.35 a.m., but snow flurries obscured it again. About midday the weather cleared when both it and Elephant Island showed up distinctly. It is hard to describe the memories which these two islands revived for those of us who took part in the *Endurance* expedition. Readers of Sir Ernest Shackleton's *South* will find a description of our arrival and landing – the first landing to be made on Elephant Island. We stood gazing through binoculars picking out old familiar landmarks, each one reminiscent of some incident that came rushing back to the memory. There was Cornwallis Island, the shape of which was so familiar, and beyond it Cape Valentine, where we landed eight years ago, a haggard, worn-out and bedraggled party, rejoicing at the sight of firm, solid land, the first we had seen for nearly two years. We had just spent eight days and nights in the boats battling with ice, darkness and storm, toiling unceasingly at the oars with brief spells of the most fitful slumber. There our old Boss, whose indomitable will had overcome every obstacle and surmounted each difficulty as it arose, lay down on the shingle and had his first sleep for eight days – slept for eighteen hours without a wink!

In the distance we could see Castle Rock, unmistakable from its peculiar shape, and beyond it we knew lay Cape Wild, though invisible just now. There I wintered with my party while the Boss went for help, living hand to mouth on penguins, limpets and seaweed. From a sentimental point of view this was the place I wished to visit more than any other, but I knew only too well that it did not provide a good anchorage, and I was anxious while the weather was favourable to find a suitable place for ballasting the ship and obtaining sea-elephants for their blubber. We therefore set course to pass between the two islands and along the south-eastern side of Elephant Island.

As evening approached there was a wonderful mirage. Looking to the south-west we saw a number of large icebergs poised high above the horizon in a sky of the purest gold, while all about and in between them were numerous whales spouting. These mirages are by no means uncommon in these latitudes, but this was by far the most extraordinary I have ever seen in any part of the world, and certainly the most beautiful. Later on the sun sank with a peculiar effect – both Clarence and Elephant Islands seemed to be afire, a rosy glare rising from each of them to the sky. Over Cape Wild lay a reddish-golden glow, and the whole appearance of the island was beautiful, giving an impression of the most peaceful calm. Any ship passing the island on that evening would have carried away a very wrong idea of the place, and I am sure that many of our party who had listened to our unqualified, or perhaps I should say much qualified, descriptions of our sojourn here must have thought we were rather drawing the long bow. However, they were soon to learn differently.

During the night we had kept a safe margin between ourselves and the shore, but with the advent of daylight we stood in more closely and kept a sharp look out for possible anchorages and suitable spots for our purpose. We saw none on this side of the island, which presents nothing but steep mountainous rocks and sheer glacier faces. As we approached Cape Lookout at the south-western end of the island we saw a small spit lying between two high rocks. The wind was blowing from the west-north-west and this seemed to offer a shelter. We approached cautiously, sounding continuously with the hand lead. As we drew near I looked carefully through binoculars for signs of sea-elephants. Penguins were present in large numbers, but I saw no sign of larger game, and I was not altogether pleased with the place as an anchorage. I therefore decided to turn round Cape Lookout and look for a better place on the western coast. Once round, however, we met strong head winds against which we could make little headway, and the coast did not promise anything better, so we returned to the spit and came to anchor in 5 fathoms.

The surf-boat was lowered and I went ashore with Wilkins, McIlroy, Macklin, Carr, Kerr and Douglas. As we approached the spit I saw several seals and sea-elephants ashore, but they did not seem to be in sufficient numbers for my purpose. There was little surf on the beach and landing proved easy. Wilkins and Douglas went off on their respective jobs, and I landed Macklin and Kerr with instructions to reconnoitre and look for seals and sea-elephants, but on no account to scare away those which were present. I went back with McIlroy and Carr to the ship to bring off more hands. On the return trip I landed on a narrow strip of beach overhung by a large glacier which abutted on the north-west end of the spit, and with McIlroy and some others walked along it to where the sea-elephants lay. This is a practice I do not often adopt, for one never knows at what moment these glaciers may calve, sending down masses of many tons' weight on to the beach below. However, nothing happened and we crossed safely.

The landing-place in its essential features closely resembles Cape Wild, being composed of a narrow low-lying spit connecting the main island with an outstanding rock. This, again, is separated from another higher outlying rock by a channel through which the seas surge with some force. At the inner end of the spit is a high shoulder of rock which bounds the glacier on this side, while on the far side of it is another similar shoulder. The main part of the island seems to be much more accessible than it is at Cape Wild, but the place seemed to be no more suitable as a site for a permanent camp, for there were signs that the spit is at times sea swept, and it is equally unsheltered from strong winds.

Penguins were present in large numbers. There were two varieties, ringed and gentoo, which had segregated into two camps, the ringed occupying the outer rock whilst the gentoos collected together on the inner buttress. The former, which derive their name from a thin but clearly defined ring round the throat, are quaint, deliberate little animals which show not the least fear of man. They are the most wonderful climbers and form their rookeries in the most inaccessible places, often on the faces of steep and precipitous rocks where the footing is very precarious. After coming in from their fishing it often takes them hours to reach their final positions, but they show extraordinary patience and perseverance as they hop from ledge to ledge and from one small foothold to another. They are often to be seen on the slopes of large icebergs out at sea. The gentoo is a larger, more brightly coloured bird, with orange beak and legs, and has a small white patch over each eye which gives it a curiously inane expression. It is more shy of man than any other of the Antarctic penguins, and when chased can travel at quite good speed and dodge cleverly. As we came up a number of both kinds were stalking slowly and solemnly along the beach. Among them moved little pigeon-like paddy birds (*Chionis alba*) which look very pretty at a distance, but at close vision are seen to have very ugly heads and beaks. They darted about with little quick steps and, like the penguins, watched us curiously, no doubt wondering what strange new creatures we might be. Dominican gulls, skuas and Cape pigeons flew all about the place, and numbers of blue-eyed shags perched on rocks close to the sea or, with necks outstretched and stiff as ramrods, flew with an intent air to their fishing in the bay.

I walked across the spit to find a beach on the other side leading down to a small bay. My mind was immediately set at rest regarding our blubber requirements, for, lying about in the shelter of rocks and large pieces of stranded glacier ice, were a number of seals and sea-elephants, including three enormous bulls, each of which weighed many tons, while on a strip of beach on the far side of the little bay was a large harem of cows. I shot those on the spit and set all hands to the flensing. I have a mind-picture of my men: McIlroy, Kerr, Carr and Macklin busily plying their knives, arms bare to the shoulders and red with blood. Soon the place resembled a shambles. I loathed having to slaughter all these creatures, but the matter was one of the direst necessity, and I had to put aside any feelings of sentiment. I have never at any time countenanced the unnecessary taking of life, and whenever it has been necessary to kill I have always insisted that it should be done in the most humane way possible, and that steps would be taken to ensure that no wounded animal should escape.

The blubber was removed in large strips from the carcasses, and a party led by Jeffrey dragged it over the beach to the edge of the water. Another party secured it to lines and towed it out to the ship.

While the flensing was in process a curious incident occurred. I had given orders for a dozen penguins to be killed. One gentoo, in taking flight, had splashed through a small pool of blood and came out with white waistcoat dyed a vivid red. He went to rejoin his fellows on the hill, but they, failing to recognise him in his new colourings, pecked at him so viciously that he at last drew away and went off, to stand disconsolate and solitary at the head of the beach. Some little while later Watts, who had not witnessed the incident, suddenly exclaimed with much excitement, 'Look, there's a new species of penguin! Quick! Somebody help me to catch him!' Taking pity on the penguin's outcast condition I drove him into the sea, from which he returned clean and white, once more a normal penguin. This time his friends received him without comment.

I pushed on energetically with the work, for I feared a change of weather, my previous sojourn here having taught me never under any circumstances to trust Elephant Island. In the late afternoon the wind came round to the south-east, and a swell began to come into the anchorage. I kept the men at it as long as possible, but at last such a surf started running on to the beach that I was compelled to take them from the flensing and put all hands to getting the blubber aboard. Before leaving I took off also a load of glacier ice for melting down to water. It was as well that I stopped the work when I did, for the surf increased so rapidly that we had the greatest difficulty in getting away the last few boatloads, and in assisting to push out from the shore I got soaked to the waist with the icy cold water. Some hours elapsed before I was able to change into dry clothes and my legs became absolutely benumbed.

On returning to the ship I found that Worsley was growing very uneasy and was anxious to get away before darkness set in, so as soon as the boat was up we heaved anchor and proceeded out to sea.

Just as we were leaving the glacier fired a salute in the form of an enormous mass of ice, which fell with a reverberating crash on to the narrow beach below and, entering the sea, caused a large wave to come out towards us. I was glad that it had not happened earlier in the day while we were walking underneath it. This was the source of the pieces which we collected from the spit. Some of them are of great bulk and weight, and, with the erratic boulders which also are of great size, give an indication of the force of gales which blow in these regions, and show clearly that at certain seasons of the year the spit is so sea-swept as to be untenable by any temporary structure which might be set up there. These pieces of ice, except when salt encrusted, are crystal clear in appearance, and when melted down form the purest of water. When we were living at Cape Wild we used to be very fastidious about our ice. It was the one thing about which we could afford to be particular.

During the night of the 26/27th we kept well out from the coast to avoid outlying rocks, of which we had seen a number when we rounded Cape Lookout. When morning broke we stood up for the north-westerly point of the island, keeping a close look out for Table Bay or any other harbour which would afford a good anchorage. The reports of whalers speak of a large bay in this locality with safe anchorage, where the landing is good, where seals, sea-elephants, penguins and all sorts of seabirds abound, and where tussock grass grows luxuriantly. It was a common expression among the marooned party at Cape Wild to say: 'If we could only reach Table Bay!' We talked of the things we would do when we got there. I remember that one man (Greenstreet [first officer of the *Endurance*]) had sketched an elaborate plan which made all our mouths water. He was going to kill a seal and, having removed its entrails, fill it up with penguins similarly prepared. The seal was to be covered with stones and a blubber fire kindled on the top. The cooking was to last a whole day, at the end of which we were to eat not the seal but the penguins, which had thus lost none of their own juices but received those of the seal as well. Can you not imagine us sitting with tightened belts listening to the proposal, with our mouths watering at the very prospect?

We were never able to make the attempt to get there, and it is perhaps as well that we did not do so, for on this occasion we saw no signs of anything resembling the paradise we had so fondly pictured. There are places at the north-west end of the island where a landing could be effected, but the coastline is composed largely of rocky bluffs and sheer glacier faces, some of them of immense size.

We started, therefore, to cruise in a north-easterly direction, and sighted a narrow beach some miles in length running along the foot of steep mountains. On the beach were several harems of sea-elephants, each containing as many as forty cows. Jeffrey, Wilkins and Douglas wished to go ashore to carry on their scientific work, and I thought this a good chance to get some more blubber. I had contracted a chill as a result of my prolonged soaking in the cold water, so I sent Macklin ashore with McLeod, Marr and Young to deposit the scientists and bring off in addition to the blubber some meat for cooking. I gave Macklin a revolver with which to dispatch the seals, and he took with him also a BSA airgun in the hope of obtaining some paddy birds, which make very dainty fare.

Shortly after midday I noticed a change in the weather and with the steam whistle signalled to the party to return. This they did, bringing a small but useful addition to our supply of blubber and some paddies.

We killed in all nine sea-elephants and about the same number of seals. There were many hundreds which we did not molest. I found on my return to England that a report had been published in which it was suggested that we had slaughtered all the sea-elephants on Elephant Island. As a result some alarm was felt by the directors of the Natural History Museum at South Kensington that these animals were in danger of extinction, and without any reference to me a protest was published to that effect.

I can only repeat what I have already said: that I have always set my face against unnecessary killing. In all the expeditions in which I have taken part I have never seen a case of wanton destruction of any animal. I believe that among explorers as a class there is much greater sympathy for animal life generally, and especially for those types which they have known in the natural state, than exists among those who know them only as stuffed specimens. I may add, however, that had it been a matter of saving the life of any one member of my party I would unhesitatingly have ordered the slaughter of every sea-elephant I could find. Without wishing to labour the point I think the following taken from Macklin's journal may be of interest:

I do not know how to explain the attraction of this life ... it is certainly more primitive ... one meets Nature on more familiar terms and learns to love her and all her works. One feels drawn into much closer companionship with the lower animals, though I am not sure that the word 'lower' is always correct ... I have no doubt that what I have written is so much Greek to the town-dwellers. One cannot explain – these things are 'felt' and are not to be learned from a book ... The English natural history museums are such hopeless failures; at any rate, in so far as they attempt to instil a love of Nature. They are so gloomy, and the stuffed, unnatural creatures in glass cases are to me positively revolting. I believe every healthy boy gets the same impression and comes from them into the fresh air with a feeling of 'escape'. This surely is bad.

My first visit to the Natural History Museum of New York brought me a revelation. The building itself is a bright, well-lighted place and contains things of the most absorbing interest beautifully set up. In the hall the whole history of polar exploration is set out on two immense half-globes; there is the sledge taken by Peary to the North Pole and the one used by Amundsen in his race for the South Pole. The specimens are wonderful and the setting of them is the work of artists who know their job, for everything is lifelike and natural. In a snow-covered forest glade there are timber wolves on the prowl after game, flamingoes stand among the reeds in a swamp where the muddy ripples seem almost to move, one can gaze into tree-tops and see monkeys on the swing from branch to branch, reptiles swarm about a pool of water in a tropical forest, and there are other examples too numerous to mention. It is a place where boys stand fascinated, and one to which they return again and again...

Space forbids the full entry, though much of which he writes is interesting and very true, for once wedded to Nature there is no divorce – separate from her you may and hide yourself among the flesh-pots of London, but the wild will keep calling and calling for ever in your ears. You cannot escape the 'little voices'.

They're calling from the wilderness, the vast and god-like spaces,
The stark and sullen solitudes that sentinel the Pole.

I now set off along the coast in the direction of Cape Wild, and about 4.00 p.m. came in sight of the large rock lying at the end of the spit. We picked out many old familiar marks about the place. The weather was looking very unsettled and I decided not to attempt a nearer approach before darkness, but to lie off for the night.

Just before dusk the wind increased, blowing up strongly from direction north-west by west, and many nasty willy-waughs came gustily down the glaciers from the hills. Worsley suggested spending the night under the shelter of Seal Rocks, to which I assented, and we crept up under their lee, feeling our way carefully with the hand lead, finally coming to anchor in 8 fathoms.

Seal Rocks is the name given to a group of very barren islets lying about a mile from the northern coast of Elephant Island. They are covered on the northern side with lichen, the only form of vegetable life which exists in these regions. They are the resting-place of a number of seabirds, and penguins go there after their fishing to sleep and digest their food. Our berth was by no means a comfortable one, for the rocks are not large and give a very imperfect shelter from the winds, while in addition there are round about them a number of small ledges and submerged rocks, the proximity of which caused me no little anxiety. I was very anxious, however, to revisit Cape Wild, as were all those who had wintered with me there, and I hoped that the weather might moderate by daybreak.

I was feeling a little feverish as a result of my chill and turned in early, having arranged that a careful watch was to be kept, and having given instructions to be called in the event of anything untoward happening. Macklin relieved Jeffrey at midnight, the latter telling him that both wind and sea were increasing, and advising him to call me at once should he get the least bit uneasy. This he did at about 12.30 a.m., to say that we seemed to be dragging anchor and asking me to come on deck.

I got up at once. The wind had come round to the south-west, so that we were no longer in a lee, and the sea had risen considerably. The rocks showed up indistinctly as black masses against scudding clouds. I perceived that we could not stay there any longer, so at once called out the hands and rang the engine-room telegraph for full steam in the boilers.

We started to get up anchor right away, but as we shortened cable the ship began to drag more rapidly, and as there was little sea room I began to fear that we might foul some of the rocks or ledges before we could get clear. I kept her going ahead with the engines, but to add to the awkwardness of the situation the cable fouled in the chain locker, so that the incoming links would not enter the spurling pipes but, piling on deck, jammed the winch. I ordered Macklin and Carr to jump below, taking with them a heavy maul and a chain hook to break open the chain locker and free the cable. Worsley had by this time joined me on the bridge, and we had some anxious moments as we waited for the signal that all was clear, peering through the darkness to where a seething line of breakers indicated sunken rocks and reefs. From the darkness we heard the weird 'jackass' call of the gentoo penguin, like a wild lament for a ship in peril – fitting properly the stormy environment.

At last the cable was freed, we brought home the anchor and were able to steam away without damage from our unpleasant neighbours. All the time the wind rose. For a while I steamed east, hoping to be able to hang on, for I was loath to give up the landing at Cape Wild and we were not yet properly ballasted. In a short time, however, the gale had increased to hurricane force and such a steep sea started running that I could think of nothing but the safety of the ship, and so ran away before the storm.

Dawn broke on a stormy scene, and our last view of Elephant Island, seen through the driving spume astern of us, was a very different one from the calm and beautiful appearance with which we were greeted on the day of our arrival. I had hoped with the coming of light to be able to get under the lee of Elephant Island, but to have attempted to put our now light and un-ballasted ship across these seas would have been fatal.

I had to make up my mind at once as to what course to adopt. We had in the bunkers sufficient coal for one day's steaming which, mixed with sea-elephant blubber, might be made to spin out three or four days. To beat back to Elephant Island was therefore out of the question. My chief object in making for Deception Island had been to obtain the coal necessary to take the ship to South Georgia, and, even under the most favourable circumstances, I should have had against me the strong current which runs out of Bransfield Strait. The hurricane, though driving me away from the desired landing at Cape Wild, was fair for South Georgia, and under single topsail, with fires banked and the engines stopped, we were making better progress than the *Quest* had ever accomplished before. McIlroy reported that he could see no sign of change of wind for some days, though a falling off in force might be expected. This was just what we required. I decided, therefore, to make direct for South Georgia under sail, reserving the fuel to enable me to steam round the island and take the ship into harbour. I called all hands to set the square sail, which was coiled in a frozen mass on the top of the deck-house. This was covered with a thick, smooth coating of ice on which no one could keep a footing. We were compelled to clamber up the stays and seize the right moment to let go so that the roll would shoot us across to the foresail gaff, to which we clung desperately with one hand while we used the other to free the sail. The *Quest* rolled and pitched in the liveliest manner. Wilkins, in casting off a frozen lashing, lost his grip and I saw a form shoot to leeward and disappear. A voice behind me shouted in my ear, 'Wilkie's gone!' and indeed there seemed no doubt that he had fallen overboard. No attempt to pick him up was possible, for no boat could have pulled back into these enormous breaking seas, and in any case to have broached the ship to would have meant losing the masts and probably the ship as well. It was with tremendous relief that I saw Wilkins appear some minutes after and go to the halliards. He told me later that he had shouted that he was all right, but the sound of his voice was swept away by the violent wind. He had grabbed the backstay and fallen to the deck, fortunately without damage.

We swigged home the square sail and felt the ship lurch and stagger under its influence, but it increased our speed and enabled us to put the miles behind us. We tore through the water, which bore down on our stern as though to overwhelm us and passed sizzling and hissing along our sides. We were swept continually. One heavy sea, coming over our stern, fell with a smash on the poop, carried away the after-scuttle, broke the skylights and filled the after-cabin with several feet of water. Dell, McLeod and Marr immediately set to to repair the damage with temporary structures, which would at least be watertight. Dell and McLeod were required for another job, and Marr carried on alone.

The work was difficult and extremely unpleasant. The seas kept coming over the stern, compelling him to grab some support to prevent being swept forward with the wash. He was soaked from head to foot, the water freezing and casing him in a solid suit of ice. I kept a watchful eye on him. He stuck gamely to his work and made an excellent job of it. If he is a product of Boy Scout training it says much for the organisation. I warn Sir Robert Baden-Powell that he will find himself hard put to it to 'skin alive' this hefty young seaman [referring to a telegram sent by Sir Robert Baden-Powell to Sir Ernest Shackleton just as we were leaving England to the effect that if the Scouts did not serve him well he would 'skin them alive' on their return].

We continued running all day and kept the sail on throughout the night.

On 29 March the wind abated a little, but it still continued to blow a full gale. The seas had not gone down and the *Quest* was thrown about like a plaything of the ocean, so that the man at the wheel had his work cut out to maintain the course and prevent her from broaching-to. I hung on, however, for we were making good progress in the right direction and saving coal.

We had irrevocably cut ourselves off from any chance of seeing our old winter quarters at Cape Wild, which was a great disappointment to us all, especially to McIlroy, who in the excitement of the rescue had left behind his diary. It was wrapped up in an oilskin covering and he had great hopes of recovering it. One writer says in his diary:

> This is a great disappointment, but one meets many in this kind
> of work, and it is no good making a moan about them ... I would
> like to have got there all the same (he adds irrelevantly).

The rest of the run to South Georgia was not marked by any outstanding incident. On the 30th we saw a school of piebald porpoises, and Worsley reported seeing a 'blackfish' about 4 feet in length, which leapt several times out of the water. Numerous birds tailed in our wake, increasing daily in numbers till we reached South

Georgia. The winds dropped a little, but continued to blow freshly from the west-south-west on to our port quarter, enabling us to set all sail. The noon observation on the 31st showed a run of 197 miles. This was the *Quest*'s record, and was made without use of the engines. On the same day we were struck by an enormous breaking sea which almost broached us to and half filling the foresail dropped in a deluge on the deck-house, pouring in through the ventilators and flooding the cabins and wardroom. Much of it found its way through the main hatch, which is in the wardroom, and wetted many things in the hold. As we approached South Georgia we noticed about the ship a number of small seabirds somewhat resembling puffins, with short tail feathers and a very quick movement of the wings in flight. Worsley recognised them as 'the same little flippity-flip-flop short-tailed birds that flew round the boat and annoyed the Boss so much', referring to Sir Ernest Shackleton's historic boat journey from Elephant Island to South Georgia during the last expedition.

On 3 April we were in the vicinity of South Georgia and expected to make a landfall about dark. Worsley, who had not been able for some days to get an observation of the sun, was unable to pick up the island and we lay off all night. A number of soundings was taken. A large school of whales surrounded the ship and we could hear their 'blowing' all about.

4 April was also thick and hazy, and Worsley made a traversing cruise looking for the island, the proximity of which was indicated by the presence of birds, which we saw in hundreds with many young ones. In the afternoon the fog cleared and we caught sight of land, which we made for under steam. Night coming on, however, we stood off till daybreak.

At dawn on the 5th we recognised Anenkov Island, and decided to make for Leith harbour round the north end of South Georgia.

During the afternoon we saw several steam whalers, a welcome sight after having had the world to ourselves for so long. At night there was a fine sunset, and out-lined against the rosy horizon to the westward these little steamers made a very pretty picture.

We entered Leith harbour at daybreak on 6 April and moored to the buoy. Scarcely had we made fast when we saw the motor-boat coming off with the familiar figure of Mr Hansen and another smaller one wearing a white yachting cap. It proved to be Hussey, whom I had imagined back in England long before this. Mr Hansen gave us a most cordial welcome, and I learned from Hussey all the news he had to tell.

CHAPTER 9

South Georgia (Second Visit)

Sir Ernest Shackleton's body had been brought back to South Georgia for burial. I insert an account written by Hussey of what had occurred since I saw him last.

> The journey up to Montevideo was marked by wretched weather. The ship's wireless was out of order, so that I was unable to acquaint the world with my sad news. We arrived on Sunday morning, 29 January, and I immediately went on shore and cabled to Mr Rowett, asking him to break the news to Lady Shackleton.
>
> That afternoon, while I was in Wilson, Sons & Co's office, a telephone message came through from the Uruguayan Government asking me if they might take charge of any arrangements that had to be made there as a last tribute to the great explorer. I acquiesced, and they immediately set about bringing Sir Ernest's body ashore. Within half an hour they had sent a naval launch out to the *Professor Gruvel* to fetch the coffin. It was met on the quay by a guard of honour of 100 marines and taken to the military hospital, where a guard of two soldiers was mounted over it day and night.
>
> Next morning the medical officers at the hospital re-embalmed the body, as it was at first intended to bring it to England for burial.
>
> That day, however, a cable came from Mr Rowett saying that Lady Shackleton was sure that Sir Ernest would have wished to be buried on South Georgia, the scene of his greatest exploit, and asking me to make arrangements to do this.
>
> The next ship to leave for South Georgia was the *Woodville*, with Captain Leaste in command. He was most courteous and sympathetic, and immediately placed such accommodation on his ship as was necessary at our disposal.

The day before she sailed a commemoration service was held in the English church at Montevideo, Canon Blount and Canon Brady, an old friend of Sir Ernest, officiating. The coffin had been transferred from the military hospital to the church on the previous day.

While Sir Ernest's body was lying in state in the military hospital the matron and one of the nurses placed fresh flowers on it each day from the hospital garden.

For the memorial service the church was packed. Many members of the Uruguayan Government were present, and representatives from nearly every country in the world either sent wreaths or came in person. The President of Uruguay came into the church and stood a few minutes in silent contemplation before the rough wooden coffin which, covered by the Union Jack, stood in front of the altar. The Republic of Uruguay also sent a magnificent bronze wreath to be placed on the grave. The French Maritime Society sent a bronze palm, and Mr Ogden Armour, representing the United States of America, brought a huge wreath of lilies. The British Minister at Montevideo came with a bronze wreath and a memorial plaque, both of which I screwed up later on the walls of the little wooden church in South Georgia.

At the conclusion of the service the coffin was carried to a waiting gun-carriage by ten British ex-Service men. Huge crowds had assembled to pay their last tribute to the great explorer, and the whole of the route from the church to the quay where the *Woodville* was lying was lined by troops. Along one part of the route women showered rose petals down on to the coffin from overhanging balconies.

On arrival at the ship the coffin was taken aboard and the Uruguayan Minister for Foreign Affairs made a short speech, in which he said that not only England but the whole world was made the poorer by Sir Ernest's death. The British Minister replied, thanking the President and the Republic of Uruguay for the way in which they had honoured the dead explorer's memory.

The coffin was then lowered into the hold, and the *Woodville* put out into the harbour.

The Uruguayan Government had asked to be allowed to take the coffin down to South Georgia in a warship, but owing to the bad ice conditions which existed at that time I considered that to take an ordinary steel ship down there would be unnecessarily risking the lives of all on board as well as the safety of the ship. So they very reluctantly gave up the idea, but when the *Woodville* left next day the warship escorted her to the 3-mile limit, fired a salute of seventeen guns – the highest possible honour that could be shown to anyone less than their own President – and steamed up alongside the *Woodville* with the marines formed up at the salute while their buglers sounded the 'Farewell', which is usually only sounded for the fallen after victory in battle. This seemed to me to be the most touching tribute of all, symbolising as it did their idea of Sir Ernest's life-struggles and his triumphant passing over.

We reached South Georgia on 27 February 1922, and in a blinding snow-storm we took the coffin ashore to the little wooden Lutheran church at Grytviken.

Sunday 5 March broke clear and calm. The managers from all five whaling stations had assembled at the church by three o'clock that afternoon, and a crowd of about 100 fishermen were present to pay their last respects to Sir Ernest. The first part of the funeral service was said in English and Norwegian, Mr Binnie, the magistrate, officiating. Then the coffin was taken by six Shetland islanders – all ex-Service men who happened to be working at Leith harbour whaling station – to a light decauville railway, and carried over tiny mountain streams formed by the melting snow, and past huge boilers and piles of whalebones to the little cemetery on the hill. On arrival there the funeral service was completed, and with the British and Norwegian flags at half-mast at the gate of the cemetery the coffin was lowered to its last resting-place.

After the grave had been filled in I had a simple wooden cross erected, and on it I hung wreaths which I had brought from Montevideo on behalf of Lady Shackleton and her children, Mr and Mrs J. Q. Rowett, and the members of the expedition.

Many more floral and other tributes were placed round and on the grave.

When the funeral service was over Mr Hansen, the manager of Leith harbour whaling station, very kindly offered me the hospitality of his house till I could get passage in a homeward-bound ship. Nothing had been heard of the *Quest*, and I was anxiously waiting for news of my companions. On the morning of 6 April Hansen wakened me with the news of the ship's arrival. We were not long in going aboard, and I reported at once to Commander Wild, giving him a full account of all that had happened. While the *Quest* was in harbour I went aboard and shared in such work as was necessary, and Commander Wild decided that I had better return to Montevideo as quickly as possible, collect all Sir Ernest's gear which I had left there in store, and proceed to England, there to report to Mr Rowett and Lady Shackleton and give them any information that they might require.

Accordingly I arrived at Montevideo on the *Neko* on 24 April, and, accompanied by the British Minister, I thanked the Minister for Foreign Affairs, Dr Buero, on behalf of Mr Rowett and the members of the expedition for the way that this great little Republic had honoured our late leader's memory.

I arrived in England on 28 May and was met at Southampton by Mr Rowett, whose many encouraging and sympathetic cables had greatly cheered me on my sad and lonely mission, and to whom I gave a full report of all that had happened since the *Quest* had left England in September, 1921.

Whilst Hussey was telling me all that happened there flashed into my mind the remark Sir Ernest had made when the Quest first entered Grytviken Harbour – 'The cross has gone from the hill-side!' When he spoke I little thought that when next we should round the headland and look across the harbour to those slopes another cross would be there to replace the one that had gone, erected this time to the memory of his own brave spirit.

Hussey was still awaiting a chance to go home, for since the arrival of the *Woodville* there had been no return steamers. The *Neko*, a floating factory belonging to Messrs Salvesen & Co., was due from the South Shetlands in about ten days, and he hoped to secure a passage in her. I was glad to see this cheery little man again, who within a few hours had settled down among us as if he had never been away.

The first work to be done after our arrival in South Georgia was the getting up again from the bunkers of all the heavy deck gear which had been placed below as ballast for the run from Elephant Island, where, owing to depleted stores and the small remaining supply of coal, the ship had become very light and top heavy. It was not at all a pleasant job, for the bunkers contained a considerable quantity of blubber, and, owing to the heavy seas, the gear had shifted about and become covered with the most disgusting mixture of coal and grease, which had to be removed from each article as it came on deck. The remaining pieces of blubber were passed up and dumped overboard, for with the heat from the engine-room they had started to become very offensive. This done, the bunkers were cleared completely and made ready to receive coal. Attention was then turned to the ship and engines, to both of which there was a good deal to be done, as may be understood, owing to the severe bumping and the continued bad weather we had experienced.

Under Jeffrey's direction, Dell, McLeod and Marr proceeded with the deck work, reset up the rigging generally, replaced all worn gear, and put everything into shipshape order ready for once more proceeding to sea. The greater part of the next portion of our journey would be in the 'Roaring Forties', which by no means belie their name, so I was particularly anxious that this part of the work should be thoroughly carried out.

Kerr and his staff had a busy time in the engine-room, where all parts of the machinery were subjected to a complete overhaul. The main pump was taken down, new parts fitted, and the whole put into good working order. The hull was still leaking badly, and all the time we were in harbour we had to keep the hand pumps going vigorously while the steam pump was out of action. It was found that the engines as a whole had withstood the unusually hard conditions much better than was expected, and credit is due to the engine-room staff for the careful nursing they gave them throughout the period spent in the South.

The contents of the hold were tallied and re-stowed, and space made to receive the mails for Tristan da Cunha, which had been deposited here in charge of Mr Hansen. While in the ice regions I kept the boats provisioned for thirty days, but I now reduced the amount to supplies for ten days only, as the larger weight is apt to make the boats unhandy.

I found it necessary to take aboard some fresh provisions, and a small amount of equipment to replace damaged gear, but our requirements in this respect were small. I was fortunate in obtaining from Mr Hansen a supply of fresh potatoes, which are, perhaps, the most valuable of all foodstuffs to people living under our conditions.

Wilkins and Douglas were set free from all work about the ship so that they might have all their time free to carry on their scientific observations.

A certain amount of carpentry was necessary about the ship, for which work the managers of the whaling stations supplied me with men. The broken after-scuttle was renewed and strengthened, and the deck-house, which had leaked badly, re-canvassed and covered with a coating of red lead.

Throughout the whole of this work I received the most valuable assistance from Mr Hansen, to whom nothing proved too much trouble. In addition, he gave us a most cordial welcome to his house, where we renewed our acquaintance with Dr and Mrs Aarberg. It was indeed 'Liberty Hall', for we came and went as we pleased; the bathroom was thrown open for our use, and there was always an unlimited supply of hot water. We certainly needed it – words cannot give an idea of the luxury of that first long wallow in the bath. I was much touched by Mr Hansen's kindly and practical hospitality, and tried many times to express my thanks, but he brushed them aside as if it were all a matter of no moment. Indeed, I was surprised at the warmth of welcome we received from everybody we met. I have an inkling that the *Quest* was regarded as far too small a vessel for the undertaking, and that the enterprise was considered a somewhat hazardous one.

While the work of the ship was going forward I made a point of allowing the members of the expedition as much time for rest and recreation as possible. The period spent in the South had proved a trying and wearing one to everybody, and all were in need of a rest and change of exercise. Time also was required for 'make and mend', washing of clothes and attention to personal gear generally, which had been impossible while the *Quest* was the plaything of the heavy southern seas.

I sent the men ashore, whenever the opportunity afforded, to walk over the island, play football, or visit the people employed at the station, of whom a number were British, chiefly Shetlanders. There was a football ground behind the station, situated at the foot of a high mountain and overlooked by a glacier; the ground was more remarkable, however, for its romantic position than for the condition of its surface. We received a challenge from the Shetlanders, which I accepted. In so small a company as ours, numbering nineteen all told, it was not easy to raise eleven footballers, for many were Rugby players, and had never played the Association game. However, we succeeded in putting out a side which, after a good game, defeated the Shetlanders by one goal to nil. Anxious for revenge, they challenged us to a return match, and beat us. Unfortunately, the opportunity for a third and decisive game did not occur.

I encouraged incidents of this nature, for they provided an entire change from the routine of ship's work and served to draw the men more closely together on a common level than the routine ship's work could ever do. Also they gave a new topic for conversation and discussion which lasted for days.

On 14 April the *Neko* arrived, and I accompanied Mr Hansen on a visit to her, when I discovered that her master, Captain Sinclair, was an old friend whom I had met in South Georgia eight years before. He readily consented to take Hussey to Rio de Janeiro, where he could transfer to a mail boat for home, and offered him the only accommodation available on board – the settee in his cabin. The *Neko* is a floating factory. Each spring, as soon as the ice opens, she proceeds to Deception Island, and thence as her captain may think fit. She is accompanied by four steam whale-catchers, which, when they have killed a whale, bring it in and lay it alongside the parent ship. She herself is provided with boilers and vats and all the apparatus necessary for trying down the blubber into oil. The pursuit of whales has changed largely since the days of the old Dundee fleet, when the actual killing was carried out from boats by means of hand harpoons and lances. Now, instead of boats, small but fast steel steamers are used, which carry in their bows powerful guns from which the harpoon is fired. Attached to the harpoon is a strong rope coiled ready for running on a small sloping platform over the bows. A bomb is fitted to the end of the harpoon and forms the point. If the aim is good, this bursts inside the animal, causing instantaneous death.

In the case of the stations located on South Georgia the process is much the same, but the shore factory replaces the parent ship and everything is on a larger scale.

The newer method of hunting is a much more lethal one – for the whale; from the catchers' point of view it is, of course, much safer and more comfortable. In the old days the chase of these huge animals was looked upon as a dangerous undertaking and might be regarded in the nature of a sport, for the whale had more than a sporting chance of getting away and the hunters stood a good chance of being drowned. Nowadays it has become a mere business. Nevertheless, the floating factories, in pushing south to good whaling grounds, take considerable risks of being crushed by the ice.

Captain Sinclair is an old and very experienced hand at the work, and in addition to his whaling activities has added largely to the charting of the South Shetlands and the Palmer Archipelago. He has succeeded also in bringing home some unique live specimens of seals and penguins, which have been added to the collection in the Zoological Gardens in Edinburgh.

On the 15th we went to Stromness harbour, where we were welcomed by the manager, Mr Sorlle.

When Sir Ernest Shackleton, accompanied by Worsley and Crean, made the crossing of South Georgia during the *Endurance* expedition, it was here that they arrived and were received by Mr Sorlle, who fed them and provided them with hot baths and beds, and was instrumental in fitting out a relief ship to go to the rescue of the marooned party on Elephant Island, getting it ready within twenty-four hours of his first hearing of the state of affairs. This relief ship, the *Southern Sky*, was unfortunately held up by the ice, and her return was dictated, not by the Norwegians who manned her – they were ready to hang on for many more days – but by Sir Ernest Shackleton, who was anxious to get to the Falkland Islands so that he might set going the preparation of a larger, properly ice-protected wooden ship.

I decided to lay the *Quest* alongside the *Perth*, a large oil transport which acted as tender to the station. A strong breeze was blowing, which made the *Quest* very unhandy to manoeuvre, and while Worsley was putting her alongside she struck her bowsprit against the steel sides of the *Perth* and snapped it off short. This might have proved a serious disability, but, fortunately, Mr Sorlle had a spar which he not only presented to us, but had cut down and shaped to our requirements.

Here, as at Leith, we received every kindness, and we had hardly made fast before a present of a pig and a reindeer – the latter shot by Mr Sorlle himself – were sent aboard. All the officers were invited to dine with Mr Sorlle at his house in the evening, and we received a dinner of six or seven courses which rivalled anything to be had in civilisation. Afterwards we spent a very pleasant evening with reminiscence, story and song. Mr Sorlle is a most charming host.

While lying in Stromness harbour we experienced one of those tremendous hurricanes which are characteristic of the southern volcanic islands. Descending from the hills without a moment's notice, it blew with such violence that the whole surface of the bay was lashed into a torn mass of driven water, the tops of the seas being snatched off and blown in a blinding spume to leeward. One of our boats lying alongside the ship was swamped, and all gear that would float, such as oars, bottom boards and fishing tackle, were swept out of her and lost. Fortunately, the painter held, and there was no damage to the boat itself.

There was no coal available at Leith, Stromness or Husvik, so on the 17th I proceeded to Prince Olaf Harbour to see if I could obtain what I required. The whaling station there is the property of Messrs Lever Brothers, and is under English management. On my arrival I called at once on the manager, Mr Bostock, who relieved my mind very much when he said he would give us what we required for our purpose. We accordingly lay alongside the *Southern Isles*, the oil transport steamer and station tender which was to supply us. Here, again, we received much help from Captain Sapp, who supplied all the labour necessary to put the coal on our decks.

While we were here Carr developed a nasty abscess of the face, and on the invitation of the company's doctor went ashore to the hospital, where he could get a bed, with clean sheets and other comforts not available on the ship. Macklin was suffering from an inflamed hand, the result of an accident while in the ice, and McIlroy found it necessary to incise it for him.

On the 19th we had completed coaling, and on the 20th set off for the Bay of Isles to study the bird life of the numerous islands dotted about it. On this day Hussey left us to join the *Neko* at Leith. He had taken his old place among us and had joined fully in all the work of the ship. His unfailing optimism and cheerfulness had done much to enliven us, and it was with genuine regret that we said good-bye. I think he felt the going. With him went Carr, who was now suffering a good deal from his face. Hussey had instructions to take medical charge of him, and if his condition became worse to take him home on the *Neko*, but if it showed signs of improvement he was to hand him over to Dr Aarberg, to await our arrival at Leith harbour.

We made first for Albatross Island, under the lee of which I lay to, and sent Jeffrey with the boat to put Wilkins and his party ashore. They effected a landing in a small cave, and, having scaled a cliff, reached the summit of the island, where they found albatross and giant petrels in large numbers.

Macklin, whose hand prevented him from working, asked permission to go with them, and I quote from his diary:

We landed on a little beach inside a cave which was occupied by a number of sea-elephants, which showed their resentment of our approach by opening their mouths very wide and making stertorous windy noises which could hardly be described as 'roaring' – 'breathing' defiance with a vengeance.

In the enclosed atmosphere they smelled horribly, for they are unclean, swinish brutes. From the cave we clambered up a steep cliff to the top of the island, which we found to be irregular in shape and covered with tussock grass. Wilkins, with the assistance of Marr and Argles, immediately set about collecting albatross for addition to the natural history collections. These birds, when seen at close quarters on the ground, prove to be much larger than one would imagine, being about the size of large geese, but with much longer legs. Their appearance on land is ugly and ungainly, and contrasts strongly with the grace and beauty they exhibit when in flight. Wilkins, by going slowly, was easily able to get within reach, when he grabbed their beaks and 'pithed' them by passing a needle through the back of the skull into the brain. He took the heads, wings and legs as specimens and made them into neat parcels for transmission to the museums. Jeffrey and McLeod had stayed to look after the boat, so, being at a loose end and remembering Worsley's ecstatic remarks concerning baby albatross, I set about collecting enough of them for a meal for all hands. The island was covered with little paths worn by the birds, which formed a regular maze among the tussocks and hummocks of grass. Here and there one came across little circular plateaux which apparently formed a meeting-place for numbers of birds, for they were worn absolutely bare to the mud. The nests of the albatross are placed on the top of small, raised, cone-shaped mounds composed of earth and tussock grass, which are nearly always situated on the windward side of the island, so that the birds when preparing for flight have merely to spread their wings to get a good take off. The inside of the nest is hollowed sufficiently deep to allow the young bird to crouch and take shelter from the winds. The young are pretty little things covered with white down, and from the highest point of the island I could see them all round me standing out in marked contrast to the dark green of the tussock grass.

The giant petrels, 'Nellies' or 'Stinkers', as they are variously called, nest in much the same way. They are most unpleasant creatures and receive from sailors none of the veneration accorded to the albatross. We had been ashore some hours when Commander Wild sent up a detonator as a signal for our recall. The cliffs on the side where we had landed are steep and overhanging, so that we had to approach cautiously, and had some difficulty in finding the way back to our cave. We at length found the spot where we had ascended. I flung my collection of birds over the cliff to be picked up below, and all of us having got safely down we rowed back to the ship.

Macklin, in speaking of 'the veneration accorded to the albatross', voices a very old superstition among seamen of the old sailing ship days. When I first went to sea as a boy this was still a common belief among sailors, but though there are a few of these old-timers left who still hold to the old romantic ideas, they are becoming more and more scarce. Romance is not dead, as Kipling says, but it moves with the times. Masefield says:

> Them birds goin' fishin' is nothin' but souls o' the drowned,
> Souls o' the drowned an' the kicked as are never no more;
> An' that there haughty old albatross cruisin' around,
> Belike he's Admiral Nelson or Admiral Noah.

I recalled the party on account of the weather, for a strong wind had blown up, the seas were increasing and there were indications of a heavy storm. I did not care to be caught with the *Quest* on a lee shore, so went back to Prince Olaf Harbour, where we found that all their own whale catchers had returned for shelter. In addition there were a number belonging to other stations which had put in here till the weather should abate. We had for dinner the next night the baby albatross which Macklin had brought off. This was the first food obtained by Sir Ernest Shackleton on his arrival at South Georgia from the boat journey, and often had we listened to Worsley's telling of the story, this much of which never varied: 'Baby albatross just off the nest – we ate them! By jove, they were good, damn good!' By one of life's little ironies he was having dinner ashore that night and so missed them; his disappointment on hearing of it was keen.

On the 22nd, the weather having abated somewhat, we left to carry out an extensive series of soundings about the north-western end of South Georgia. This we accomplished in spite of very bad weather. The *Quest*, as usual, behaved abominably, having a most uncomfortable motion as we butted into the head seas, which sent the spray in clouds high over the yards.

We returned to Prince Olaf Harbour on the 25th. There was still much to be done, and Mr Bostock kindly lent me his shore carpenter for some jobs that were still outstanding on the ship.

On the 27th we said good-bye to our friends and left for Leith, passing *en route* the *Woodville*, which was coming up the coast, and presented a fine sight as she dipped her nose deeply into the swell.

We arrived in Leith harbour in a blinding snow squall which made mooring to the buoy a difficult matter. The *Quest's* engines were of such low power that manoeuvring in close spaces was an extremely difficult matter during the squalls, which came out of the mountains with hurricane force and startling suddenness.

On the 29th Mr Hansen was able to make room for us alongside his little pier, where we proceeded to take in water. Owing to the low temperature the water in the hose froze solid and it became necessary to clear the galley to thaw it, the process being carried out section by section till all was clear. Green had the dinner in process of cooking, and was quite perturbed when he had to sweep away all his pots and pans to make room for the hose – such is an example of what a cook has to put up with at sea.

On 1 May we took aboard what stores we required and the mails for Tristan da Cunha. We received from Mr Hansen some final presents in the form of a pig and several small but useful sundries, and from Captain Manson of the *Albuera* an additional two crates of fresh potatoes.

On the 2nd we said good-bye to Leith harbour, which we had regarded as our South Georgia home and where we had received so much kindness, not only from Mr Hansen, the manager, who had done everything in his power to assist us, but from Dr Aarberg, who had looked after Carr while we had been carrying out the soundings about the island and had been of assistance to the surgeons in many ways. Our thanks are due to Mrs Aarberg also, for with much kindly thoughtfulness she had asked us to entrust to her care such articles of clothing as might require the 'stitch in time'.

As a result of our stay we were refreshed and full of vigour, for the spell ashore and in harbour had done us all good. Thanks also to the various managers we had been able to vary the diet from our own preserved provisions to fresh food in the form of pork, reindeer and whale-meat, which provided a most pleasant change. We were able to catch also Cape pigeons and albatross, which when properly cooked make quite good eating. The former have an oily taste which can be largely removed by soaking them for twenty-four hours in dilute vinegar.

I seized every chance of sending away the boats to catch fresh fish, which are found in great quantity about the coast. Macklin, Jeffrey, Green and Hussey (while he was with us) were those most often engaged in this work, which was not always pleasant. An entry in one diary reads:

> Some people fish for fun, some consider it a sport, others fish because they have blooming [for the substitution of the adjective I apologise to the entrant] well got to. I am one of them. Down here the job is often anything but a joyous one in cold driving wind and snow, fingers so cold that one can scarcely remove the hooks from the fishes' mouths. Sometimes the blizzards sweep down and it is all we can do to fight our way inch by inch back to the ship...

Macklin writes in this connexion:

> The fish here are of excellent quality and have the peculiarity that when cooked they do not taste fishy. Green usually fries them in olive oil and they are particularly good. The best spots for finding fish are in belts of kelp close to the edge where the tides sweep in and out. Whale meat (not blubber) makes a good bait and a spinner (or any piece of bright tin) helps to attract the fish. One can usually moor the boat to the strands of kelp, but it is advisable always to have on board a small kedge anchor and a good length of line in case of being swept away by the blizzards which blow from the hills with strong, sudden blasts.
>
> Green is a great enthusiast, and is always willing to come, whatever the weather...

There is no sport in the actual fishing, for the fish abound in great quantities and are very sluggish. The chief art lies in knowing just where to go for them. There are two kinds, which we speak of as 'ordinary' fish and 'crocodile' fish. The first, as the name implies, have nothing peculiar about them. The latter have immense mouths with crocodile-shaped jaws and look hideous. The tail is small, and indeed it may be said that there is more mouth than anything else.

The trip to Grytviken was uneventful and we arrived there the same day.

Before leaving South Georgia we had rather a sad duty to perform. For a long time I had desired to erect some mark which would serve to perpetuate the memory of Sir Ernest Shackleton. We had no time to do it before we left for the South, for every day was precious and it was essential that we should get away at the earliest possible moment. After some consideration I decided that the mark should take the form of a cairn surmounted by a cross, and I selected as a site for it a prominent spot on the headland which stands out from the lower slopes of Duse Fell, at the entrance to Grytviken harbour. I determined that it should be the work of his comrades, something which we ourselves could create without help from outside sources. Everyone on board was anxious to have a hand in the building, so I arranged things that they might do so. On the night of our arrival the temperature fell very low and the surface of the harbour froze over, not sufficiently to permit of walking but enough to make it an extremely difficult matter to get the boat to the shore. Also snow fell thickly. We broke a way through the ice and proceeded to the headland, where we made a search for suitable building stone. There was none convenient, and to obtain it we had to go some distance up the hillside to where a shoulder of rock jutted out through the tussock grass. Having removed the snow we bored the rock and blasted it with sabulite, afterwards breaking away suitable pieces with crowbar and pick. For sledging it down the hill we had to make special box-containers; even then with the steepness of the declivity and the roughness of the track it was a difficult matter to prevent the loads from falling off. The work was awkward and hard; on several occasions the sledges broke away and careered down the slippery hillside with the men clinging desperately behind. No one grudged the labour and time spent, for it was the last job we should do for the Boss. The foundations were laid and the cairn began to grow. There were no expert masons among us, but the work when completed had a most pleasing appearance. Into the stone we cemented a brass plate on which was engraved very simply:

Sir Ernest Shackleton
Explorer
Died Here, January 5th, 1922.
Erected By His Comrades.

The cairn is solid and will stand the ravages of frost and blizzards for many years to come.

It will be the first object picked out by any ship entering the harbour, and to anyone looking back as the vessel steams away it will stand out in lonely prominence long after the station has disappeared from view. It can be seen also from every part of the harbour.

Our last act before leaving was to pay a visit to the Boss's grave, for which purpose I gathered together all those who had served under him on the *Endurance* and had shared with him all the trials and vicissitudes that followed her loss in the ice. There were, in addition to myself, Worsley, Macklin, McIlroy, Kerr, Green and McLeod. That I included none of the newer men who had known him for so short a while casts no shadow of aspersion upon them. My feelings in the matter are hard to describe. We were joined to each other and to him by ties so strongly welded through the long months of common danger and uncertainty that I felt there would be something wrong in introducing anything in the nature of a less intimate element.

So our little party rowed across the bay, walked to the little graveyard and gathered for the last time round his grave. It was deeply snow-covered. We carefully removed the snow and disclosed a number of bronze wreaths: from Lady Shackleton and from numerous friends and relatives at home. There were others from the Uruguayan Republic, the British residents in Uruguay, the Freemasons of Uruguay and the French Maritime Society. Two others hang in the little church, placed there by Hussey: one from

His Majesty King George V and the British people, the other from his old school-fellows resident in South America. There was also the flower wreath placed with such kindly thought by the doctor's wife, Mrs Aarberg.

The graveyard is a simple little place. In it are already a few crosses, some of them very old, mute reminders of forgotten tragedies. Four of them mark the resting-places of officers and men of the sailing ship *Esther*, of London. They had died of typhus fever and were buried here in 1846. There is one inscribed to W. H. Dyke, Surgeon, who in his devotion to duty in attending the sick had also contracted the disease and died. There are some newer crosses erected to Norwegian whalers who had lost their lives in the arduous calling which brings them to these stormy waters. All of them are the graves of strong men.

It is a fitting environment. Grytviken is a romantic spot. All around are big mountains, bold in outline and snow-covered. Below lies one of the most perfect little harbours in the world, at times disturbed by the fierce winds from the hills and lashed by the gusty squalls to a mass of flying spume and spindrift. Often it lies calm and peaceful, bathed in glorious sunshine and reflecting in its deeps the high peaks around, while the seabirds, 'souls of old mariners', circle in sweeping flights above its surface and fill the air with the melancholy of their cries. An ideal resting-place this for the great explorer who felt, more than most men, the glamour of such surroundings.

So we said good-bye to the 'Old Boss', and I who have served with him through four expeditions know that if he could have chosen his own resting-place it would have been just here.

Here – here's his place, where meteors shoot, clouds form,
Lightnings are loosened,
Stars come and go! Let joy break with the storm,
Peace let the dew send!
Lofty designs must close in like effects:
Loftily lying,
Leave him – still loftier than the world suspects,
Living and dying.

Robert Browning

We had still some work to do before finally setting course for Tristan da Cunha.

Before leaving Grytviken I entrusted our last lot of letters and messages for home to Mr Binnie, the magistrate, who, together with the other Government representatives on the island, had been very helpful to us in many ways.

We went alongside the little pier where we hardened up [a sea term, meaning that we filled the tanks full to the top] the water tanks. Mr Jacobsen paid a last visit to the ship and presented us with a parting present in the form of a fine young sow, which was carried aboard in a box, receiving the excited attentions of Query. I did not kill her at once, intending to keep and feed her up so that we might have some fresh meat when at sea. Someone gave her the name 'Bridget', and so she was known until her demise some weeks later at the hands of Dell, who did our butchering.

We received also from Mr Jacobsen some packets of dried Swedish oaten cakes, which were of particular interest in that they had formed part of the stores of Filchner's German expedition which had come to grief and been abandoned here. They were still, after eleven years, in excellent condition.

We left on 7 May and had been some hours at sea when we discovered a stowaway aboard. This was 'Micky', a small black-and-white dog belonging to Mr Binnie, the magistrate. He was discovered by Macklin who, while descending into the hold, stepped in the darkness upon something which moved and yelped and which proved, upon being dragged to the light for inspection, to be this animal. We lavished upon him no loving remarks, but knowing that Mr Binnie set great store by him I put back and in the small hours of the morning sent Jeffrey with the boat to put him ashore, having previously tied to his neck a message to Binnie, explaining his disappearance and requesting him as a magistrate to award a punishment of at least three days' jail for having caused us so much trouble and loss of time.

On 8 May we visited Royal Bay and Moltke harbour, where the German Transit of Venus expedition had had a station in 1882. One of the huts then set up is still standing.

The glacier running into this harbour is of great geological interest because in the last forty years it has advanced about a mile and receded to its original position. I sent the boat ashore with Jeffrey, Macklin and Ross to find suitable landings for the scientific parties. There was a heavy surf running which made the operation difficult, but they succeeded in putting Douglas with Carr and Argles on to a steep rocky beach which ran along the side of the harbour. Marr, still very inexperienced in boat work, fell overboard during the process and was rolled over and over in the surf, to be eventually cast upon the beach; but he escaped with nothing worse than a ducking – which is not a joke in these temperatures. Wilkins, who with Marr had wished to land on the beach at the side of the glacier, was unable to do so.

I sent Macklin, McIlroy, Marr and Green to catch as many fish as possible for taking away with us. Finding a suitable spot at the edge of a belt of kelp, they secured a good haul and brought back enough to last for several days, for in these temperatures there was not much fear of its going bad.

Shortly before dark I recalled all hands, who were picked up and brought off safely.

Before leaving, Worsley took a line of soundings along the front of the glacier. This was our last work in South Georgia.

This remote island has drawn to it scientists from all nations, yet there remains much to interest the investigators of to-day. During our stay we made a great number of observations and collected a mass of data which when sorted and worked out fully will, I hope, be of great interest to the scientific world.

We now put to sea and set course for Tristan da Cunha. As we left the bay the moon came out – a big golden moon which cast a broad pathway on the sea and bathed the huge glaciers and the snow-covered mountains and valleys in a soft golden glow. Our last sight of South Georgia was a very beautiful one, and my last thoughts as I gazed back over our rippling wake, gleaming in the moonlight with brighter phosphorescence, were of my comrade who stayed there, and I hoped for his sake that our completed enterprise would be the success that he himself would have made it.

CHAPTER 10

The Tristan da Cunha Group

From South Georgia we proceeded first in a northerly direction in order to get into the belt of prevailing westerlies which would give us a fair quarterly wind for Tristan da Cunha.

While still in the vicinity of the island a number of soundings were carried out by Worsley and his assistants.

From the first we had bad weather, and the winds increased in force during the next few days until, on Friday 12 May, so fierce a gale was blowing that I was compelled to take in sail and heave to. We had a most uncomfortable time, though we could expect nothing less since we were now in the 'Roaring Forties'.

Macklin's diary of 13 May is fairly descriptive of conditions about this time:

Had the middle watch. Heavy seas were running and the wind was strong with violent squalls of rain and snow. It was a dirty night. The *Quest* rolled worse than anything I have ever known, with staggering jerks that made it impossible to let go a support.

At times the ship sagged down so heavily to leeward that my heart was in my mouth, for it seemed as if she could never recover herself. Peering to windward as the great seas bore down upon us I was reminded of Kipling's

Be well assured that on our side
The abiding oceans fight,
Though headlong wind and heaping tide
Make us their sport to-night.

which is comforting to know. He always seems to catch just the right expression, as:

> Out of the mist into the mirk
> The glimmering combers roll.
> Almost these mindless waters work
> As though they had a soul –

However, as the Boss used to say: 'When things are bad any change is likely to be for the better.' We pour some vile epithets upon the head of poor old *Quest*, but she really does not deserve them, for she is always at her best when things are bad. Commander Wild says she is like a woman, quoting something about 'Women in our hours of ease, perfidious, fickle, hard to please!' I suppose he knows all about it. Anyway, she has brought us through what might well have caused many a more stately ship to founder. Things have remained much the same during the day – water keeps coming over the gunwales in huge masses and hundreds of tons pass hourly across 'The Rubicon', as we call the wash of water in the waist of her. Occasionally big green seas come aboard *en masse*, flooding the whole ship, and find their way everywhere, through cracks in the doors, spirting through the keyholes and through the ventilators, which, with all the ports tightly closed, must be kept open.

Macklin places in my mouth an incorrect rendering which I would never apply to the gentler sex, but which is certainly very appropriate to the *Quest*.

'Bridget', the pig which was presented to us by Mr Jacobsen on leaving South Georgia, had a very miserable time, and I was almost giving instructions to have it killed right away. It was totally unable to keep its footing on the slippery deck and it was very sea-sick. I handed it over to the care of McLeod, who found it a snug berth in the bathroom, where it quickly recovered its spirits and began to develop an insatiable appetite.

In passing I may mention that the bathroom, so-called, was a small recess containing a tub situated at the side of the engine-room and opening into the starboard alleyway. It was always warm from the heat of the engines and we used it chiefly as a drying-room for clothes. It was used occasionally also on very cold nights as a warming-room for chilled night-watchmen. We possessed nothing so luxurious as a real bathroom, and, sinking modesty, we bathed ourselves from a bucket on deck. In the very cold weather those who were able to ingratiate themselves with Kerr, the chief engineer, could sometimes take their tub in front of the furnace fires. This was a real luxury.

I was glad to notice on 14 May a falling off of both wind and sea, and McIlroy predicted a spell of finer weather. On the 15th it was distinctly calmer and we were able to continue the work on deck, which in a ship at sea is interminable, but which the heavier weather had compelled us to suspend temporarily. 'Bridget' emerged from her retreat and started to move about the deck, where she quickly made friends with Query. It was highly amusing to watch the antics of the two of them. She also started to make friendships among the hands – notably with Green, whom she quickly learned to regard as the source of her food supply. At times she became too friendly, for she began to take an interest in the cabins and wardroom. Another bad habit was that of moving about the decks at night, where she had repeated collisions with the men working the sails.

In spite of the improvement there was still a big enough sea to cause the *Quest* to roll heavily, and on the 18th we nearly had a nasty accident.

I had set a party, composed of Macklin, McIlroy, Jeffrey, Carr and Marr, to hoisting up from the lower hold a number of sacks of beans which had got wet and become offensive. The work, which was hard and difficult on account of the awkward motion, was being carried out, and to clear a space Macklin had sent up a large heavy ice-basket full of sundry stores, the whole weighing many hundredweights. Carr was on deck, and had received the basket when the ship gave an unusually heavy lurch. Both he and the basket were shot to the opening, and though he was able to save himself the basket fell with a crash into the hold where the men were working. Carr yelled a warning and they managed to leap clear, receiving the impact of some of the cases but escaping a direct blow. This is but one example of many 'incidents' of the kind that occurred throughout the trip.

Worsley, Jeffrey, Carr, Macklin, Kerr and Green all at separate times fell through the hatch, and that none of them received serious injury is remarkable. I was fully prepared on any day to witness some accident, and that so few occurred can only be due to the special Providence that guards children, drunken men and sailors. 'There's a sweet little cherub that sits up aloft, looks after the soul of poor Jack' (sea song).

Leaving the 'Roaring Forties', the air became milder and the temperature rose, so that we were able once more to go about without heavy clothing and could cast aside mufflers, mitts and woollen caps.

We sighted Inaccessible Island just after midnight on 19 May. It appeared as a high mass with dimly marked outline obscured at the top by dark banks of cloud. As we came abreast of it the moon came out, creating a very weird effect. The island itself stood out in deep, almost Stygian, blackness, and from its summit smoke seemed to be belching in great rolling masses. High above all was the moon, showing fitfully from between scudding clouds, and in front, accentuating the effect, was a rippling silvery pathway. It reminded me of a scene from Dante's *Inferno*.

I now set course direct for Tristan da Cunha, where we arrived about daybreak.

The summit of the island was entirely obscured by heavy clouds and rain fell thickly, so that everything had a dreary aspect. As the light increased we were able to pick out the little cascade which gives a good mark for the anchorage and dropped our anchor in fathoms. Looking ashore I saw a number of small, thatched houses situated on a piece of flat ground bounded on the side of the sea by short steep cliffs. This was the settlement where the whole population of the island lived. As we saw it now, on this soaking early morning, it might have been a dead village, for there was no sign of life, either beast or human, not a wreath of smoke ascended from the chimneys, and nothing at all stirred. To attract attention I blew a blast on the steam whistle, when there was an immediate change. The people came running from their cottages and the settlement sprang to life. The men launched their boats and came off to us. The sailor's eye was at once attracted by the boats, which are made of canvas over a wooden framework. The men themselves were an uncouth lot. They were very excited and talked a great deal in thin jabbering voices.

They hastened to board us and started at once to ask for things. They proved to be a great nuisance, so I sent them all ashore, retaining only one man, Robert Glass, who seemed to be the most intelligent of them. I learnt from him that the islanders were very destitute. He asked in the name of the community for our help and, realising that they were indeed in a bad way, I determined in the name of Mr Rowett, who I felt sure would sympathise with my action, to give them all the relief I could.

I gave instructions to Worsley to see what could be done for them in the way of deck gear, nails, canvas, rope, paint, etc., things of which they were in great need, and told Macklin to find out what could be spared in the way of food and general equipment.

We had brought fifteen bags of letter and parcel mail from England for these islanders; we had on board also a large number of packages and cases which Macklin, who had been compelled to find room for them in the sorely restricted space at his disposal, was pleased at the prospect of being able to hand over. They included a large gramophone, a gift from the Æolian Company, and some Bovril sent by the firm as a present to the islanders.

As I was anxious to learn all I could about these people, their ways and customs and mode of life generally, I detailed Macklin to go ashore for this purpose. I also gave him instructions to take a complete census, which might be of use to the Cape Government. He remained there while the ship visited Nightingale and Inaccessible Islands, and as I have asked him to write his own account, to avoid repetition I will refrain from any further description of Tristan da Cunha itself.

The Tristan da Cunha group of islands includes the three just mentioned and two smaller islets known as Middle and Stoltenhoff respectively. They lie roughly in latitude 37' S and 12' W longitude, and they are approximately 4,000 miles from the Cape of Good Hope. Tristan is probably the most isolated inhabited island in the world.

The group was discovered by the Portuguese admiral whose name they bear, in 1506. The Dutch, at the time of their settlement in the Cape Colony, examined it with a view to making it a naval station. The East India Company also sent a ship to see if it would be worthwhile forming a settlement there. No one lived there, however, till early in the eighteenth century, when a man named Thomas Currie landed and decided to remain. He was joined by two American whalers, named Lambert and Williams respectively. There is a vague report, too, of a Spanish boy having somehow or other joined the party. Lambert and Williams were drowned while making a visit to Inaccessible Island. What happened to the other is not clear. The history of the present settlement is dealt with in the following chapter.

A British naval officer, named Nightingale, visited the group in 1760, and the crew of a sealing vessel, under command of John Patten, spent six months about the islands, collecting the skins of fur seals. The first accurate survey was made by the hydrographic staff of the *Challenger*, which in the course of her historic voyage round the world spent a short time here in 1873.

All hands having been recalled from the shore, we left Tristan da Cunha at 7.30 p.m. on 20 May and proceeded in the direction of Inaccessible Island, which loomed up in the dark ahead of us about midnight. We reduced speed, waiting till daylight should give us a chance to see what we were doing.

I took with me on the *Quest* three of the inhabitants of Tristan da Cunha to act as pilots and guides about the islands. They were Bob Glass, his brother John Glass, and Henry Green.

In the early hours of the morning the wind increased and blew from the north-east with very heavy rain squalls. A landing on Inaccessible Island seemed quite impossible, so I ran for shelter under the south-west end of Nightingale Island, which we reached at about 7 a.m. I put out the surf-boat and sent ashore a party, composed of Wilkins and Marr, for natural history work, and Douglas and Carr for geological purposes. Jeffrey was in charge of the boat, and I sent with him Henry Green and John Glass. They effected a landing on the south-east corner of the island, at a point where the rock rose sheer from the water, but where there was a rough ledge, on which they managed to get a footing and place their equipment, which consisted of theodolites, guns, pickaxes, bags, etc.

Here the parties separated, John Glass accompanying Wilkins, while Henry Green acted as guide to the geologists.

Marr writes in his diary:

We climbed a short way along the jagged rocks with our baggage and came to a flat table-like area backed by high cliffs with gigantic boulders at their base. The other party went right on up a narrow gully with the intention of inspecting a guano patch at the far side of the island. We remained here for a short space whilst Wilkins shot a number of birds and then followed up the hill. From the ship we had thought that this would be easy going up a grassy slope. We were sadly disillusioned, however, for the grass was rank tussock and grew high above our heads, from 6 to 10 feet in length, and was extremely difficult to break through. Underfoot the ground was rotten and soaking, and at every step it gave way and we sank knee-deep and further. Mr Wilkins kept shooting birds on the way up, but we had great difficulty in finding them in the grass. We were drenched to the skin by the time we arrived at the top, where there was open land covered with small trees and loose rocks and a peculiar round-bladed grass which grew in close tufts very difficult to walk upon. Here more birds were shot, and we started on the return journey, sliding down the soaking rotten earth, stumbling blindly through the long grass and slipping into the holes.

On reaching the bottom the party returned in the boat to the ship without waiting for the geologists. The latter had crossed the col to the northern slopes, finding, like the others, that the going was very hard on account of the tussock grass. 'These (grass reeds) grow to about 8 feet high,' says one of the party, 'and are about half an inch in diameter, and are so dense that a man 5 feet away is invisible.' Examinations were made and survey work was carried out, and when it was finished the party set off back to the landing-place. Douglas writes:

Upon reaching a small eminence we saw the *Quest* steaming around the north-east point. This was one of the few occasions when she added to the picture and not, through the ugliness of her lines, detracted from it. In the brilliant sunshine as she came into the mouth of the passage between Nightingale and Middle Islands, gently dipping in the north-east swell but still rolling, she made a very pretty picture.

I suppose Douglas is right when he remarks that the *Quest* is not a beautiful ship, for her lines certainly cannot be described as yacht-like. Yet as my affection for her grew she appeared more and more beautiful in my eyes, till, thinking of her in retrospect, I have almost a feeling of resentment at any such criticism. After all, beauty is largely a matter of what we are educated to regard as such, and our ideas change, as witness what are to us to-day the extraordinary 'fashions' of only fifty years ago! The *Quest* is neither stately nor graceful, but she certainly has a beauty of her own. What 'she' has not?

The geological party also was safely taken off, and we lay off for the night about a mile from the land. In the morning I brought the ship closer in and, feeling my way carefully with the hand-lead, proceeded to the north of Nightingale Island. I was anxious to put Douglas ashore on Middle Island, and sent off the boat with Jeffrey, Dell and the three islanders. Douglas and Henry Green effected a landing, and in the meantime I dropped anchor in the passage where we were in shelter, the wind having come round to the west. While waiting here we fished for sharks, which abound in considerable quantity and of which we caught several. They were of little use, but I have the sailor's hatred of these rapacious brutes and had no compunction in destroying as many of them as my men could catch.

During the afternoon a strong wind blew up, and Jeffrey and Dell had the greatest difficulty in getting in to the island to pick up the party. During the more violent squalls they shipped oars and clung to the kelp which grows about here in long, strong strands. Dell describes this as the worst row he had ever experienced. They succeeded eventually and returned with the party to the ship.

Weather conditions at this time of year are not very suitable for carrying out an extensive survey and examination, and I was unable to allow Douglas any great opportunity for accurate work. He made good use of his few chances, however, and his observations are likely to prove of value.

A landing (was effected) at the south-east corner (of Nightingale) where a platform of lava extends from the foot of the low col which forms the easiest passage to the north of the island. The island is rectangular in plan, about one mile by three-quarters. The south shore is bounded by fairly high cliffs, except for one or two small platforms. The east shore is also high, and the highest point of the island rises here in very steep slopes. The col above mentioned is the low feature joining the high peak with the other high points to the west and interior of the island. It is probable that the island was once a volcano, as the central depression and various agglomeritic occurrences would testify. From the centre the island slopes down gradually towards the north, ending in low cliffs of about 30 feet high.

Nightingale Island has a single sharp peak about 2,000 feet high. Middle Island lies to the north, and is separated from it by a passage half a mile in width. Douglas says:

The island owes its existence to two causes – first the lavas from Nightingale ... must have extended well to the north, and secondly, there has been local out-welling of lava. The latter lava is extremely hard and has formed the col which has resisted the action of the sea. The first lava is so soft that it is easily worn away, which accounts for its separation from Nightingale. The island is comparatively small, being less than half a mile on its longest axis. Being close to Nightingale its flora is similar. The island does not rise higher than 200 feet, and is girt with vertical cliffs on the west, north and east sides. The landing is at the south-east point, and there is a large cave at the most southerly point.

The island of Stoltenhoff, a little more than half a mile distant, is a huge flat-topped rock rising from the water for 200 feet. No landing possible. The island is probably an extension of 'Middle' to the north, but may represent another separate centre of activity.

We remained at anchor for the night in the passage between Nightingale and Middle Islands, and sailed at 4 a.m. for Inaccessible Island.

This island has been the scene of several shipwrecks, including that of the *Blendon Hall* in 1821. It does not belie its name, for as we approached it certainly looked inaccessible enough. No low land is apparent, and the whole rises sheer from the sea on every side. The weather was so uncertain that when sending the party of scientists ashore I gave instructions that stores sufficient for several days should be taken in the boat in case it should be impossible to pick the men up when we wanted to. The party took also biological and geological gear, surveying instruments, two good Alpine axes and a coil of good Alpine rope.

A landing was effected near the north-east corner, largely through the help of the Tristan islanders, whose intimate local knowledge proved of the greatest value during the whole time we spent about these islands. The beach was steep and stony, and big curling seas were breaking on it. Intervals of comparative calm occur, and by taking advantage of them a boat can be fairly easily beached. The landing effected and the gear removed, the boat was hauled up while the party went about their work. The beach is about a mile long and forms a very narrow strip, behind which the cliffs rise vertically for an average height of from 300 to 400 feet. Half a mile to the south-east of the landing-place a narrow waterfall drops in a cascade over the edge of the cliff about 350 feet up and has hollowed out a deep pool below. The ascent to the summit lies beyond this, and here Douglas, with John Glass and Henry Green, started the climb. These two islanders are strong, active, nimble men and wonderful climbers. Douglas gave them the greatest praise, and said that but for their assistance he could never have attained the summit. On one occasion during the descent they had to lower him over a particularly steep part with the rope. Douglas writes:

Inaccessible Island is pear-shaped, the longer axis being about 3 miles and the shorter 2½ miles. The land rises around the island in almost vertical cliffs about 500 feet high. On the south and south-east there is a gradual slope up to the highest point, which is about 1,500 feet above sea level. On the north and north-west sides the rim continues to rise to about 1,300 feet, and then it slopes down towards the interior and the foot of the slope of the central cone. In fact, it is a great caldera, with the southern side blown out and having a central small cone.

The interior is really a beautiful landscape of broken country, clad in verdure with a stream running through it.

Wilkins, assisted by Carr and Marr, carried out natural history investigations on the lower slope and shot a number of birds for preparation as museum specimens.

During the years 1871–73 two brothers, Germans named Stoltenhoff, lived here. They gave their name to Stoltenhoff Island. Nightingale Island derives its name from the British navigator who visited it in 1760.

All the islands of the Tristan da Cunha group have a similar flora and fauna. They are covered in parts with tussock grass (*Spartina arundinacea*) and bracken. One small tree, the 'island tree' (*Phylica nitida*), grows at levels up to about 2,000 feet. The smaller plants include twenty-nine species of flowering plants and twenty-six ferns and lycopods. Numerous seabirds nest on the islands, including mollymauks, terns, sea-hens or skua gulls, prions, black eaglets, 'Pediunkers', and several kinds of petrel. On the rocky beaches we saw a number of small land birds, one species of which resembled a thrush and the other a finch. They were very tame and could be easily caught. The islanders showed us several rookeries where rockhopper penguins congregate in large numbers during the nesting season. The rockhopper is a pretty bird with a crest of yellow and black feathers. Its call is rather deep and harsh – 'Aloh-ha!' as nearly as I can write it.

But for the difficulty of landing, Inaccessible Island would be almost as suitable a spot for a small settlement as Tristan da Cunha. A few cattle are kept there. The islanders from Tristan make frequent visits in their boats. Experience has taught them what are the most suitable weather conditions for effecting a landing. It appears that the winds follow a fairly definite cycle, and the islanders can predict with some degree of certainty the conditions likely to be met with in the next few days.

One has to give the islanders credit for their boatmanship, for their craft are frail and require the most careful handling to prevent their being stove in.

Of the men taken with us on the *Quest*, Henry Green and John Glass had never been away from the islands. They were really two extremely nice men. Douglas writes of Henry Green who accompanied him:

> Henry proved to be a delightfully refreshing character. His simple outlook on life, facts being facts to him and needing no reason, the pride he took in his ability to climb and find his way over the islands, notwithstanding his years, and his love of his own hearth, marked him out as one of the best, if not the best, of those who live on Tristan.

What a strange life they lead, passing day after day of their long lives in this restricted environment with the same outlook, among the same people and with only occasionally the sight of a new face, which passing, never returns, for no one ever goes back to Tristan. As Macklin shows, their longevity is remarkable; few seem to die under ninety years of age.

I returned to the settlement via the southern side of Tristan to enable Worsley to carry out a series of soundings, and arrived there at daybreak on 24 May. We proceeded in through the kelp and came to anchor.

I allowed most of the hands ashore for the day, and detailed a party to install a portable wireless receiving apparatus which Mr Rogers, the missionary, had brought from Cape Town. One of the masts for the aerials broke while being erected, and the pieces fell among a crowd of islanders who had gathered to watch proceedings, causing them to scamper wildly in all directions. Mr Rogers told me that he had not learned the code, and as there are several mechanical details to be mastered it is doubtful if the apparatus is likely to be of great value.

I was up before daybreak on 25 May, to find that the wind had come round to the west and a strong swell had started to run into the anchorage. I saw that the sooner we were off the better, and blew the steam whistle for the recall of those who had spent the night ashore.

When I had told Glass on our arrival that I would be able to leave a considerable amount of general supplies for the islanders, he had said that he did not think they had stock enough on the island to pay for it. When I replied that I did not require any payment, he was most agreeably surprised, and promised to send us two or three good sheep and some fresh potatoes. I had also asked for a number of geese and poultry with the idea of placing them on Gough Island in the hope that they would settle there and breed.

The blowing of the steam whistle caused the most marked excitement among the islanders, who came rushing to their boats, which they launched, and, having rowed out to us, crowded aboard in dozens. Immediately there was a noise like babel let loose. Many of them approached Bob Glass, saying: 'Can't you get nothing more out of them, Bob?' As I had emptied the holds and stripped the ship of everything I could spare, and in the name of Mr Rowett given all the relief I could to these people, I was not very well pleased at their attitude. On my asking for the sheep and potatoes and the livestock for Gough Island they suddenly remembered that they owed us something in return, and dragged up from the bottom of the boat what looked for all the world like two large and skinny rabbits. They proved to be sheep, the most miserable creatures I had ever set eyes on. They dumped aboard also two bags of potatoes which in size resembled marbles and some very indifferent-looking geese and poultry. They seemed to lose all restraint and begged for anything which caught their eye or their fancy, each man trying to get in his request before his neighbour or endeavouring to overshout him. There were no longer any requests on behalf of the community, each man trying to scrounge what he could for himself. A boatload containing some of the steadier men brought off six bags of mail, six bales of feathers and about nine bags of potatoes. These were dumped over our rail, and when I sent Macklin to find out what it was they had put aboard, they replied that they were parcels which they wished delivered to their friends in Cape Town who would send them something in return. These casual folk had made no arrangements and had not even addressed them sufficiently.

Rain had started to fall and Macklin, who knowing nothing of their coming had not prepared a place for them in the hold, turned to a group of the islanders and asked for some help to put the bales in the shelter of the alleyway, where they would be protected from the rain. Not a man stirred, each saying it had nothing to do with him. Macklin had to search out each man in turn to help with his own bag for none of them would touch anything that did not belong to him personally. We were all thoroughly disgusted with their behaviour, and on this last morning they undid any good impression we had gained of them while ashore.

One group of men brought me some bundles of whalebone which they asked me to buy for £20. As I had no idea of the value of the stuff I could not do it, but offered to take it to Cape Town and hand it over for disposal and have the value sent them in general goods. This arrangement they regarded with suspicion and tried hard to induce me to barter with them. It was a curious thing that all the islanders seemed to think that we had a mysterious bottomless store from which we could go on supplying quantities of pipes, tobacco, foodstuffs, etc. etc., in exchange for the most valueless trash. Knowing that as a community they stood in great need of copper nails for their boats I offered them a 7-lb bag, our all, which we could ill spare. No one man would burden himself with this on behalf of the community and it was finally left aboard.

I made full allowances for the limitations of these people, but at last they became so troublesome that I ordered them back to their boats and got ready to put to sea. Just before the last lot left some of the older men came to me and thanked me for what we had been able to do. They included Henry Green, John Glass, Tom Rogers, Old Sam Swaine and Lavarello, the Italian. I told them that they must not thank me altogether, for they owed what I had given them to a man named John Rowett far across the sea in England. John Glass said in his high piping voice: 'You will see Mr Rowett again? Then tell him that he is the koindest man that I ever know.' I promised I would. Bob Glass also brought me a letter which he wanted me to send to Mr Rowett for him. In return I thanked them, etc. etc. Just before leaving I received a long letter from the missionary Mr Rogers, in which he expressed the appreciation of the islanders and sent a message of gratitude to Mr Rowett.

Though very disgusted at the time with the behaviour of these people, I felt on more mature consideration that one could not fairly judge them by instances like this. They are ignorant, shut off almost completely from the world, horribly limited in outlook, and they realised that at this moment there was slipping away from them the only possible source of acquiring the many things they so badly needed. Indeed, looking back on the whole visit to Tristan da Cunha, I am surprised that they were not much more wild and uncivilised than we found them, and they were, I believe, at any rate the older men among them, really grateful for what we had been able to do.

I think their characters may be somewhat roughly summed up by describing them as 'a lot of grown-up children'.

CHAPTER 11

Tristan da Cunha (By Dr Macklin)

We arrived at Tristan da Cunha on 20 May 1922, just as dawn was breaking. A fine rain was falling and all the upper part of the island was shrouded in mist. The islanders seemed to be still in bed, for we saw no signs of activity until Commander Wild blew the steam whistle, which brought them running from their houses in haste, evidently very excited, for we saw them pointing towards us. The men ran down a steep winding path leading to a beach of black sand where a number of boats were drawn up. They launched the boats and came out towards us as fast as they could row.

At first sight the people presented a curious spectacle. They were rather a wild-looking lot, and were clothed in every conceivable kind of male attire, which seemed to be the cast-off clothing of sailors who had called at the island. One man in particular was wearing the queerest mixture: an evening dress jacket, striped cotton shirt, dungaree trousers, while on his head was an officer's peaked cap!

The majority of them were white, but many showed signs of a coloured ancestry in a dusky complexion and features of a distinctly negroid type.

Their boats attracted our attention, for they are made of canvas over a framework of wood. These are ingenious pieces of work and built on very shapely lines. The canvas is begged from passing ships. The cross-pieces are made from the branches of small, stunted apple trees which are grown on the island, but for the pieces which form the keel and the main part of the frame they are dependent on chance bits of driftwood thrown up on the beaches.

On this day there was a considerable swell running, which made it dangerous for more than one boat to come alongside at a time, the others lying off at a safe distance. It was apparent that the islanders did not care to submit their frail craft to any more bumping than was necessary. In their excitement they made a tremendous noise, shouting to each other in voices which were curiously thin and high-pitched.

As soon as the first boat came alongside a strong active man with a cheery face leapt on to our gunwale and clambered aboard. He told us his name was John Glass, and he seized those of us whom he could reach in turn by the hand, exclaiming in a piping voice that contrasted strangely with his powerful frame: 'I'm glad to see you all. How are you? Have you had a good trip?' Another man, taller and more slimly built, quickly followed him and made his way to the bridge. He was wearing an old khaki overcoat, and was shod on one foot with a worn-out leather boot and on the other with a sort of moccasin made of cowskin. Several others came aboard and started at once to ask for things, saying: 'Say, Mister, you ain't got an old pair of boots, have you?' or 'Mister, I'm building a boat – can you spare a few nails?' 'Mister, can I have a piece of salt beef?' – always the prefix of 'Mister', said in a most ingratiating tone. The requests were made to anybody whom they encountered, no matter how busily engaged.

When told to 'wait a little and we'll see what can be done', they would say, for example, 'Well, my name's Swaine – young Sam Swaine, son of old Sam Swaine. You won't forget, will you?' Often two or three of them bombarded one man at the same time, when they raised their voices, both in volume and pitch. They made themselves such a general nuisance in this way and, together with those in the boats, who kept calling continually to those aboard, raised such a pandemonium that Commander Wild approached John Glass and asked him if there was a 'head-man' of the island or recognised representative of the community.

John Glass promptly replied, 'I am!' but continued in the same breath, 'There ain't no head-man now. Bob Glass, my brother – that's him on the bridge – he's head-man. Anyways, he's the best one for you to talk to. He's got the larnin'!' Having 'got the larnin'' meant that he could read and write.

Bob Glass was told to remain on the ship. The rest were packed off into their boats and sent ashore to await the blowing of the steam whistle as a signal for their return. Glass, the tall, slim man who had made for the bridge, proved to be an intelligent fellow. We asked him to have breakfast with us. He accepted the invitation without embarrassment, and showed himself much more at ease than one would have expected from anyone living in so remote a part of the world.

From him Commander Wild learnt that there had been only one ship to the island in the last eighteen months – a Japanese steamer, which had brought a missionary and his wife, but which had immediately proceeded without letting them have supplies of any kind. Glass had made his way to the captain in the hope that an explanation of their needs and of their peculiar situation might induce him to allow them some stores, but he was promptly ordered off the ship. The captain, relenting a little at the last moment, gave him as a personal present a bundle of coloured postcards, all of them with the same picture – a very highly coloured impressionistic view of Fuji-yama, the sacred mountain of Japan! They had received quite a considerable mail from people in the outside world who took an interest in this isolated community, but, as Glass remarked contemptuously, 'Chiefly clothes for the womenfolk.' The missionary had brought some supplies, but, according to our informant, hardly enough for himself and his wife. The people were at the present time very badly off and were, indeed, destitute of what elsewhere might well be considered absolute essentials, such as articles of clothing, cooking and table utensils, wood, canvas for the upkeep of their boats, nails, tools, rope, wire, etc. For a long time they had been without luxuries in the way of food, such as tea, sugar, flour or biscuit, and commodities such as soap, candles, etc.

In the old days, said Glass, the settlement had been much better off, for ships had appeared within reach of their boats many times a year, and with them they had bartered livestock and potatoes, produced on the island, for what they themselves required in the way of general commodities. Nowadays, ships seemed to have entirely left the ocean, and they were in a bad way.

He and his brother, John Glass, are direct descendants of Corporal William Glass, who founded the settlement. He accounted for his 'larnin'' and general knowledge of conditions by the fact that he had been away from the island for eighteen years, had apparently travelled a good deal on one job and another, and mixed with people. During the South African war he had served with Kitchener's Scouts, and had received the Queen's medal. We gathered that he was not lacking in common sense and had a pretty shrewd knowledge of the value of things.

Of the truth of his statements with regard to the condition of the community there could be little doubt, and a visit to the settlement made later in the day showed that he had not exaggerated. They made an earnest appeal to us for help, and Commander Wild decided to do all that was in his power to alleviate their hardships.

We had, fortunately, on board a considerable quantity of bulk stores in the way of biscuits, flour, Brazilian meal, beans, etc., which had been kept in reserve in view of the possibility of our being frozen in and compelled to winter in the Antarctic. These Commander Wild offered to Glass, with as much as could be spared from our stores of a wide variety of foods, such as tea, sugar, coffee, cocoa, dried milk, Quaker oats, lentils, split peas, jam, chocolate, cheese, tinned meats, tinned fish, salt beef, candles, matches and soap. We gave them also from the deck stores a quantity of planking, rope, wire, nails, paint, canvas, and two good spars.

In addition to this we had brought with us in the ship a large letter and parcel mail and numerous packages sent privately for the islanders, including several sent in gratitude by a sailor who had been shipwrecked there and who had been very kindly treated. We had a busy day getting all these goods out of the hold and stacking them along the ship's side ready to be placed in the boats. When all was ready we signalled the return of the others, who, as soon as they had approached to within a measurable distance of the ship, started shouting innumerable questions to Bob Glass. The purport of them all was: 'What are they going to give us?'

Glass clambered on to the gunwale of the ship and started shouting back in a high, piping voice. We saw their faces, which had worn a look of anxiety, suddenly break into smiles when they heard what we could do, and they became like a lot of schoolboys informed of a holiday, shouting gleefully to each other and singing snatches of song. Indeed, these people are very child-like in many of their ways.

The loading was an awkward job. Everything had to be lowered slowly and carefully over the side and placed gently in the boats, for, being made of canvas and frail craft at best, anything dropped into them with a bump would assuredly have gone through the bottom. The difficulty was increased by the swell and the rolling of the *Quest*, which caused the boats to rise and fall and surge in and out in the most awkward manner. We were interested to note that many of the islanders who came aboard were sea-sick, but recovered when they clambered back into their own boats. Evidently they were used to the short, quick motion of the smaller boats, while the more pronounced roll of the *Quest* upset them. They plied to and fro till everything was ashore, where it was stacked in an imposing pile at the top of the beach.

After lunch I went ashore with Worsley and some others of the party. We went in an 'island' boat. Worsley, known among the South Sea Islanders as 'Tally ho', from his habit when approaching through the surf of shouting the well-known hunting call, 'Yoicks! Tally ho, tally ho, tally ho-ooo-oh!' insisted on taking the steer oar, and as the boat neared the beach raised his cry, to the amusement of the crew and the people on shore. They enjoy little jokes. On the beach there was a scene of activity. The goods were being loaded into small carts, each drawn by two bullocks. They were rough and primitive affairs. The wheels were made from sections of a tree which had been blown up on the island some years previously. The oxen were small but strong looking.

The way from the beach led up a winding rocky pathway to the top of a cliff, and thence along to the settlement, distant about half a mile.

Tristan da Cunha, in the greater part of its extent, is very mountainous, but on the northern side there is a stretch of flat land about 6 miles long and from half to one mile deep. Behind it rises the mountain, sheer and steep, to a height of from 2,000 to 3,000 feet, from where it slopes more gradually to the summit. In front cliffs, 50 or 60 feet high, drop abruptly to the sea, but are broken here and there by beaches of black sand.

The settlement, composed of a number of small stone cottages, is situated on the eastern end of the flat land, which is grass-covered and strewn with boulders. The western end provides good grazing ground for sheep and cattle, and in the sheltered spots small portions are set aside for growing potatoes.

On the way we met several women and children. The women were well built and healthy looking, and wore, like the men, a variety of clothing. They also showed differences of colour and feature, one whom I noticed being quite blonde. The children are attractive, very quiet and demure in their deportment – what the islanders themselves call 'old fashioned'. I do not think their demureness was altogether due to the presence of strangers among them, for before I finally left the island I had had a chance to observe them in their play and made friends with a number of them, but I never saw anything approaching boisterousness.

In many respects the settlement differed little from an Irish village. Geese waddled about the common and showed their resentment of too close an approach with the usual hissing and stretching of the neck. All about were little pigs – long-nosed and lean-flanked, obviously not far removed in type from the original 'wild pig' – which were rooting up the earth with their snouts. Each had an attendant fowl which accompanied it in its movements and picked at the newly turned earth. There are a number of dogs on the island, mongrel curs of which one would grudge even the admission that they were 'just dog', and there seems to be a regular feud between them and the pigs. Whenever a dog, accompanying his master on a walk, encounters a pig, it rushes up, barking furiously, and only desists when the pig, squealing violently, is stretched at full speed. The pig gets very angry, but immediately after goes on rooting. There was something very ludicrous about this little piece of byplay, which always provoked a laugh from us. On the slope behind the settlement a flock of sheep, numbering a hundred or so, was grazing. Here and there about the common I saw donkeys, all of them very diminutive.

At the entrance to the settlement we came to a brisk little stream of clear water, which we crossed by a ford.

We were met by Mr Rogers, the missionary, who had recently come to the island.

There are in all about twenty completed houses and others of which the walls have been built, but which, from lack of material, have never been roofed over. The first one we came to belonged to Henry Green, a small, self-reliant man whom we had already met on the ship. He gave us a cordial invitation to come in at any time we cared. He had a small flagstaff, from which flew a Union Jack that had been presented to the islanders.

Commander Wild had detailed me to stay on Tristan da Cunha while the ship proceeded to Nightingale and Inaccessible Islands, and I now made inquiries as to where I could stay. Bob Glass said immediately: 'You come right 'long to my house, and I'll tell my wife she got to look after you and give you everything she got, which ain't much, I may tell you.' He now led me to it, and introduced me to his wife and family, which numbered eight – six boys and two girls. His wife, who was a second wife and not the mother of any of his children, was a very pleasant woman, with quiet, natural manners. She told me she would be glad to put me up for as long as I cared to stay on the island. The members of the family varied in age from a young man of twenty-two years – who was married and had two children of his own – to a bright lad of eight. The girls, aged twenty and seventeen respectively, seemed to be very pleasant, but had little to say, being, I think, rather shy and bashful in the presence of a stranger. Bob Glass said to me after: 'That gel Wilet,' – Violet, the elder – 'she's a foine gel; me and she never had a cross word. But that there Dorothee – she's wery loively.' Quite what form the liveliness took I never learnt, but his words led me to believe that Miss Dorothy was a less dutiful and obedient daughter than Violet.

This house resembles all the other houses of the settlement, which are erected to more or less the same design, being long, low, oblong structures built of stones of considerable size and weight. The side walls are usually a little more than 2 feet thick, and the end walls are heavily buttressed. They all face the same way, so as to be end on to the prevailing winds, which blow at times with great strength and with sudden violent gusts.

The roofs are composed of wooden beams, and are thatched over with tussock grass, which is made into bundles and lashed securely to the beams so that they overlap from above downwards. A layer of turf is placed to cover the apex where the two sides meet. The ceilings and floors are made of wood – odd pieces begged from ships, taken from packing cases or found along the seashore – collected only with much patience over a period of months or years before enough is accumulated for the purpose. Much of the planking in the older houses has been derived from ships wrecked on one or other of the islands. In the house of Mrs Repetto there is a piece from the stern of a small vessel bearing the name *Mabel Clarke* which had gone ashore forty years previously. The insides of the stone walls are faced with wood in the same way. The space left between thatch and ceiling is used universally as a store room. Windows, except in the case of one of the houses, are on one side only, and face the sea to enable a good look out to be kept for passing ships. The exception is in the house just mentioned, that of Mrs Repetto, whose husband (deceased), an Italian sailor, survivor of a ship wrecked on the island, must have been a man of much ingenuity and practical ability, for the house is much better equipped and furnished in every way than any other in the settlement.

Taken on the whole, the houses keep remarkably dry and are durable, though the tussock thatch often requires renewing in patches and the turf is often lifted away in the fiercer gales. They are divided, in the majority of cases, by a single wall, into living-room and bedroom, but a few have an additional room. There is a fireplace at one end of the living-room made of stone, with two or three pieces of iron let in. In some of the houses the cooking is done in these fireplaces, but in others, especially where the family is a large one, an annexe is built on to the end of the house to act as a kitchen. In one or two of the better houses a separate kitchen is included in the main building. Each house boasts a table and some chairs, often very rickety, and most of them have also a wooden settee, or 'sofa', as it is generally called. Some possess tablecloths and sofa covers and have a few bright pictures on the walls. Others are lacking in these luxuries, the walls being bare or adorned only with one or two tracts. As a rule the houses are kept clean, but in this they vary very much, depending upon the occupants. One must understand some of the difficulties they have in this respect. Brushes and brooms are a rarity; they use whisks made from the 'island tree', which answer only moderately well. They are often without soap, and when there is any on the island it has to be used with the greatest economy. Taking everything into consideration, I think they are to be congratulated upon what they achieve in this way.

Rats came ashore from a ship called the *Henry B. Paul*, wrecked on the back of the island. They increased and multiplied so rapidly that they have overrun the place and are found in the lofts of every house. To combat them a few cats are kept, but while I was living ashore I preferred the company of the rats to that of the cats, which are most unpleasant brutes and more than half wild.

Fleas swarm all over the settlement, and none of the houses seem to be wholly free from them. As a doctor, I had occasion to examine many of the people. Nearly all of them were extensively flea-bitten, but some seemed to have escaped their ravages. I found no trace of other body parasites.

Any man starting to build a house here sets himself a difficult task. The stone is fairly easily obtained and set up. Boulders carried down from the mountain strew the lower slopes, and there are plenty in the neighbourhood of the settlement. They are brought in by securing them with chains to which bullocks are attached, the number of animals varying with the size of the boulder. They are dragged bodily over the ground, the work, however, being the easier in that most of the distance is downhill. Soft boulders are selected, and are cut to shape with small axes. A number of men sit or kneel about the boulder to be cut, chipping away little pieces in turn with rapid strokes of the axe.

Wood presents to the prospective builder a much harder problem, and many a young man anxious to marry or a young married couple eager for their own home have to spend long weary months, or even years, in accumulating the wood necessary to make the roof, the ceiling or the floor. The shores, not only of Tristan da Cunha, but also of Inaccessible and Nightingale Islands, are eagerly searched for driftwood. Especially is it difficult to collect the crossbeams, those in existence having come from wrecked ships. The islanders regard it as a regrettable fact that 'wracks' are becoming more and more scarce. Many of the occupied houses are only partially ceilinged over, and have holes in the floor which their occupants are unable to complete or repair for lack of the necessary wood. The holes in the floor, if not too large, are covered by boxes in which belongings, the *lares et penates*, are kept.

When completed, the houses make snug little dwellings and adequately meet the needs of the islanders.

As Commander Wild was not leaving for Inaccessible Island till next day, I slept that night on the *Quest*, but told Mrs Glass that I should come ashore the next day to stay. I felt that my board might be a bit of a burden to her, and was anxious to bring with me sufficient stores amply to cover my stay.

The next day (20 May) was beautifully fine, with bright sunshine. Commander Wild sent ashore the scientific staff, with assistants, to carry on their special work. Jeffrey verified the position of the settlement and took bearings of all the more salient points on the northern side of the island. Wilkins took his cameras and cinematograph machine, and had a busy day photographing the people in the various stages of their work, family groups, cottages and, indeed, anything of interest. Carr made observations of the flat land to the west of the settlement with regard to its future usefulness as a landing-place for aircraft. Douglas made an ascent to the peak of the mountain for geological purposes, while McIlroy seized the opportunity of discussing with Mr Rogers, the missionary, meteorological work and observations.

The most interesting event of the day was a parade of the Tristan troop of Boy Scouts, which was turned out for Commander Wild's inspection. The troop was instituted by Mr Rogers on his arrival, and was, of course, still very raw. It was surprising to note how well these boys looked and how altered in appearance they were after changing from their nondescript garments to the smart new uniforms. After considerable manoeuvring, they were finally drawn up on parade, when Marr, in full Scout uniform with kilt, formally presented a Scout flag specially sent out by Sir Robert Baden-Powell for this purpose. The boys felt a little bit overcome by the occasion and responded indifferently to the words of command, but under the circumstances any but the most friendly criticism would be unfair. The boys appeared to be keen, Mr Rogers was keen, and it is probable that the next people to hold an inspection will see a very different turnout. Everyone on the island witnessed the ceremony, and all the women donned their best clothes for the occasion. I had thought that they would have taken a greater interest in the kilt, but they seemed hardly to notice it – unlike the women of France and Italy, who during the war were so fascinated by the Highland uniforms. Mr Rogers and Marr had quite a lengthy talk on Scout matters.

The islanders very hospitably looked after all who had come ashore, which included most of the crew of the *Quest*, inviting them to their houses for meals. Jeffrey and I had both lunch and dinner with Bob Glass, waited upon royally by Mrs Glass, 'Wilet' and 'Dorothee' while a large number of peeping faces grouped themselves about the door and windows.

After the parade of Scouts, Commander Wild went back to the ship. He permitted the others to stay longer, but gave instructions that they were to go aboard before dark. There was some delay, however, and to hurry them up he fired a detonator, which burst with a loud report and a spangle of stars and reverberated in numerous echoes from the hillside. The effect was extraordinary. Every living thing on the island was thoroughly startled; dogs bolted and yelped, girls and children screamed and ran for the houses, while sheep, pigs, geese and poultry scampered in all directions in the wildest confusion.

Soon afterwards I saw the lights of the *Quest* passing out in the direction of Inaccessible Island. With her went three of the islanders whom Commander Wild had taken to act as pilots and guides. They were Robert and John Glass and Henry Green.

I had spent the day in seeing sick people or people who thought that, seeing a doctor had come to the island, they might just as well get him to have a look at them. The men came to see me at Robert Glass's house, and later Mrs Glass conducted me on a tour of the settlement to see a number of women patients. There were numerous minor ailments: sprains, old fractures, or 'brocks', as the islanders call them, which had reunited with serious deformity, rheumatism, and a condition they call 'ashmere', meaning asthma. This seems to be the most prevalent complaint on the island. Taken on the whole, however, they are a very healthy little community.

I had with me in my medical equipment a small portable electric battery. In the evening a man named Tom Rogers, who had received an injury to his arm some time before, came for treatment, and I gave him some electrical massage. He was delighted with the sensation, and made everyone who came to the house take the terminals and feel it also. I got several of them to join hands, and passed the current through all of them at one time. Tom Rogers kept sending for more and more people to 'feel the electricity' until the house was full. Finding that the current passed through any part of the body that was touched, he determined to play a joke on a new-comer, suddenly touching his ear while a strong current was passing. The newcomer, Gordon Glass, who had never seen such a thing before, was considerably startled, to the great joy of all the others, who thoroughly appreciated the joke and retailed it all over the settlement, to my undoing, for I had to demonstrate the experiment again and again.

I found that these islanders, when gathered together, were a genial, pleasant lot, very good tempered, and quick to see humour. Though intelligent in many respects, most of them had absolutely no interest in anything happening outside the island; but, considering their isolated position and lack of communication with the rest of the world, together with their inability to read, this can easily be understood.

Bob Glass had given his family instructions to put me in his bed and to clear out of the house and leave me to myself. Goodness knows where they went to. I turned in and quickly fell asleep, to awake very soon with a sensation that all was not well. The trouble proved to be a countless host of small marauders, which were very persistent and voracious. I had no more sleep that night.

The next day (Sunday, 21st) I was up early. Mrs Glass brought me a cup of very strong black coffee without sugar or milk. Acting probably on her husband's instructions, she brought me also some hot water for shaving. This accomplished, I sallied forth to the clear brook and started sponging down, to find myself, much to my embarrassment, an object of interest to sundry small children of both sexes.

Breakfast was served to me in solitary state, which was a disappointment, for I had hoped to sit down with the family. The meal consisted of mutton and potatoes, as did all the meals I had while remaining on the island. Mrs Glass would have fed me on her share of the stores from the *Quest*, but I told her I was tired of ship's food and wanted a change.

The weather had changed; it was raining hard, and the wind having come round to the north-west, from which direction it blew up strongly, it looked as if a landing would not be effected on Inaccessible Island. I wondered what the *Quest* was doing – at least, I knew very well what she was doing, and felt glad I was on terra firma.

I called on the Revd and Mrs Rogers, and later went to church, the service being held in the little schoolroom. It was well attended. One side of the room was filled by the women, who left their husbands to get in where they could. They looked well in their best cotton dresses, with bright-coloured handkerchiefs tied over their hair. This form of headgear is very picturesque, very practical, and eminently suited to this wind-blown island. I was accompanied by my hostess, and hoped to get a back seat where I could see all that was going on; but room being made for me on the front bench, I was bound to accept. I regret to say that I was guilty of many turnings of the head. The service was short and simple. I was surprised at the hearty way in which everyone, both men and women, joined in the hymns, which, as most of them could not read, they must have learnt by heart. I was told that the wife of a previous missionary had taught them a number of the best-known hymns, and that the 'New Missus' (Mrs Rogers) was bringing them up to scratch again in their singing. A larger place is necessary, for the room was filled and several people hung about the door unable to find a seat. All the missionaries who have been on the island have tried to persuade the people to build a church for themselves, but without success.

After church I called on Gaetano Lavarello, one of the shipwrecked sailors from the *Italia*, a Genoese by birth. I spoke to him in his own language, which he understood, but found when he attempted to reply that he had lost the fluent use of his mother tongue, having for nearly forty years spoken nothing but English. He expressed himself as quite content with life on the island. He had married a Glass, and had several children. He said the thing he felt the lack of most was tobacco. He had not had a smoke for a long time, and asked me if

I could give him some plug or a stick of hard tobacco, offering in exchange a sheep. He said: 'I have the largest flock and the best sheep on the island, and I will give you a good one.' Unfortunately, I had no tobacco, but told him I had no doubt that Commander Wild would give him some when the ship returned, and would not require the sheep.

I then called on Mr and Mrs Rogers. They are known by the islanders as 'Reverend Rogers' and 'The Missus', which names I adopted, for there are so many 'Rogers' on the island as to be confusing. They asked me to have lunch, during which they told me of the difficulties and heavy expenses they had been put to in order to come out and take up their work on this island. Apparently it was an entirely individual enterprise, and the Church organisation had taken no part in it at all. The first assistance of any sort which they had received was at Cape Town, where considerable interest is taken in this little outpost.

The 'Missus' was only nineteen years of age, and had had no previous experience to guide her in her preparations for the life she was to lead. It takes a lot of pluck for a woman to cut herself off from all home connexions and bury herself in a small spot like this, shut off entirely from the outside world, without guidance or counsel in the changes and chances which fall to the lot of every married woman. I admired the courage and enthusiasm with which she faced her self-imposed task, which included not only the instructing of the unwilling youth of Tristan da Cunha in cleanliness, morality and the 'three Rs', but also such multifarious duties as nurse, midwife, scribe, reader and general adviser to the womenfolk.

In the afternoon I again visited some of my patients. One woman was really very ill and in need of hospital attention. I did my best to persuade her to go to Cape Town. The husband, on having things represented to him, was agreeable, but there were numerous objections. I asked 'The Missus' to use her influence to persuade her to seize the chance of a passing vessel to go. It must be admitted that this reluctance to leave the island is natural. These people have no money and are not well off for clothes (I believe this was the chief objection in the mind of the good lady herself), and the leaving of the island to those who have known nothing else resolves itself into a great adventure into an unknown world.

Commander Wild had asked me to take a census of the island, and this I proceeded to do, visiting the houses in turn. There was considerable vagueness about ages, and in many cases about names also. On more than one occasion a man (it was always the stupid male sex) did not seem clear about his own name, sometimes contradicting himself or appealing to bystanders for confirmation. As may be gathered from the history of the settlement, with comparatively few exceptions everyone on the island is either a Glass, Green, Swaine or Rogers. Consequently, individuals are better known by Christian names than by surnames, which probably accounts for their vagueness. It is rather remarkable that with so few names among them the new chaplain should be a Rogers.

The history of Tristan da Cunha is interesting. The island was discovered in 1506 by a Portuguese navigator, Tristão da Cunha, from whom it takes its name, and though individuals on different occasions lived on it for short periods at a time, for 300 years it remained nobody's property. It was formally annexed by Great Britain in 1816, and a garrison, consisting of about 100 men, placed there, with the object of resisting any attempt by foreign Powers to use it as a base of operations for the rescue of Napoleon from St Helena. The garrison remained for a year only. Corporal Glass, of the Royal Artillery, a native of Kelso, in Scotland, asked for, and received, permission to stay. He had married a coloured woman from Cape Colony, and had at the time two children. It was no doubt the possession of this black wife that chiefly influenced his decision. He was joined by Alexander Cotton and Thomas Swaine, two members of the relief ship. This little party was augmented by some shipwrecked American whalers, but none of them remained long, the only names persisting today of the original settlers being Glass, Swaine and Cotton. Some twenty years later Pieter William Green, a Dutchman, was wrecked on Inaccessible Island, and having made his way to Tristan da Cunha, elected to remain. About the middle of the century two American whalers, Rogers and Hagan, also settled there, and more recently, within the present generation, two Italian sailors, Andreas Repetto and Gaetano Lavarello, survivors cast upon the shores from the wreck of the sailing ship *Italia*, were so determined never again to risk their lives upon the ocean that they also threw in their lot with the islanders and stayed.

Of the original settlers, only Glass was married. The others obtained wives through the good offices of the captain of a whaling vessel, who brought five women from St Helena. It was a funny way of choosing their mates, and the islanders of today speak of the incident as a great joke, guessing at the feelings of their great grandsires when they went to meet their brides and speculating upon the methods adopted in the selection. Occasionally the settlement has been temporarily augmented by other shipwrecked sailors, who seized an early opportunity to get away in some passing ship. There is evidence to show that they introduced a certain amount of new blood among the islanders, for some of them had children which were born after their departure. No new names were introduced, however, for the children adopted the names of the mothers. This factor must be taken into account when considering the effects upon the present generation of intermarriage and consanguinity.

The original garrison brought to the island a considerable quantity of livestock in the shape of cattle, sheep, pigs, geese, poultry, donkeys and goats, and were responsible for the laying down of the 'potato patches', small walled-in potato gardens situated about 2 miles to the west of the settlement under the lee of some high mounds. The livestock throve, and there are representatives to-day of every species except the goats, which took to the hills, but were destroyed by the heavy torrents which rapidly form and sweep down the gullies whenever there is heavy rain.

From time to time attempts have been made to introduce corn, maize and vegetables of different sorts, but owing to the violent winds which prevail they have never been a success. Practically the only vegetable grown in useful quantity to-day is the pumpkin, and this is in no great abundance. In the sheltered gullies at the back of the island there are some very stunted apple trees which produce small crops of apples.

The herds, from which they derive their supply of meat, milk and butter, and the potatoes have met the chief food requirements of the islanders, but for everything else they have relied upon trade with passing merchant ships and whalers.

In the days, not very remote, when a number of sailing ships were making the Australian passage round the Cape of Good Hope and during the period of whaling activity, the islanders throve, for the ships were glad to obtain fresh meat and potatoes, and gave in exchange things of general value, such as clothes, tools and materials, and flour, sugar, tea and soap. With the establishment of fixed whaling stations ashore and the rapid disappearance of sailing ships in favour of steamers, which are more or less independent of winds and follow fixed routes, carry refrigerating plants, and to whom delay means loss of money, this trade by barter has languished and died away. They are a prolific people. The population has increased and is likely to increase more rapidly with every generation, so that their needs today are greater than they have ever been since the foundation of the settlement.

For this history of the island I am indebted to Miss Betty Cotton, an interesting old lady of ninety-five years, to whom I paid many visits. In spite of her age she is still very bright and active, with a clear memory for past events, of which she took a pleasure in narrating to me the salient facts I have set down, together with a wealth of more intimate detail which might well fill a volume. In everything which it was possible to verify I found her to be very accurate. Indeed, she was really a wonderful old lady, for she still moved actively about the settlement on fine days. She regretted, however, that she was no longer able to face the fiercer gusts of wind and her sight was very bad. She asked me to give her some pills, not because she felt ill, but had, I suppose, the general impression that some pills would do her good.

It is extraordinary how all the inhabitants carry their age, many of those who should normally be entering the 'sere and yellow' being still bright and active and in appearance middle-aged. Many middle-aged people, in the same way, give the appearance of youth. This applies to both sexes, but more particularly to the men.

Certainly in this island, situated 'far from the madding crowd', there is little of the nerve-racking wear and tear of modern civilisation. Freedom from epidemic diseases, the impossibility of over-indulgence in tobacco, alcohol or faked-up foods, the pure atmosphere and the healthy open-air life which they are compelled to lead are, no doubt, factors in producing this longevity.

Again during the night I was attacked by marauders, which allowed me little rest. In the morning, after breakfast, I took a walk out along the bluff to see if I could pick out through my binoculars any signs of the *Quest* at Inaccessible Island. It was too misty to get a clear view, but as there was a strong nor'-westerly wind and a heavy swell with much surf, which would have made a landing there quite impossible, it did not seem likely that they would be successful. I was followed out from the settlement by the husband of the woman whom I wanted to go to Cape Town. He was anxious to discuss further the possibilities. Poor fellow! he was very concerned for his wife's welfare. I went with him to his house, which is one of the cleanest and neatest on the island, situated some little distance from the rest of the settlement, to see my patient again. Some mischievous though probably well-meaning body at home had sent her a large supply of pills, with which she had been drugging herself heavily.

The morning was wet and squally, so I did not go far from the settlement, but walked about watching the men and women at their work and inducing the children, by sundry small bribes of chocolate, to come and talk to me. They were wonderfully free from shyness. Later, I called on 'Reverend Rogers' and 'The Missus.'

At 12.00 noon the day cleared, and so I set off with Frank Glass, one of Bob Glass's sons, to climb the mountain face. My companion, aged seventeen years, was a bright, cheery youth with a firm belief that there could be no place in the world like Tristan da Cunha nor such an all-round lot of fine fellows as the 'Tristanites'. He expressed, however, a willingness to leave the island and see something of that other place, 'the world', but would seize an early chance to come back again.

We crossed the settlement and the land lying behind it, passing at the foot of the mountain the springs from which the water supply is derived. In this respect the people are well off, for the water is good and beautifully soft. The original garrison, in order to divert the water past the houses, had built a canal, which in some places passed through little tunnels in the hillocks, and was quite a small feat of engineering. The volume is considerable, and the water running to the cliff edge falls to the beach in a good-sized cascade, which makes a useful mark for ships looking for the landing-place.

The ascent of the mountain lay first up a steep, grassy, boulder-strewn slope, from the top of which we made a traverse across the face of the mountain to a ridge where the climbing was steep, but where there was good hand- and foot-hold. We zigzagged up this for several hundred feet. There was abundant vegetation, numbers of ferns, including a species of tree fern, tussock and other forms of grass, mosses, lichens and the 'island tree' (*Phylica nitida*), a gnarled and stunted tree which is found all over the island and which offers firm holding for climbers. There were also on the lower slopes a number of field daisies, or marguerites, and a species of wild geranium bearing a small flower with a pleasant aromatic smell. To another plant my guide gave the name of 'dog-catcher', because during the summer it grows a sort of 'burr' which catches in the hair of the dogs and is very hard to remove.

Our route followed a faint but definite track which is used constantly by the islanders in their search for wood to burn, and in the season for the eggs of mollymauks and other seabirds which nest there. Even the women make this ascent.

We crossed several bold rocky bluffs and gullies. Nowhere was there any danger, provided reasonable care were used, but in one or two places one crept along dizzily poised ridges where a false or careless step would have been sufficient to precipitate one to a drop of 2,000 or 3,000 feet.

Near the top we were enveloped by dense mist accompanied by squalls of rain. Everything was obscured, and so we returned to the scrub, where we built a shelter from branches of the 'island tree' under which I sat and talked with Frank Glass. For one with such a limited outlook, this young man had very advanced ideas on life in general. He told me quite cheerfully that the island was faced with starvation and ruin. He also remarked that it would not do to go on marrying each other, and that they needed new blood. I recognised many of his expressions, however, as those of his father, Bob Glass.

Our shelter after a while ceased to be effective, and the water started pouring through in little rivulets. There were no signs of the weather clearing, so we descended some distance and made a traverse to a high projecting rock known as 'The Pinnacle'. This is a high, straight mass crowned with a little vegetation. It is inaccessible except by a tunnel running up the middle and emerging at the top, up which we scrambled with free use of elbows and knees. Here we were out of the mist, and had a fine bird's-eye view of the flat part of the island and the settlement. The sea, edged with a long irregular line of white where the surf was breaking on the shore, stretched like a flat board to a dim, far-distant horizon.

We were now in bright sunshine, and I felt quite content to lie, chin in hand, gazing at the tiny objects far below; but while I was enjoying the view the mist came down the hill and again enveloped us. We therefore descended to the settlement, where we arrived soaked to the skin.

I noticed a large crowd collected about one of the houses, and so, having put on dry clothes, I approached to see what was happening. I found that the islanders were engaged in dividing up the goods we had sent ashore into approximately equal lots.

They have a system of their own for dealing with common stores. When the boats go out to a ship barter is first of all carried out in the name of the community for such stores as tea, sugar, flour, etc. Each family in turn provides whatever goods are necessary for these exchanges in the way of cattle, sheep, geese or potatoes. When this has been done, the individuals who have manned the boat may barter with their own goods for any particular article which they or their families may require. This includes articles of clothing, general household utensils, knives, wood, nails, etc. In exchange they can give of their own livestock or polished horns, mats made from penguin skins, socks knitted by the women, shells and other curios. The goods brought ashore in the name of the community are divided equally among the families irrespective of the size of the family, so that a man with eight or nine children draws no more than a man who has none.

Everything that is divisible is divided up even to the smallest amounts, so that one family's share of rice, for example, may amount to no more than one spoonful! One single piece of soap has been known to be divided into eight pieces! Things which are obviously indivisible, such as stone jars, baskets, pots and pans, tins or sacks, are made up into little batches of as nearly as possible equal value and allotted by the system of saying 'Whose?' In carrying this out one person points in turn to each batch, saying 'Whose?' while another, blindfolded or with back turned, answers the name of one of the families. It is a very fair system. Supposing that there are only twelve lots and twenty families to draw, the caller shouts 'Whose?' twenty times, occasionally indicating a blank by pointing at the ceiling or floor. No name, of course, is called twice. The women adhere very rigidly to this division of goods, even to the extent of quantities which are valueless. The men, on the other hand, occasionally decide to own things jointly, such as spars, chains, tools or implements, or where a thing is obviously of use to one man only – e.g. an empty cask – they will agree to take turns in acquiring it. Also, a man who is collecting wood for his house will be allowed to have for his own use one or more packing-cases on the understanding that he must compensate in one way or another later on. No written note is made, but they seem to have tenacious memories in this respect.

Again, in the case of an article which has been blown up on the island too heavy or bulky to be dealt with by the finder alone, such as a large tree or a stranded whale, those who help to bring it to the settlement participate equally in what profit may result from it.

This system was evolved by the patriarchs of the community, men such as Corporal Glass, the founder, and Pieter William Green, each of whom was for long the virtual head of the island. On the whole it is a very fair one, and even though it seems unjust that the large families should share equally with the small ones, it must be remembered that the small family, when it comes to its turn to find the goods for barter, has to bear an equal brunt with the larger. Children also are not regarded as a handicap, but as an asset, for from the time they are able to run about and drive sheep or geese they work for their living. In England one's income does not vary with the number of children, and a bachelor employee receives the same wages as a married man if he does identical work.

On this particular occasion the work of dividing was going on merrily, and the young people and children were kept busy running to and from the houses with the shares. The missionary and his wife were acting as umpires at the 'sheering' (they pronounced long 'a' as 'ee'). When it was over I returned with Mr and Mrs Rogers to their house, and sat talking for a while. They brought their house with them from England, cut in sections all ready for putting up. It is small but snug. Their chief fear in connexion with it is that it may be lifted and carried away by some of the fiercer gusts of wind, and they were proposing to have it walled over with stone. They were very wise in bringing their own dwelling, for the housing problem is as difficult in Tristan da Cunha as it is in England in these post-war days.

While I was sitting and talking darkness set in. The wind outside was blowing hard, with sharp rain squalls. Mrs Glass, accompanied by one of her family, thinking I might be lost, set out on a pilgrimage round the settlement in search of me, and was relieved when I was discovered to be all safe and sound. She said that getting about was awkward for a stranger, and thought I might have walked past the house (which is the lowest of the settlement) and fallen over the cliff. She said: 'You stop now and finish your talk with the Missus, and I'll tell Tom Rogers (who lived nearby) to bring you down when you are ready.' The latter had supper with us. He is a pleasant, talkative fellow. Mrs Glass says he will talk all day to anyone he can get to listen to him. 'Usually,' she says, 'grown-ups is too busy, so he has to talk to one of the children.'

In the course of conversation Tom Rogers said that he was going to the back of the island to 'turn over' his cattle. By 'turn over' he meant drive them from one pasturage to another. I asked if I might accompany him. He was willing, but thought that I might find it a bit far, as it entailed a considerable walk and a good deal of climbing. I smiled to myself, thinking that I could hold my own well enough with any islander, more especially as Gordon Glass, a slim-looking young fellow, was also to join the party. I was to have my eyes opened, however.

After Tom Rogers had gone 'Wilet' and 'Dorothee' came in. Mrs Glass went to the door and called into the darkness: 'Come in, don't be shoi; no one ain't going to hurt you; come in, they'se both in!' Whereupon after a good deal more urging two very sheepish-looking youths entered, and planting themselves down on a form said no word at all but gazed across at the two girls. It seemed to me that I was very much *de trop*, and not wishing to be in any way a spoil-sport, I made some excuse to go out. It was not a pleasant night, being cold, and there was a slight drizzle. After about half an hour of stumbling blindly into every quagmire on the common, crossing the stream at its deepest and most slippery part, and causing all the dogs in the settlement to bark, I decided that I had been 'sporting' enough and returned to find them in exactly the same attitude as I had left them. Later on, touching on the subject to Mrs Glass, she remarked: 'Oh, they'se been coming every night like that for years, but Mr Glass he ain't going to let none of the gels marry till they'se twenty-one.'

I had with me in my medical equipment a small bottle of essential oil of lavender, and with it I plentifully sprinkled my bedding in the hope that it would keep away the fleas. I believe they liked it, and the only result achieved was that I acquired a distaste for the smell of lavender which will probably last my lifetime! However, as a result of my exercise in climbing, I slept well.

In the morning at 8.00 a.m. Tom Rogers, Glass and I set off for the back of the island. The road, a mud track, ran westwards, and led across a deep gulch which had been cut some years previously by a torrent from the mountain. We had a stiff wind against us, which, in a narrow passage between a big bluff and the side of the mountain, blew in gusts, against which it was hard work to force a way and which occasionally drove us back a step or two. Behind the bluff were several pyramidal grass-covered mounds, in the shelter provided by which are the 'potato-patches'. They consist of small walled-in areas, the walls serving to protect the plants from the force of the winds, which have a very deleterious effect upon the 'tops'. This is amply demonstrated by comparing those in well-protected areas with those which are more exposed, the latter being stunted, dry and withered looking. The potatoes are planted in September and early October, and taken up in February. They are small in size, but otherwise of good quality. At the time of my visit (late May) the islanders were engaged in collecting seaweed from the shore and conveying it in bullock-carts to the patches, where it is allowed to rot, mixed with sheep manure, and placed on top of the potatoes when they are planted. The manure is obtained by corralling the sheep and leaving them closely penned in for twenty-four hours. We passed across several more gulches and encountered some broad patches of stone which had been swept down out of the hills during the rains.

The soil in this part of the island is better than that at the settlement, and provides a flat grassy plain, giving good grazing for the sheep and cattle which are dotted all about its surface and climb up into the lower slopes of the mountain. Both are small, but of fairly good quality, the meat which I tasted on the island being tender and of good flavour. A number of the cattle had calves, which were pretty little creatures.

On this part of the island the land ends in short cliffs, at the foot of which are numerous narrow beaches on which, as we went along, a heavy surf was breaking, looking pretty in the sunlight and having a pleasant sound.

About 5 miles from the settlement the flat ground ends in a high straight bluff running steeply down to the sea. To get round this we had to ascend the mountain, having a steep climb of about 2,000 feet. The cattle and sheep, to get to the back of the island, have to make this climb, and there is a narrow track, worn by them, which zigzags upwards, passing across places where one single slip would mean destruction for the animal. I am told that very few of them fall. They must be amazingly sure-footed.

On several occasions as we wound along my companions pointed out to me in some of the sheltered gullies what they called 'orchards', little clumps of apple trees so small, bush-like and stunted as to be almost unrecognisable. Nevertheless, each year they get small crops of apples from them. I tasted some, and found them to have quite a good flavour. It is from these trees that the cross-pieces for their boats are made. The vegetation in the gullies is very luxuriant, and the grass, being sheltered from the winds, grows lush and long. Far below the clefts ended in little bays, where we caught glimpses of the surf breaking in creamy ridges against the shore. We continued upwards, and came suddenly to a sharply defined ridge above a steep precipice across which the wind blew strongly. We threw ourselves on our faces and peered over the edge, and got a view of the 'back of the island'. Far below us was a flat grassy plain with many cattle grazing, and away out to sea we saw Inaccessible and Nightingale Islands. I carefully scanned their base lines through my binoculars for any signs of the *Quest*, but the day was too hazy to permit of a clear view.

Tom Rogers proposed to descend from here to the plains to 'turn over' his cattle, but, having climbed so far, I was anxious to continue up till I could get a clear view of the top of the mountain, so he good-naturedly put off the job to another day, and we went on upwards, laboriously working through long tussock-grass and thick masses of tree fern.

These men with whom I had thought to hold my own so easily seemed to be absolutely tireless, and they took a keen interest in the outing and in showing me all things of interest.

Here and there we came across little bundles of branches cut from the 'island tree'. These were loads in process of being collected to be taken finally to the settlement for firewood.

Some of the branches which went to the formation of these bundles had to be dragged for a considerable distance across the face of the cliff, often only with the utmost difficulty. They are collected eventually at a point above a gully which will give a clear drop to a point thousands of feet below, where they can be gathered up and loaded into bullock-carts for taking home.

Through my binoculars I could see men at work all about the ridges, and I was deeply impressed by the hardihood of the life they must lead in having thus to fare abroad for their daily needs.

Gordon Glass had with him his dog, which occasionally discovered a 'Pediunker', a species of seabird which frequents the island and about this time of year is preparing to nest. They lay in holes in the hillside, and a search was made for a chance egg, though it was still early in the season for them. We allowed the birds to go free.

We reached at last a point where the heavier vegetation ended and the hill was covered with a rather coarse grass interspersed with patches of moss. It was very damp. From here we had a fine view, and the air was keen and cold. We descended by another route, which led eventually to a cattle track where the going was easier, but the steepness and tortuosity of which again impressed me with the remarkable climbing powers of the animals.

Reaching the plain again, we set off at a good round pace for the settlement, where I arrived, I am not ashamed to say, pleasantly fatigued with the day's outing, while my companions seemed to think they had done nothing out of the way. I mention this particularly because it has been stated from time to time by visitors that these islanders are becoming a decadent lot and are suffering from the results of intermarriage and consanguinity. That they are physically decadent is not true. Taken on the whole, they are of medium height and slimly built, but they are very tough and wiry. John Glass, whom I have already mentioned as having been the first man aboard the *Quest*, is a powerful man. Some of the elderly men of fifty years or thereabouts are wonderfully nimble and active. They are hardy walkers and climbers, and in their attempts to reach passing ships are often compelled to row long distances against heavy winds – a procedure which requires plenty of stamina.

Speaking of them collectively, they are not good workers, and attempts to get them to work together in an organised way for their mutual profit have not been successful. An attempt was made some years ago by a Cape Town firm to introduce a fish-curing industry and to get them to export sheep, but the islanders did not pull together and the scheme failed. They themselves give as a reason that they were being exploited and that the return was totally inadequate.

It is possible that due consideration was not given to their insularity and limitations of outlook, and that the use of a little more patience and diplomacy might have met with better results. I doubt very much, however, whether these islanders would ever settle down to a daily routine of work, having all their lives been more or less their own masters and able to decide when they shall or shall not work. Nevertheless, the necessities of life compel that the days spent at home be few, and the qualities of hardihood to which I have referred are not developed by doing nothing.

It has been stated also that through intermarriage there are numerous signs of deformity and mental degeneration. There are very few of these signs. As to mental degeneration, I considered these islanders to be very intelligent. They are uneducated, limited in outlook, and generally 'insular', but how could they be anything else in their peculiar circumstances? They are bright, quick to see humour and enjoy a joke, and are morally much sounder than many civilised peoples. They live on good terms, with little quarrelling, crime is unknown, and petty misdemeanours are rare.

One youth is dumb and is peculiar in manner, but works and carries out ordinary duties with quite average intelligence. Of deformities: one old woman (the island midwife) has two thumbs on each hand, but is otherwise normal. One man, a particularly noticeable case, has stunted arms, with ill-developed hands and absence of some fingers. Otherwise, he is strong, level-headed and intelligent, works as a shepherd, and in his duties roams far and wide over the hills. There are no other signs of mental or physical degeneration. The man with the stunted arms is able to do wonderful things, can carry small packages, hold a cigarette, feed himself, and, most extraordinary of all in this community of illiterates, can write. He was taught by a former missionary to the island, Mr Dodgson (brother of Lewis Carroll, author of *Alice in Wonderland*). It is surely a triumph of patient teaching. In carrying it out, the paper is placed on the floor and the man lies down. Though the writing is large and scrawly, it is legible.

I devoted as much time as possible to conversation with different people, trying to learn what I could of their manners and customs.

In religion they are mostly Protestant, but there are some who were baptised as Roman Catholics at Cape Town. There is, however, no distinction made between the religions, and they intermarry. There have been several Protestant missionaries on the island at one time and another, but never a Roman Catholic priest. Young men and women wishing to marry select their own mates by mutual agreement and are uninfluenced by their parents. The marriage service is conducted (in the absence of a missionary) by Bob Glass, who reads it from the Prayer Book. There is generally no fuss and no sort of function, but occasionally they have a dance afterwards in one of the houses. All the women go to hear the marriage service read, and such of the men as are about and have nothing better to do. I noticed in talking of weddings that the women spoke with an absence of enthusiasm and showed none of the interest that such a subject would arouse among civilised feminism.

Frequently it happens that a couple do not become married until after a child has been born; often a considerable period elapses. They are not, however, 'marriages of necessity'. A young man in Tristan da Cunha is very peculiarly placed. There are no jobs or trades or form of employment in the ordinary sense. There is no currency. If any individual wants help, his neighbours give him a hand, during which time he is expected to feed them. A young man, therefore, can acquire nothing except as a gift from his parents. In many ways it may not suit his parents to allow him to marry, for it means, first of all, another family on the island drawing a full share of common goods. It means also the loss of an adult worker. Again, they may not be in a position to spare him anything in the way of household goods, and, if he has not already built a house, it means a wife and any family he may have quartered upon them. So the young couple use compulsion, for with the advent of the child the parents think it is time to make a move, and present the pair with a cow, a sheep or two, and a few household necessities to enable them to make a start. Until the formal marriage takes place, the child takes its mother's name, and so it occasionally happens that a bewildered tot of three or four years of age suddenly finds one day that, instead of being Tommy Green, its name has become Tommy Swaine, or vice versa, as the case may be.

Promiscuity is not common and morals, on the whole, appear to be remarkably good, though to the casual observer the reverse might seem to be the case. The remarks in *Sailing Directions* seem to me to cast an unfair stigma upon the islanders.

In some ways they are very casual. Appointments are rarely kept punctually, and they are apt to put things off for another day.

In the hours of rising and going to bed they are governed by the sun. The only form of artificial illumination known to them is candle-light, and frequently they have no candles. They have, as a rule, three meals a day, which they take at times convenient on any one day. The men seek to avoid going out to work in wet weather, but at times – for instance, in the potato season – they fare forth before dawn so as to be ready for work the moment daylight appears, and do not return till dusk. On these occasions it is the duty of the womenfolk to take them out their meals.

There is an island custom that when the men have been engaged on an arduous piece of work at some distant part of the island or have had a heavy day in the boats, the women come out to meet them on their return with something hot to drink. Indeed, the women are by no means idle, for they have all the inside housework, cleaning, cooking, mending, sewing and washing of clothes to do. They card the fleece from the sheep into wool and twist it into strands, using for the purpose old-fashioned wheels which are manufactured with much ingenuity from all sorts of odds and ends of wood and metal. They knit excellent socks of pure wool, which are soft and comfortable to wear. Usually, also, they take charge of the geese and poultry, and, of course, have the children to look after. They frequent each other's houses a good deal, but there are one or two who keep to themselves and do not encourage visiting.

Sanitation is very much neglected. Closets do not exist, and the present clergyman had the greatest difficulty in getting one built for his own house. Animals are slaughtered in close proximity to the houses, and no proper steps taken for the removal of entrails and offal, which are left for the dogs to eat. Nothing is done to protect the water supply, which is derived from open streams that have been diverted to pass close to the houses, and the water becomes fouled before it reaches the lower parts of the settlement. Nevertheless, the settlement compares favourably in this respect with many of the remote villages in European countries.

The people are very free from sickness of any kind, which is probably due to their simple mode of life and the absence of any epidemic diseases. They escaped the widespread epidemic of influenza. It is likely that any infectious disease introduced would run rapidly through the whole community. They say that almost invariably when a ship has visited the island 'colds' run the round of the settlement.

Maternity cases are dealt with by an old midwife, who adopts the wise policy of leaving things very much to Nature.

This strange little community is run without any laid-down system of government. There are no written laws. In the early days of the settlement Corporal Glass, Pieter Green and William Rogers in turn ruled in patriarchal fashion, all disputes being referred to them for settlement.

By a process of evolution certain customs and unwritten laws have come into use and are, perhaps, more rigidly adhered to than any definite written rulings. Crime does not seem to exist. In the history of the island there has been one case of suicide. Petty thieving is said to occur occasionally, but in so small a community, where everyone knows everybody else so well and their goings and comings, any stolen article would be quickly recognised, so that their honesty in this way may be enforced through certainty of detection. Sheep are occasionally missed, and it is thought that theft may account for some of them, the depredations being carried out at night and the animal immediately skinned and cut up so that it is unrecognisable in the morning. There is no policeman, no jail, and no system of punishment for offenders. It seemed to me that they lived very harmoniously together, with much give and take and very little quarrelling.

It is curious that the minds of visitors to this settlement have been mainly struck in two very different ways. To the first class this island community seems to have approached the ideal. The French captain, Raymond du Baty, who visited the island in 1907, says:

The social status of Tristan da Cunha is a commonwealth of a kind which has been dreamed of by philosophers of all ages and by our modern Socialists. There is no envy, hatred or malice among them; everything is done for the common good; they render each other brotherly service; they are free from all the vices of civilisation; they worship God in a simple way; they live very close to Nature, but without pantheistic superstition; greed and usury are unknown among them; there are no class distinctions, no rich or poor. Truly on this lonely rock in the South Atlantic we have a people who belong rather to the Pastoral Age of the world than to our modern unrestful life, and who, without theory or politics or written laws, have reached that state which has been described by the imaginative writers of all ages, haunted by the thought of the decadent morality of the seething cities, as the Golden Age or the Millennium.

I have often wondered as to what place the fleas, the rats, the offal outside the window and the fouled water supply take in the Golden Age.

The second class of people are struck at once by the extreme poverty, the squalor and lack of comforts, the illiteracy and ignorance and the extreme isolation. The captain of a steamer who had once called to drop mails said to us:

> They are a greedy lot of beggars and thieves. When they come aboard they ask you for everything they see, and if you do not give them what they want they will try and pinch it. When it comes to a matter of a bargain, they give you diseased sheep and bad potatoes, though they have good enough stuff ashore.

The question which arises to the mind of everyone is: What is to become of these people, with a rapidly increasing population and a decreasing touch with outside civilisation owing to lack of shipping? The pasturage on the island will support only a limited number of livestock, which soon will be insufficient for the increasing number of mouths.

I inquired of many of them, especially the younger ones, as to whether they would leave the island and settle elsewhere if they had the opportunity. The reply in most cases was: Yes, provided they were given a chance to make a decent living. They realise, however, that without money and knowledge of its use and value, without experience of outside ways of working and living, without education and unable even to read or to write, they are likely to be at a disadvantage in a hard, workaday world.

Robert Glass and some of the others who have spent some time away from the island fully realise that there is a day of reckoning to come, and they feel that, were it possible, it would be a good thing for the young men when they have reached a certain age to go away and work for a while at Cape Town or elsewhere. They could then decide whether they would return to the island or not, and, if they did, it is likely that they would bring back wives from the outside, thus periodically introducing new blood to the community. Glass himself says he would like his boys to serve a period in the army or navy, where they would have a more or less sheltered life and to a certain extent be cared for and looked after.

It is not likely that any offer of a wholesale transference of the community to another part of the world would be accepted when it came to the point – at any rate, by the elder people. After all, this is natural enough, for how many people in England, told that the population was getting too big for the country, would consent at a day's notice to make a sudden shift to Canada or Australia?

Nevertheless, I gathered from conversation with many of the young men that there is deep down a seed of unrest and a desire to see something of the outer world, where there are so many more opportunities to get on and acquire greater wealth, including such things as wristwatches, electric torches, and boots of real leather. For this Robert Glass is largely responsible. The seed, however, requires cultivation. A missionary, by throwing himself into the interests of the islanders and becoming to some degree one of themselves, might effect considerable good by holding out continually in his daily talk and conversation prospects and mind-pictures of a greater world where opportunities wait for the young men who can grasp them. Equally good results might be effected by influencing the women in the same way. A missionary, however, to obtain a good influence on these people must be a man of broad mind and sound common sense. One previous missionary, for example, undid much good work by an attempt to stop them going out to passing ships on a Sunday, a maxim which they must necessarily reject when the chances of trade on any day at all are so few and the taking of them so vital a matter to the whole community. Mr Rogers, the present missionary, who replied very frankly when I asked him his views on the subject, agreed that much harm might be done by holding too narrow a view and trying to force a bigoted religion on these people. He has an uphill fight in front of him, for he has to undo a feeling that the observance of a religion is a bugbear which entails a number of things that may not be done.

Unfortunately, the chances of leaving the island, even if an individual has made up his mind to make the venture, have now become very scarce. There is no regular communication, and consequently arrangements for a job cannot be made beforehand,

and as there is no money on the island those who do find a passage cannot maintain themselves until work is found.

It so happens, however, that there are people in Cape Town who take an interest in Tristan da Cunha and who would be willing to give temporary help.

It is hardly likely that the Government will ever again do anything for the relief of these people, though all that is required is a small vessel to make the journey once a year from Cape Town [I learn on going to press that HMS *Dublin* is to visit the island in the near future]. It should be prepared to spend at least a week at Tristan da Cunha. Unfortunately, there is no good shelter, and on many days a landing could not be effected. Bad weather might compel the ship at any moment to leave her anchorage, and so she should have some power other than sail.

The best time of year to make the trip is January, when bad weather would least likely be met with. A vessel of 100 tons' burden would be adequate.

This is but a tiny portion of our Empire, but who knows, with the development of flying machines, of what use it may not ultimately become. Carr, our flying officer, late of the Royal Air Force, says there is a good site for an aerodrome, and the island is on the direct route from Cape Town to Buenos Aires.

The Church organisation also could do a vast amount of good by arranging for a permanent mission changeable, say, every three years, and thus ensure an unbroken education to those growing up. Much money is collected yearly for missions – for instance, to the Esquimaux – but there is evidence from the Arctic to show that the introduction of Christianity to these primitive people, who are not sufficiently evolved to receive it intelligently, has not always been productive of good, and in some cases has done much harm, whereas the value to Tristan da Cunha of a good sound practical religion combined with good schooling cannot be doubted.

CHAPTER 12

Diego Alvarez or Gough Island

On 26 May the wind was fair for Gough Island and we made good progress. Our ship had become a floating farmyard, for our livestock included sheep, geese, fowls, pig, cat, and, to stir them up and make things lively, our own dog Query, who had never before had so many interesting real live things to play with. The sow Bridget and the geese wandered all about the decks and got in the way generally. One gander was quite a character. He was blind of one eye and had a curious knack of standing with head on one side, quizzically regarding anyone he encountered. Regularly about once an hour he uttered a loud and very startling goose-call. We called him Nelson, and his mate, who followed him like a shadow wherever he went, was known as Jemima. Worsley in his watch below was being continually wakened by Nelson's harsh noises, and on one occasion I saw his head appear through his port and heard him shout: 'Be quiet, you silly beggar, you are not saving Rome now. That happened years ago!'

Bridget was a tyrant; she would not let the sheep alone, but rooted about in their grass feed, and having collected it into a nice bed for herself, lay down on it in stertorous sleep while the sheep looked on, advancing now and again to take an apologetic nibble at their own grass. Dell, who had taken in hand the attempt to fatten these poor animals, drove her off relentlessly to the accompaniment of much squealing.

We had a busy day squaring up after our upheaval at Tristan, and in getting ready the camping gear for use on Gough Island.

On 27 May at about 12.00 noon the island showed up. In spite of the comparatively short run we had had some difficulty in picking it up on account of winds, strong tides and no sun, which made it impossible for Worsley and Jeffrey to locate exactly our position, and the visibility was so poor that we could see less than a mile in any one direction. About noon, however, it appeared as a high mass crowned with mist.

This island lies about 250 miles south-south-east of Tristan da Cunha. It was discovered by Portuguese navigators in the sixteenth century and received the name Diego Alvarez. In 1731 Captain Gough in the *Richmond* sighted an island which he placed on the chart as lying to the east of Diego Alvarez and named Gough Island. For many years two separate islands were believed to exist, but now there can be no doubt they are one and the same. The name in most common usage is Gough, which seems hardly fair to its original discoverers.

In 1811 it was sighted by HMS *Nereus* under Captain Heywood. He effected a landing, described as being safe and easy, and discovered the remains of two huts which apparently had been set up some time previously by sealers. The height of the summit of the island was estimated by him at 4,380 feet. American sealers landed in 1825 but soon left. Morrell visited it in the *Antarctic* in 1829, and came to anchor in 12–14 fathoms in a cove on the north side, where he was able to water his ship. HMS *Royalist* arrived in 1887, and a survey was carried out by Lt J. P. Rolleston from which the Admiralty Chart (2228) was made. Towards the end of the same year an American schooner, *Francis Alleyn*, left a party of five sealers for six months who met, however, with little success. Among them was George Comer, who kept a diary. He seems to have been a keen observer very interested in natural history, and his diary contains a complete daily record of weather conditions during his stay. One of the party was frozen to death while attempting to cross over the island, and his grave was marked by a board bearing the inscription, 'Jose Gomez perished in the snow.' Another sealer, the *Wild Rose*, visited the island at the beginning of 1891 and landed a party which remained for about a year. They had little luck in the sealing. A harbour known as Snug Harbour is described by one of them as being situated at the southern end of the island lying between two large rocks known as Castle and Battery Rocks, suitable, however, only for small vessels and boats. Landing is said to be not difficult, and the higher ground easily accessible at this point.

On only one occasion previous to our arrival had scientific investigators landed: in 1904 Dr Bruce and members of the staff of the *Scotia* succeeded in effecting a landing. They were ashore for one day only, and bad weather and the necessity of 'standing by' for a sudden recall prevented their going far afield. Nevertheless they made full use of their time and succeeded in collecting a number of new specimens of both animal and plant life. Accounts had shown the island to be difficult of access, but I was particularly anxious to allow the naturalist and geologist with their assistants as many chances as possible for the collection of specimens and the examination of its natural features. This being mid-winter I feared that weather conditions might not be altogether propitious.

We passed along the coast, keeping a close look out for an anchorage for the ship and good landing-places for the boats. Through binoculars we saw that the island was covered with vegetation, of which tussock grass, tree ferns and island trees were the most distinguishable. In most places the land rose steeply from the sea, and down the face of the cliffs numerous waterfalls, long and thin, resembling mare's tails, fell in long cascades. Every now and then they had the appearance of being cut abruptly in half, the wind in strong gusts catching the lower portions and blowing them away in fine, almost invisible, spray. The rocky outline of the island was marked with numerous caves and chasms, and striking features of its formation were pinnacles which stood up distinct, bold in outline, some smooth and tapering, others jagged and irregular. Steep rocky islands, sharply cut off from the shore and separated from it by narrow channels, rose sheer and straight from the sea, some bare, some crowned with a mass of vegetation, most of them so steep as to be quite inaccessible.

Of bird life we saw very little as we passed along the coast. A few sea-hens flew out at our approach, while here and there on the rocks, usually near the entrance to some cave, we could distinguish the white bodies of terns.

We rounded in turn West Cape, South West Cape, South Cape and South East Cape. Snug Harbour on the east side of South West Cape much belies its name, for 'snug' it is not. Indeed, it can hardly be said that there is a harbour there at all. Although it offers a lee and a useful anchorage during high westerly winds, with no swell from south or west, to obtain any real shelter it is necessary to lie very close in to the shore, closer than is safe for any but the smallest of craft. As we passed there was a heavy swell and strong surf which made it quite unsuitable.

In the 'Glen Anchorage' on the east coast we found shelter and dropped anchor in 12½ fathoms.

Just about this time the light began to fail, and in the gathering dusk the island had a most romantic appearance. The glen forms a deep cleft at the back of which the island rises to a height of several thousand feet, marked here and there by bold outstanding masses of rock. Most remarkable of these is the 'Apostle', a lofty solid crag which from its commanding position overlooks and dominates the glen. High up on one side is a long narrow obelisk, rising straight and steep. On the other side facing the harbour is a heavy broad mass with straight, clean-cut face crowned at the top with buttresses resembling a mediaeval castle. The glen itself was in black shadow, and the last rays of the setting sun lit up the summit of the island on which was gathering a rolling mass of sombre clouds. The whole setting was very beautiful and held us momentarily spellbound, none caring to speak. Fancy carried thoughts back to the tales of childhood when gloomy keeps and dungeons, knights and fiery dragons – the myths of later years – had not ceased to be haunting realities.

I did not feel altogether at ease in this spot. Fierce winds blowing gustily down the glen caused the ship to swing continually in different directions. There was a considerable swell running in from the sea, and I knew that a change of wind blowing strongly round South East Point would make our position a very uncomfortable one. There was no moon and the night was black as pitch. I had a sharp watch set, and as it was difficult to get good bearings of the land ordered that soundings with the hand lead be taken every half-hour.

I had already arranged for a party to go ashore the next day: Wilkins and Marr to make natural history collections, Douglas, Carr and Argles to do geological and survey work, and Naisbitt, whose steady work on the ship had earned him a run ashore, to act as cook. Wilkins, as being the most experienced of these, was placed in charge. I warned them to be ready at daybreak.

The next day was fortunately fine. I took the boat ashore with Macklin, McIlroy and Kerr at the oars.

At the mouth of the glen there is a narrow beach of large boulders. On the south side a stream runs into the sea. 'Archway Rock', a large rock 85 feet high with a tunnel obviously drilled by the running stream, gives an imperfect protection to this side of the beach. A strong surf was running, but I managed to effect a landing under the lee of the rock, and after two journeys succeeded in putting the party ashore with their equipment. This was not accomplished without considerable wetting. A strong wind was blowing down the glen, and I was able to let the boat lie off and with the boat's crew go ashore also. Owing to the changeable conditions I did not care to go far away from the landing-place, but I sent Macklin up the glen to get a general impression of the higher parts of the island and if possible obtain some photographs, while with the others I explored the parts around the landing-place and the glen.

The scientific party had brought with them two tents, one of which they started to set up. The other was not required, for we found on the flat piece of ground above the beach two huts, one of wood and corrugated iron, the other built of boulders from the beach and thatched with tussock grass. Both of them were in fairly good condition, and showed that the island had been recently inhabited by someone. Mice swarmed; they were very tame and showed little fear of us. All around lay instruments for mineralogical examination; picks, shovels, hand pump and hose, washing pans, mortar and pestle, rope, axes and many other things. In the huts were cooking utensils and a few unopened tins of preserved food, some of which were badly 'blown'. I found on one of the shelves a half-used box of matches, and testing one I was surprised to find that it ignited readily. There was a little cave to the right of the huts above which a stone had been affixed, bearing the following inscription:

F. X. Xeigler, R. I. Garden, J. Hagan,
W. Swaine, J. C. Fenton, Cape Town,
1/6/19.

The carving had been done by someone who knew his job for it had been very neatly executed.

At the back of the hut and along the sides of the stream were numerous trenches and excavations, apparently where examinations had been made. One had the impression that a search had been carried out for diamonds or precious metal, but that nothing having materialised the party had just dumped down their tools and decamped.

Vegetation appeared to be very luxuriant, tussock grass growing in large clumps covered the flat ground. Close to the beach and along the side of the stream there were numerous wallows, which from their shape and from the smell which emanated from them showed that sea-elephants frequented the island in large numbers during certain seasons. I discovered two young bulls lying in the stream close to the sea. Ferns of many kinds grew everywhere. The slopes were covered with masses of tree fern, and among the smaller varieties was a very pretty maidenhair. There were several clumps of wild celery. The only trees on the island were island trees, which apparently never grow to great size, but many of which were larger and thicker than any I saw on Tristan da Cunha.

Birds resembling thrushes but of a yellowish-green colour flew down and hopped about close to us. They seemed to be quite unafraid, and were so tame that if one kept still for a few minutes they would perch on one's feet and could be easily caught by dropping a hat over them. Sea-hens flew about overhead showing a marked interest in the invaders, or, perched on some near point of vantage, regarded proceedings with a watchful eye. They did not allow anyone to approach very close, but Argles, with a well-aimed geological hammer, succeeded in knocking over two of them, which proved a useful addition to the cooking-pot. Every now and then I heard coming from the slopes the occasional 'chuck-chuck' of landrail, but the birds remained hidden in the vegetation.

I went for a walk up the glen, following the course of the stream. Foothold was bad owing to the rocks being covered by a slimy deposit brought from rotting vegetation on the slopes. The water was coloured slightly green by the products of decomposition, but was used by the shore party for drinking and cooking purposes, apparently with no ill effect.

In spite of the luxuriance of growth there is a great deal of dampness and dank rottenness of the vegetation which takes away much of its attractiveness. It is possible that this is most marked at this time of the year, i.e. June, mid-winter in the southern hemisphere, and that in summer things are drier, fresher and more pleasant. As I went along I caught an occasional glimpse of the landrails with their bright red combs, shiny black bodies and yellow legs. These flightless birds have little runways among the grass where it would be almost impossible to catch them alive. To draw them out I tried a trick which I had often carried out with success on Macquarie Island, imitating their 'chuck-chuck' by knocking two smooth stones sharply together, but though I heard their answering calls drawing nearer they showed a great reluctance to venture into the open.

This is an island where a marooned or shipwrecked party might live in comparative comfort. Instinctively, while taking in all its possibilities, my mind reverted to Elephant Island, the grim and barren spot where I wintered with my party during the last Antarctic expedition, short of food and fuel, bitterly cold and devoid of everything that makes life endurable. Here there is abundance of food and plenty of wood to burn, driftwood from the beach and the island tree wood. In addition to the animal life we saw about us, the sea swarms with fish of excellent quality, and crayfish can be easily caught from the rocks. There are also large rookeries of rockhopper penguins (as we saw later) which provide good meat and in the season abundance of eggs. Small weather-proof dwellings of the type used on Tristan da Cunha could be built from the numerous small boulders on the beach and roofed over with tussock grass. True, too long a sojourn might produce some of the disquietude of Alexander Selkirk, but there would at least be no fear of starvation, and compared with Elephant Island the place is a perfect paradise. I returned to the landing-place, and with McIlroy and Kerr put off in the boat and rowed into the belt of kelp where I was anxious to see what kinds of fish could be caught about the island. It was unnecessary to bait the hooks, a spinner bait or bright piece of tin was sufficient. The fish bit readily and we quickly collected all we required for food. The variety found in the kelp and about the shore is a reddish-coloured fish with strong horny spines. It is excellent to eat. From the ship with strong lines and hooks we caught 'blue-fish' weighing up to 40 lbs, which also make good eating. Watts and Green, who are tireless disciples of Izaak Walton, were responsible for many of these catches. Crayfish were obtained by lowering a weighted net baited with fish. Usually we hauled this up full of them with others clinging to the outside. They were to us a great delicacy.

In the afternoon Worsley and Jeffrey, with the assistance of Dell and Ross, carried out a series of soundings from the boat with a view to charting accurately the anchorage. Later they went ashore and measured the height of Archway Rock.

I sent in the boat to be put ashore three of the geese which we had brought from Tristan da Cunha. As the boat neared the beach they did not wait to be lifted out, but jumped over the gunwale into the water. They swam round the Archway Rock and made a landing at the foot of the small glen which opens to the sea there. We did not see them again, but I was in hopes that they would settle and breed.

Jeffrey, who is a keen observer and takes a close interest in things generally, discovered a very pretty maidenhair fern, a number of which he assiduously set about collecting with roots complete for taking home. On returning to the ship he placed them carefully in a large pot. Having inadvertently left this on deck, he returned to find that Bridget had discovered them and with much appreciation had eaten the lot.

Before returning the party picked up Macklin and brought him off. He had followed the main glen to where it divided into two, taken the one to the right till he reached the grass-covered higher slopes of the island, made a traverse to the base of the 'Apostle' and returned by the other glen. The following description is from his diary:

After leaving Commander Wild I set off up the glen, following as far as possible the course of the stream. To appreciate the keen enjoyment of a walk like this one must have spent many weary months knocking about at sea in a small ship. The little stream was very beautiful as it wound down the glen with its deeps and shallows and little torrents. Every turn produced a new and attractive picture, and the setting behind with the Apostle standing out dominant and high was really magnificent. One had to proceed carefully, for the stones and boulders were very slippery. Sometimes it became necessary to leave the stream and take to the bank, but nowhere was the going good. Having passed several waterfalls, I came to a long straight stretch running between steep sides covered over with branches of island tree to form a long tunnelled archway. I waded along this to encounter a high waterfall up the sides of which there was no way. I was compelled to take to the bank, climbing a steep mossy slope, and plunged in among the trees and tree ferns which grow in thick masses on either side of the glen, running upwards from the edge of the stream to a height of about a thousand feet. The going was now very difficult, for the waterfalls became too numerous and steep for one to continue following the stream. I forced my way with difficulty through masses of fern and island tree all soaking wet, much of it rotten and thickly covered with lichen and other forms of parasite.

The glen divided into two and I chose the one to the right, working my way laboriously till I reached at last the upper edge of thick vegetation and emerged on to grassy slopes, which were very sodden and covered with numerous grasses and mosses. The air blew pure and fresh, rather cold, but a welcome change from the stuffy atmosphere of the thicker vegetation. I was now able to get a look round. The island certainly had a curious formation with its rugged rocky pinnacles and ridges. I was attracted by the huge mass of the Apostle and determined to make for it. This necessitated descending into the glen, crossing the stream and climbing again through the thick belt. I chose wherever possible the course of small tributaries, but these dropped very steeply and had many long thin waterfalls which fell over smooth rock covered with moss, which readily came away and afforded no hand- or foot-hold. I reached a ridge which rose in a series of thin sharp rocky pinnacles, and working along this at last reached the grass land at the foot of the Apostle. I made an effort to climb the mass from the front, but was not successful. The time limit allowed me by Commander Wild was now up and I had to make my way down again. The geological party, Douglas, Carr and Argles, who came here later found an easy way up by walking round to the back.

I descended into the other glen and attempted to work down the stream, but found myself in a narrow gorge between high, smooth walls of rock and, coming to the head of a high waterfall, could find no way down, so that I was compelled to go back out of the gorge and come down through the vegetation on the banks. This was almost as hard work as going up, and long before I reached the bottom the climb had ceased to be a pleasure and had become mere hard work, increased by the fact that I had overstayed my time and had to hurry. The fresh upland air was changed again to the hot stuffiness of the valley, and when I arrived at the landing-place I was soaked to the skin as much with perspiration as with wet from the outside. Anyone working through this vegetation at this time of year must be prepared to get wetted through, for everything is sodden.

Through being late I had to wait some time for the boat, and cooled so rapidly that I was soon shivering. Naisbitt had kindled a fire of driftwood, and I was glad to sit in front of this. He also made me a cup of tea which helped to warm me up.

A number of small and very tame mice came out to regard me curiously; they must have been introduced by the people who built the huts. One very old one crept up to the warmth of the fire – it had very shaky limbs and moved slowly and carefully – rather like a doddery old man. I was taking a great interest in it when Query came up to me, and catching sight of it sitting in the fireglow casually bit it, killed it and dropped it. The utter thoughtlessness and callous cruelty of the act! – and all the time he slowly wagged his tail, oozing with friendliness and good nature...

It is probable that anyone visiting this island in January would find conditions much more pleasant, and to a botanist especially it should appeal as a fertile field for research.

The early part of the night was fine. All round us was a beautiful phosphorescence, the sea being covered with waves of flame. Anything thrown overboard caused ripples and splashes of liquid fire and the cable was a chain of living light, the whole being accentuated by the intense blackness of the night.

While passing along the port alleyway I noticed just opposite the galley a weird luminous glow emanating from two large spots set closely together. They were like the eyes of a large animal and produced momentarily a creepy feeling. Closer examination revealed two crayfish as the source of this phenomenon. The flesh of these creatures is brightly luminous, and wherever there are chinks in the horny coating and where it is thin the light shines through.

Towards daybreak of the next morning the wind increased and a strong swell started running into the anchorage. Not caring to take any undue risks with such an unpleasant lee shore, I heaved anchor and steamed out past South East Point, keeping close into the island to enable Worsley to carry out a series of soundings.

The land along the south side of the island slopes much more gradually to the summit than it does opposite the Glen Anchorage, and the vegetation which is the greatest bar to climbers is much less dense. Getting ashore would be less easy than at the glen. There are places where in fine weather a boat landing could be effected, but the beaches are very narrow and unfit for camping on. It would be necessary also before the slopes are reached to surmount a short steep cliff up which in many places a man un-handicapped by gear might with comparative ease find a way, but where the hauling up of camping equipment would be more difficult. Soundings were carried on throughout the day, and Worsley and Jeffrey made a rough running survey of the coast, mapping as accurately as possible the most salient points and headlands. The wind coming more westerly we returned at night to the Glen Anchorage.

The next day I intended putting Worsley and Macklin ashore and set off in the boat with McIlroy and Kerr at the oars. There was, however, a much bigger surf than we had encountered the previous day, and a landing at the beach was quite out of the question. I succeeded in putting the boat alongside the outer edge of the Archway Rock on to which they scrambled. This side is very steep and they were unable to reach the top which is overhanging. As a matter of fact, we discovered later that there is a way up by a 'chimney' at the point nearest the beach, but it was so thickly covered with tussock grass as to be invisible from below. Up this an active man carrying a coil of rope would have comparatively little difficulty in making his way, and a landing could be effected by this route when it would be impossible at the beach.

Not willing to give up the attempt I took the boat to the far side of the beach where a considerable swell was running, but where the surf was to some extent broken by a thick mass of seaweed. The swell, however, in spite of the weed was so high and steep that we narrowly escaped being capsized and had to abandon this also. I therefore gave up the attempt for that day and rowed along the coast examining rocks and entering numerous small caves. The water was beautifully clear and the bottom easily visible, with growths of beautiful seaweed and all manner of fish and crayfish.

During the next three days the swell increased, and though we tried each day to land, the attempt was attended with so much risk of damage to the boat that on each occasion I gave up the attempt.

The beaches are composed of large and irregularly placed boulders, and many rocks but little submerged and often awash complicate the approach. Our surf-boat was very lightly built, and under circumstances like this there was a danger of her bottom being stove in against the boulders. There was also a risk should she get across one of the outlying rocks of being capsized and swamped by the inrushing swell. We found that the seas were so steep that when they had passed under our bottom the boat came down heavily on the water with such a resounding smack that had she struck something hard she must have immediately been stove in. Indeed our attempt at landing provided us with no little excitement, but I was fortunate in having with me among the crew a number of cool and capable oarsmen, and we escaped damage.

Another factor which adds to the difficulty of landing at Gough Island is the force of the gusts which blow down the glen. They come in whirls so that the boat is blown violently first in one direction and then another, and at this time of year are bitingly cold.

Examination of the records of other explorers who have visited this island shows that there has always been a difficulty in landing.

The time spent lying off an island in an exposed anchorage is a trying one for all concerned, especially for those on whom lies the responsibility of action. One has to be continually on the watch for signs of change of winds. At this time there was no moon and it was difficult to fix the position of the ship by objects on shore. The fierceness of the squalls and their continually changing direction with consequent swing of the ship created a danger of dragging the anchor. By bringing the ship closer into the shore we escaped some of the effects of wind and swell, but there was less room in which to manoeuvre in case of accident. We had always to keep the sounding-lead going, and I gave orders to Kerr that he was to maintain the fires so that at fifteen minutes' notice there could be a full pressure of steam in the boilers.

I began to feel uneasy about the party on shore, for unless we were very fortunate we might have to wait many days before we could take them off. At any time we might be driven by stress of weather away from the island, and in a ship of such low engine-power as the *Quest* getting back might be a matter of difficulty. I had also to consider the question of coal expenditure. I determined, therefore, to seize the first opportunity of picking them up.

During the night we had vicious hailstorms, and the squalls which blew off shore out of the mouth of the glen increased in violence.

In the morning, with McIlroy, Macklin and Kerr, I took the boat in to the beach, and using a stern anchor was able to effect a landing close to the Archway Rock. I shouted to Wilkins to get together his party and equipment and come aboard. Unfortunately Douglas, Carr and Argles had gone out the previous day and had camped for the night farther up the hill, and Wilkins did not expect them back till late. I therefore took off Naisbitt and him, with as much equipment as was not necessary for the night. I left Marr behind with a message that all were to be ready to come off as soon as possible. Getting the gear aboard was a ticklish matter, for seas came heavily over the stern, and fierce squalls with hail blowing in our faces from the hills helped to make things more unpleasant. Macklin and Kerr leapt into the sea to assist with the loading, and no one escaped a good soaking. We got off without mishap, however, and returned to the ship. During the night the gusts at the mouth of the glen had been so violent that the tent was blown in and the party compelled to move to the hut. Wilkins writes:

> During a violent squall of hail and sleet our tent was literally blown from the ropes, leaving us exposed beneath the skeleton of ridge pole and guys. The wind, although not blowing a continuous hurricane, sweeps down the gullies and over the cliffs in terrific gusts at the rate of more than a hundred miles an hour.

As a matter of fact, the party, none of whom apparently were accustomed to tent life under these conditions, were asking for trouble, for they had pitched the tent broadside to the gusts and had left guys and skirting very slack. It is important in high winds to cut out all shake and flutter or the canvas will eventually tear itself to ribbons.

I had a good look round for any signs of the geese which we put ashore, but saw nothing of them. They should have no difficulty in finding ample food.

In the afternoon Worsley, with Macklin, Dell and Watts, took the boat to look at a cave farther along the coast. On entering they found that it had a large shaft open to the sky down which a cascade of water was pouring. Worsley carried out some more soundings with the hand-lead, taking a line across the mouth of the bay.

Next morning the upper slopes of the island were covered in white, the result of the hailstorms.

I saw that landing would be no easy matter, but determined to make an attempt to take off the rest of the shore party. I attempted the beach landing, but had to give it up. I therefore told the party to carry their equipment to the top of Archway Rock, taking with them a rope to lower themselves to the rocks at the bottom, from which it would be possible to pick them off. Rain and hail squalls blew all the time and waiting in the boat was very unpleasant. They had a difficult job but succeeded in massing the gear at the top. Carr descended, having secured the rope to an island tree. He discovered the chimney which had been invisible from below. It is situated on the bay side of the rock close to the corner nearest the beach. Twice Marr nearly stepped over the overhanging edge, but was warned in the nick of time by our shouts. Query, who accompanied the shore party, was lowered in a sack. Ultimately we got the whole party safely off and returned in violent squalls to the ship.

We left the Glen Anchorage and proceeded in a north-westerly direction to a sheltered spot close to the high rounded column of 'Lot's Wife', certainly well named for it forms an unmistakable mark. We anchored opposite a waterfall in 8½ fathoms, and Worsley, Macklin, Wilkins and Douglas went ashore. At this point there is a narrow beach with a small piece of flat land behind it from which the island rises steeply to a summit crowned with a mass of rock. Between the waterfall and the point there is a large penguin rookery, deserted at this time of the year except for a few rockhoppers, whose lives were claimed on scientific grounds. Wilkins added a number of specimens to his collection, and Macklin caught a landrail alive, which was found to be blind of one eye, this no doubt being the reason why he was able to stalk it. He materialistically designed it for the pot, but as it was a perfect specimen Wilkins asked if he might have it for his collection.

We lay at anchor for the night, and at daybreak next morning, 3 June, set off for Cape Town.

Wilkins and his party during their stay on the island had accomplished some very good work. Assisted by Marr, who thoroughly enjoyed his camping experience, he made a large collection of animal and plant life and obtained a number of photographs. Unfortunately the light was not good. Douglas, Carr and Argles made a rough survey of this part of the island and carried out a geological examination of the glen and uplands. They reached the highest point, which proved to be 2,915 feet in height. To do this they spent a night in the open covered only by a floor cloth. It was bitterly cold but the vegetation was far too damp to enable them to start a fire.

Douglas, though not a botanist, made a very interesting observation. In the 'Little Glen', just to the south of Archway Rock, he discovered a grove of trees which he describes as 'growing as if planted in an orchard', attaining a height of 13–14 feet, and covering ground of about 12 feet diameter. It differs in many respects from the island tree, and Wilkins considers it to be a species of sofhora which is found in New Zealand and parts of South America. Its features are intermediate in type between those of the trees found in these respective places.

Naisbitt took charge of the camp and acted as cook, which duties he seems to have carried out well.

The party left behind a considerable quantity of preserved provisions, which they carefully stored in the hut, for they had taken ashore a larger supply than was necessary for their own needs. I hope if it is the lot of any to be compelled by accident to sojourn on this island that these stores will add something to their comfort, though with all the equipment and shelter left by the mining party and the abundance of natural resources I would have no fear for their safety.

As much hydrographical and survey work as possible was carried out on the ship. An examination of anchorages, one on the north coast, one on the south coast, and two on the east coast showed that shelter might be found from northerly, southerly or westerly winds. There are no sheltered bays, each anchorage being an open roadstead. None of them can be considered safe for ships without steam, and the latter should at all times be prepared to get under way at very short notice. The Glen Anchorage affords good holding ground.

The positions of Penguin Island, the Glen Anchorage and Lot's Wife Cove were definitely established.

A good rough survey was made of the eastern and northern coasts and a rough running survey of the rest of the island. Soundings and examinations were made for all dangers and rocks round the coast. The height of several rocks and cliffs on the eastern coast was accurately determined.

There are no outlying dangers about Gough Island.

Jeffrey carried out tidal observations during our stay.

There is no doubt that the work of the scientific parties and the observations taken on and about Gough Island, when fully worked out, will prove most interesting.

CHAPTER 13

Cape Town

On 3 June we set course for Cape Town, where I should be able to get into communication with Mr Rowett. We had had a pretty hard and trying time, but I should have liked to have one more season in the Enderby Quadrant. The *Quest* had her faults – too many – but yet I had learned to love this little ship for all her waywardness. I had come to believe that much might be accomplished by making Cape Town our starting point and setting out early in the season.

On mature consideration, however, I realised that it was inevitable that we must return home, for I knew that we had almost reached the time limit arranged by Sir Ernest Shackleton. There was still much work to be done, for we had to call at St Helena, Ascension Island and St Vincent. If time permitted, I intended to include South Trinidad Island also. I was anxious for Douglas to make a geological examination of these places so that he might be able to link them up with the islands we had already visited.

After leaving Gough Island we had had head winds and seas, and consequently made little progress.

We slaughtered Bridget and cut her up, Dell being the murderer. She was very fat and in excellent condition, and made a welcome change of fare.

The wind fell off a little on 4 and 5 June and came abaft the beam, enabling us to shut off steam and proceed under sail only. We were now short of coal and had to economise so that we should have a supply sufficient to take us into port. The ship also was very light, as a result not only of the depleted bunkers, but also from the lightening of the fore-hold of the mails and stores which were put ashore at Tristan da Cunha.

I was now proceeding to enable Worsley to look for a reef reported by the whalers of South Georgia as seen in the neighbourhood of position lat. 35° 4' S. and 5° 20' W. long. (350 miles east by north of Tristan da Cunha). Captain Hansen, of the *Orwell*, was very positive on the matter, stating that while proceeding from Cape Town to South Georgia he had seen breaking water and strands of kelp in this position. We took a series of soundings, which showed no signs of shoaling, and the snapper revealed bottom specimens of white clay.

On 6 June we started cleaning up the paint-work in an endeavour to make the ship look moderately respectable for our entry into Cape Town, but I am afraid that as a result of the hard battering which she received in the South she still had a very weather-beaten appearance in spite of any efforts we made in this way. Dell again had some butchering to do. He skinned one of the Tristan sheep, which proved to be very scraggy.

We spent the day making a traversing cruise, looking for the reported reef, but saw absolutely no indications of its presence in this position. Three successive soundings showed not less than 1,900 fathoms, with the same globigerinous ooze bottom we had found since leaving Gough Island.

On 7 June we still traversed in search of the reef. We made another attempt to obtain soundings, but the wind and sea increased so much that it was impossible to keep the ship over the lead. Dell, at the Lucas machine, had a trying time, for he was continually being immersed. After 580 fathoms of wire had been run out I ordered him to reel in, and we headed off direct for Table Bay. The wind continued to increase in force, and, coming ahead, blew up from the south-east with heavy squalls of rain.

On the 8th and 9th we had a strong gale in which the now much lightened *Quest* flung herself about in the most lively manner, and much water came over our rails.

On the 9th the *Quest* excelled everything she had ever done in the way of rolling, and though we were by now well accustomed to her little ways, it was only with the greatest difficulty that we could move about the decks, passing quickly from one support to another.

On this day Query was washed overboard. He had become so confident and sure-footed that we had long ceased to have any fears on his behalf. Dell had just finished skinning our second Tristan sheep, and was in process of hanging it to a stay on the bridge deck.

Query, taking as usual an active interest in the proceedings, had followed him up. The ship was struck by a heavy sea, which caused her to throw herself violently to leeward, and Query was carried under the griping spar of the port life-boat. Jeffrey, who was on watch, immediately stopped the engines and attempted to wear ship, but in these heavy seas any attempt at a rescue was impossible. Poor Query! he must have wondered why the usual helping hand was not forthcoming, as it had so often been on previous occasions to help him out of his scrapes. His loss caused a real hurt.

On the 10th conditions were much the same, with heavy squalls at intervals. The wind hauled a point, and at 2 p.m. we set the foresail and stopped the engines. We logged 5 knots as an average, and 6 to 7 during the squalls. In the middle watch at night I saw a perfect lunar rainbow stretching in a big arc across our bows.

On the 11th and 12th the wind fell light and we had fine weather. I set all hands to cleaning up, for this work had been suspended during the bad weather. We could do nothing to the outside of the ship, which was so scratched and scarred as to make hopeless any attempt to improve it. We managed, however, to brighten up the wardroom and cabins a little. 'Old Mac' scraped the foremast – a difficult job on account of the heavy rolling – but it greatly improved our appearance. This fine old seaman is a product of the old-time sailing ships, a real sailor of a type only too rare to-day. He has made three voyages to the Antarctic.

The rest of this portion of the trip was uneventful till, on the 17th, we sighted on the horizon the Cape of Good Hope and saw Table Mountain appear from behind the clouds. We entered Table Bay early in the morning of Sunday 18 June.

At Cape Town we were met by our agents and Mr Cook, who was acting as Mr Rowett's representative. They brought us a big mail. It was interesting to see the members crowd round till they had received their letters, when each man sought out a quiet corner to which he might retire and read them undisturbed by anyone.

After the usual formalities had been gone through, we were piloted to a snug berth in the Alfred Dock. It was not until I had seen the comments in the Cape Town Press that I realised how much battered our little ship had been in her arduous struggle with the heavy seas and ice. One paper spoke of her as 'small, unpretentious, but grizzly looking, and bearing signs where the ice had scored furrows in her planks'. Another described her as

> a black, stubby little boat, steaming into Cape Town unknown, unannounced ... the leaden skies, the cold green waters of the harbour, the sullen murkiness of the distant sea, the little furtive showers of rain, all seemed to claim the little ship as part of themselves, catch her up and absorb her into them as an essential part of the picture...

All were amazed at her size, and few believed that so small a craft could have accomplished so much and covered so great a distance. We had the warmest of welcomes from the people of South Africa, and during our stay were so lavishly entertained by these hospitable folk that each one of us must carry for ever a warm spot in his heart for Cape Town and its inhabitants.

We were received by the Prime Minister (General Smuts) and entertained by him and his wife at their beautiful house at Groote Schur.

The ship was visited by many of the prominent people of South Africa, including members of the House of Parliament, which was then in session. All of them took a very keen interest in the regions we had visited, especially in Tristan da Cunha, the islands about it, and Gough Island. Much sympathy was expressed at the state of destitution in which we had found the people of Tristan da Cunha, and the *Cape Argus*, an enterprising and very efficiently staffed daily paper, immediately started making arrangements for a relief ship to visit them, and asked our advice as to the most suitable type of vessel for the work. It was hoped that she would be able to sail about the beginning of January, that being the most suitable time of year for effecting a landing on the island.

The Enderby Quadrant of the Antarctic is also of special interest to South Africans because the climatic conditions there have a large bearing upon the weather of Cape Colony. The Meteorological Office of South Africa was anxious for a preliminary report of our meteorological work, which McIlroy gave them.

I gave Douglas permission to spend his time in Johannesburg, for as a geologist he was very anxious to visit the mining areas. He was accompanied by Wilkins.

Invitations poured in for the various members to visit the different parts of the country about Cape Town, but though I much regretted having to decline them, I was unable to give any further leave, as the different members were required for work about the ship.

As is common on the occasion of the return of an expedition from the Antarctic, most of the party were attacked by 'colds in the head'. Influenza was prevalent in the town and found two ready victims, first in Macklin, who contracted it soon after our arrival, and, later, myself.

Much repair work and general overhauling was necessary on the *Quest*. I had it put in hand at once. The engines, which under the careful nursing of Kerr, Smith and their staff had withstood the hard conditions remarkably well, now required an overhaul before we could again put to sea. The rigging was reset up and all necessary repairs completed. The ship received a new coating of paint, which completely transformed her battered appearance and made her once more a smart-looking little vessel. Fresh stores were taken aboard, and, the work completed, we left next day for the naval dockyard at Simonstown. Several of our friends made the trip with us, including a number of Boy Scouts who had been assisting aboard the ship, but the *Quest*, reverting quickly to her old antics, made them wish they had stayed ashore.

We were most kindly received by Admiral Sir William Goodenough, who gave us a snug berth in the harbour. I am much indebted to him for his kindness during the time we remained in Simonstown. Here again we received every kindness from the officers of the ships attached to this base, especially those of HMS *Lowestoft* and *Dublin*, who welcomed us with the proverbial open-handedness of the Navy.

On 13 July, the day of our departure, we had the honour of a visit from the Governor-General, HRH Prince Arthur of Connaught, who, accompanied by Admiral Sir William Goodenough, made an inspection of the ship and took a keen interest in everything he saw.

My attack of influenza had been a very severe one and left me feeling very weak. I was fortunate in making an uncomplicated recovery. My best thanks are due to Mr and Mrs John Jeffrey, old friends with whom I stayed during my illness and whose many kindnesses I shall not easily forget.

In order not to delay the sailing of the *Quest*, I re-joined her earlier, perhaps, than was advisable, and on arrival at the dockyard felt so exhausted that I was compelled to take to my bunk at once.

Before finally leaving we swung the ship to adjust compasses. This was again done for us by Commander Traill-Smith, RN, who had so kindly performed this office on our leaving Plymouth, and who had since our departure been transferred to this base.

CHAPTER 14

St Helena–Ascension Island–St Vincent

For the first few days at sea after leaving Cape Town I was obliged to keep my bunk, but the care of the doctors, the solicitous attentions of Green, who went to all sorts of length to produce delicacies for me, and the good salt air worked wonders, and I began to regain strength and was soon up and about.

As I was in bed the following is quoted verbatim from Macklin's diary:

14 July.

A lovely sunny day with smooth sea, and the *Quest* behaving better than she has ever done before. Surely this is a prelude to something wicked – I do not trust the *Quest* when she is good.

Worsley took the ship close in to Sea Point to enable us to signal good-bye to our many friends there, after which we put out to the open ocean. We passed close to a small fishing boat and called her alongside to enable one of our members to pass over a letter for his latest best girl. A sailor, of course! with a girl in every port, but I omit his name. I took the opportunity of buying some fresh fish, for which I exchanged some tobacco and ship's biscuits.

It was a lovely afternoon, and all about the ship were numbers of seabirds – gulls, albatross and shags. In the water were penguins (a type not found in the Antarctic), seals, turtles and sharks. This part of the ocean must simply teem with life to support all these large animals.

About 5 p.m. a big Castle liner passed us homeward bound, and Wuzzles changed course to enable us to give a shout to Cookie, who was aboard. The skipper, however, must have been watching through his glasses, and, seeing what a crowd of toughs we were (Wuzzles prominent on the bridge), sheered widely off and passed us too far away to distinguish individuals.

Commander Wild is very limp. He had a very bad attack of 'flu'. He's a hard case, and it takes a lot to upset him. A few of Green's egg-flips and the salt air will soon set him on his feet again.

Sunday 16 July.

Yesterday was a fine day, most of which I spent below hatches making, with Marr's assistance, a final stowage and getting things ready for sea.

To-day has been perfectly lovely. Had the 4.00–8.00 a.m. watch, and Dell, Mick and I had just scrubbed down decks, and made a jolly good job of it too, when the stokers started cleaning pipes and simply covered the whole ship with soot and ashes. We blessed them fervently for this good beginning to a Sabbath Day, the rest of which we spent trying to get our cabins and living quarters clear of the mess they had made.

Commander Wild is much better, though he is not yet all right, as he seems to think. I allowed him up to sit in the sun for a little while.

The *Windsor Castle* passed and signalled us, 'A pleasant voyage.' We dipped ensigns. There is something rather nice about these sea courtesies.

Bosson, Green's new mate, entrusted with a carving knife, succeeded in nearly severing one finger.

19 July.

Weather has continued fine, with fair, following winds. Commander Wild improving steadily and eating better than I have ever known him to do. He has a good deal to make up, for he lost a great deal of weight in Cape Town.

Yesterday I stowed some cases for Jeff and bound them with pyrometa wire. Today Jeff and Dell removed the wardroom stove, which we shall no longer need, thank goodness, for with the down draught from square sail and topsail the smoke nearly always went the wrong way.

20 July.

Engines stopped, and we lay to for a bottom dredging. We wound in the line by hand. Good old man-power! – we always come down to it in the end. The whole job took about eight hours; it is good exercise, but towards the end becomes a bit of a toil. While stopped we were surrounded by albatross, and Green and Watts succeeded in catching some alive. Good-looking birds were passed to Wilkins, the poorer specimens were set free (this is subject for a moral).

The next few days were uneventful. I had by now quite got over my illness and begun to go about as usual.

On 27 July we arrived at St Helena, which was of interest to me because in my first voyage as a boy in an old sailing ship we had called here and I had not been back since.

This island has a most interesting history. It was first discovered in 1592 by Juan de Nova Castilla, one of the enterprising Portuguese navigators of those days, who claimed it for Portugal. Since then it has two or three times changed hands. The East India Company used it as a port of call for a long time, but handed it over to the British Government in 1833. Under the company's administration the island prospered exceedingly. The famous navigator Captain Cook, who visited the island in 1775, speaks of finding its people 'liying [sic] in delightful little homes amongst pleasant surroundings', and describes them as the nicest people of English extraction he had ever met. The Government, on taking over, seemed to have a much less sympathetic understanding of the island and its people, for since that time its prosperity has steadily declined. It was used and is chiefly known to the world as the prison of such men as Napoleon, Cronje and others.

From the sea the island is very unprepossessing, rising steeply from the water's edge and looking bare, hot and dry. Jamestown, the port, lies in a valley which runs backwards and upwards from the sea in a straggling and ever-narrowing line. From the anchorage one gets a refreshing glimpse of green on the inner slopes. One of the first things that catches the eye on looking ashore is a huge ladder, nearly 1,000 feet long and over 600 feet high, which passes from

Jamestown to the summit of Ladder Hill. It contains 700 steps, to the top of which, in days gone by, a postman carrying his bag of letters used to run without a halt.

Having passed through the usual port formalities, I got ready to go ashore. While preparing to leave, the ship was called up from the 'Observatory', and I received an invitation from HE the Governor to lunch at his house, together with two or three of my officers. I took Worsley, McIlroy and Macklin with me.

Jamestown is protected from the sea by a wall, and we entered through iron gates which no doubt in the days of Napoleon always had an armed guard. There is nothing of that sort today, and, indeed, St Helena is an island that has 'seen better days'. At one time a flourishing settlement and an important military station famous as the prison of Napoleon, it is now almost forgotten by the rest of the world.

We procured a carriage, drawn by two small but sturdy horses, and set off for the 'Plantations' at the summit of the island where the Governor's house is situated. The climb was a stiff one, and to ease the horses we walked up most of the way. At first the road was bare and dry, cut from rocks of obviously volcanic origin, the only vegetation an occasional dusty cactus growing here and there. As we mounted, however, we entered a greener area, with vegetation which increased in luxuriance till, at the top, we saw that the inner parts of the island were really very fertile. The air also was purer and more fresh. I was struck by the appearance of the 'mina' birds, which have a pretty dark brown and white colouring, and at first sight resemble magpies. They were introduced to the island for the purpose of killing insects.

We had a most pleasant lunch with HE the Governor (Colonel Peel) and his wife. The house has a very fine outlook down a valley to the sea, and is situated in very beautiful grounds which contain a number of interesting trees: oaks, Scotch firs, spruces and Norfolk pines, and a tree with dark foliage and brilliant scarlet blossom. Numerous white arum-like lilies grow in profusion, and many other flowers, including a beautiful small blue flower with a pleasant fresh scent. It was a very happy change from our sea life. We were introduced to a huge tortoise, reputed to be 200 years old, which sometimes leaves the grounds for the road and causes all the horses which encounter it to shy. When this happens a cart is sent out to fetch it home. It takes six men to lift it off the road.

After lunch we paid a visit to the tomb of Napoleon and the house at Longwood where he lived while on the island. The tomb is in a deep hollow, and for so great a man is very unimposing. It is covered with a large marble slab, blank, with no inscription of any sort. Sometime after his death his body was exhumed and taken to Paris, when it was laid finally in Les Invalides, where a magnificent and more fitting tomb has been erected to his memory. The house at Longwood also is unimposing. One can imagine how his restless spirit must have chafed at its confinement. The rooms are kept spotlessly clean, but are bare except that in the small chamber where he died there is a bust set on a long pedestal hung with a few bedraggled pieces of tricolour ribbon. It contained also, when we were there, a baby's perambulator, but was otherwise empty. The sight of this house caused me to feel a great pity for its prisoner.

I learned from the Governor that while alive he had been well treated, having had an allowance from the English Government of £12,000 per annum.

The island inland from the sea is very hilly and divided into numerous ridges and valleys. There is not a really good piece of flat land anywhere. The valleys are very fertile. Owing to the steepness of the roads we proceeded most of the way on foot, leaving the paths, which zigzagged, and making straight traverses across the fields. Brambles grow profusely, and at this time a number of blackberries were ripe. Gorse and broom covered the hillsides with yellow. The chief industry of the island seems to be the growing of New Zealand flax and the making of it into fibre. During the war they obtained the most phenomenal prices, which, however, have since dropped to normal. The flora generally of St Helena is very interesting, for there are over sixty native species of plants, nearly all of them peculiar to the island. Every now and then we caught glimpses of pretty little residences situated in gardens of their own. We met numerous people, including a number of British folk, driving in their carriages – it seems to be the custom here to greet everyone one meets.

The natives we met showed unmistakable signs of a very mixed origin. In the days of the East India Company labour was imported from India and from China, and on frequent occasions natives of different parts of Africa have been introduced. The African type predominates.

We next visited the station of the Eastern Telegraph Company, where we met the manager and his wife. They have a very nice place, situated in beautiful grounds containing masses of bougainvillaea, geranium, scarlet hibiscus and many other kinds of blossom. They have bananas and guavas in abundance, but oranges do not grow well.

They told me that the natives of the island, of which there are about 3,000, are very badly off, for there is practically no work for them to do. Some of them look half starved. A lace industry was started about twenty years ago by an Englishwoman. The lace is said to be of good quality, but I did not have the opportunity of seeing any.

We returned to the ship about 6.30 p.m., and immediately set off for Ascension Island.

In the meantime Douglas had made a brief geological examination of the main features of the island. There was not time to do more.

Bosson, the new hand taken on at Cape Town, whom I had allowed to go for a run ashore, fell into a cactus bush, and did not forget the fact in the next few days.

We had an uninterrupted run to Ascension Island, where I intended to take in coal. As we approached we saw hundreds of birds, which flew squawking overhead, but were apparently intent on their fishing, and took very little notice of the ship. We arrived and dropped anchor about 8 p.m. on 1 August.

From the shore we received a signal to ask if we had a clean bill of health, and soon after the officer commanding the station came off to visit us in a boat pulled by several hefty bluejackets. He announced that at the moment of our arrival an interesting and unusual event had taken place: the birth of a child. I learned from him that I could get what coal I required to take me on to St Vincent.

2 August was a rather muggy day. The ship was surrounded by thousands of fish of a dark purple colour with white patches on their tails. They rushed at anything edible that was thrown overboard,

and the water was lashed into foam by their efforts to get at it. It was really a wonderful sight. They could not be induced to take a hook and fought very shy of anything with a line on it. Green, the enthusiast, tried all morning to catch some, but without success. He succeeded, however, by putting out more line, in catching a red spiny variety at a deeper level. He also caught a shark.

I sent ashore the scientists, and later went myself with McIlroy and Macklin. On landing, Macklin saw an officer of marines to whom he said: 'Your face is familiar to me. Where have I seen you before?' Apparently they had met somewhere in Russia. It was rather extraordinary meeting again in this out-of-the-way little spot in tropical mid-Atlantic. We went on to the 'Club', where we met several more officers of the station and a number of the Eastern Telegraph Company's officials.

The island is bare, sandy and desolate looking. The barracks and officers' quarters are at sea level. The latter consist of neat little bungalows, about which some pretty blossom has been induced to grow.

The troops and naval ratings wear solar topees, khaki shorts and shoes. Usually they have no stockings. The soldiers have khaki shirts, and the ratings white jumpers. There are a number of women on the island. They wear light cotton dresses and often have no stockings – a sane and healthy fashion for this part of the world.

After lunch Macklin went off to see one of the sights of the island – the nesting-ground of the 'Wideawakes'. He writes:

After leaving Commander Wild and Mick, I walked out to 'Wideawake Valley', so called because of the number of birds which nest there. It is an extraordinary sight. There are millions of them, covering the ground for acres. They lay a single egg, about the size of a bantam's and spotted. Many of the chicks had hatched out. If one goes too near they rush frantically about and lose their parents, and if they intrude too much on their neighbours sometimes get pecked to death. Many of the birds rise up and come flying, with raucous din, all about one's head. The noise is maddening. Having seen what I wanted to see, I was glad to get away. I left the track I had come by and returned across country.

The going off the tracks is very bad indeed, the surface of the island being much broken and covered with a short dry grass amongst which were numerous stones and boulders, which tired one's feet very much. The heat, too, was considerable, and I was glad when I reached the club and obtained a long, cool drink, which was very comforting to my parched throat.

During the afternoon the *Durham Castle* came in. This is a bi-monthly event, and throws the whole island into a fluster. I took Worsley, McIlroy and Macklin aboard, when we met the captain and the ship's doctor. I dined in the evening with the commandant.

On 3 August preparations were started for the coaling. The coal is of the poorest quality, consisting of dust and slag, and the price we were charged was exorbitant, but I was obliged to the commandant for being at pains to give us the best he could under the circumstances.

Scientific work was continued, and Macklin and Kerr went off in the boat to another part of the island to obtain some different varieties of fish.

In the evening we dined at the mess of the Eastern Telegraph Company, where we had a very merry evening. Most of us slept ashore, being kindly put up by members of the telegraph company. Douglas and Marr, who had ascended to the high part of the island, were very kindly accommodated by Mr and Mrs Cronk at their pretty house on the hill.

Coaling was continued on the 4th. The coal is put into bags at the dump and loaded into lighters, which are taken off by a tug and laid alongside the ship. The work is often awkward on account of the swell. It was a messy business, and the ship soon became covered in every part of her with dust. It took us many days to get really clean again. In order to keep an eye on things, I stayed near the scene of operations. Macklin ascended to the summit, and the following account from his diary is fairly descriptive of the island:

I went ashore early with Wilkins, who had with him his camera and cinematograph machine. He was going off with the commandant in a pinnace to an island where there was a large number of birds.

I first of all walked about the station and took a number of snapshots, after which I set off up the dusty track leading to Green Hill. It was a blazing hot day, and I wore nothing but singlet, shorts and shoes, and had a good sun hat. This garb was cool and gave a delightful sense of freedom in movement, but it proved, to my cost, to be an inadequate protection from the sun.

I passed *en route* the wireless station, which has been abandoned. Its six immense poles are cemented and stayed in such a manner as to make the removal of them not worth the labour. The track led up a gentle slope over sandy ground that supported a few low-lying shrubs but very little else. Farther towards the summit the vegetation increased a little, with cactus plants and a few aloes. Still farther up an attempt had been made to plant trees along the sides of the track, and, considering the dry, hard nature of the earth, they were growing not badly, but gave little impression of greenery. I continued along the main track till I reached eventually a point marked by the two halves of a boat which had been set up on either side of the road. The gentle slope was now replaced by a more steeply rising mountain face, up which the main track zigzagged so much as to make the total distance a very long one. I accordingly left it for a steeper but straighter track. The air was now fresher, and the higher one climbed the more abundant became the vegetation, which included trees – palms, pines, firs, eucalyptus – and a tree with bright yellow flowers which I did not recognise. There were ferns of several sorts, small flowering shrubs, thistles with a yellow flower, and, higher up the mountain, a species of scarlet hibiscus.

Grasshoppers were numerous. They hopped off the ground in much the same manner as an English grasshopper, but were capable of a certain power of flight. I saw also a number of beetles, rats and land-crabs, but animal life generally is scarce.

Near the top of Green Mountain there are a few little residences situated in very pretty gardens. Indeed, the whole of the island above a certain level is very beautiful and a paradise as compared with the hot, dusty garrison at the base.

Near the summit I came to a house surrounded by a picturesque garden containing many trees and shrubs with bright blossom. I learned that it belonged to the 'Farm Superintendent'. At this point a corporal of marines approached me, and remarking that I looked hot, asked me if I would like a glass of beer. I was hot, and the suggestion was too alluring to be refused, though I had doubts as to the wisdom of it, seeing that I had still many miles of hot walking ahead of me. There is a small signal station here, and the corporal took me to his quarters, from where I had a magnificent view of the slopes of the island and of the sea, covered with twinkling points, stretching like a flat board to a far distant horizon. There is a small farm which supplied the station with fresh meat, milk, etc. I had a look at the cowhouses, which literally swarmed with rats of enormous size. There are also some hen-runs and pig-sties, and a number of sheep graze on the hills.

Thanking the friendly corporal, I pushed on over a grassy slope dotted about with trees, and finally reached the summit, where there is a thick plantation of bamboos, the stems of which rattled in the strong south-east trades. In the middle of it there is a pond of very stagnant water. The view from the top is wonderful, every part of the island being clearly visible. All about the upper slopes are asphalted watersheds leading to storage tanks. All the water for the garrison and the other buildings at the base of the island comes from the summit, and is conducted there by pipes.

Descending the farther slopes, I came to the entrance to a long narrow tunnel cut through the hill. It had been dug by the military detachment many years before, quite for what purpose I did not learn. It is low, narrow and pitchy black, but there is a hand-wire by using which as a guide one can go steadily forward. It emerges in a corner of the farm superintendent's garden.

I had lunch on the summit with Mr and Mrs Cronk. They have two pretty children. Mr Cronk has been farm superintendent for twenty-five years. It must be a funny life in this remote spot. He is responsible for all the vegetation, and takes a great pride in his work – certainly he has made his mark on the world. The whole garrison is being removed, and is due to leave in a few months. He goes too, and regrets that no one is being left to carry on the work he has so carefully inaugurated. He has had to overcome many difficulties, and is disappointed that the labour of so many years will be thrown away. The big plants grow all right and do not require much attention. The young ones must be shaded from the fierce sun, and unless this shade is provided artificially the only seeds that flourish are those which fall beside the parent plant and derive shade and a certain amount of moisture from it. The summit of the island, being often clouded in mist, is very damp, and those who live there for any length of time suffer considerably from rheumatism.

I descended towards 'Wideawake' Plain again, visited the circular crater of a volcano, and crossed it to enter a belt of loose, broken pieces of cellular lava. The inside was covered with sand, was bare of vegetation, and had round it a circular track which gives it the name of the 'Devil's Horse-ring'.

On my way back I passed again over a sandy plain, where I saw a number of small rabbits. I enjoyed my day immensely and was pleasantly fatigued after my climbing. I suffered badly from sunburn, which will probably get worse in the next few days. My neck and legs are chiefly affected. Marr, who had spent the day with Douglas on a geological expedition, was also badly burned, and had a temperature of 103° F. I had to put him to bed...

The coaling was completed during the afternoon.

We had many visitors to see us off, and left finally at 4.30 p.m., setting course for St Vincent.

The next part of our journey proved uneventful. We crossed the equator to run into hotter weather, the sun being near its northern limit of declination. With a light following wind there was no draught, and the ship was covered daily with dust and ashes from the very dirty Ascension Island coal. So bad did it turn out that Kerr and his staff had the greatest difficulty in maintaining a sufficient pressure of steam, and the work of the stokers was consequently very hard. Young, Ross and Murray (a new hand taken on at Cape Town) stuck splendidly to their work during this uncomfortable and trying stage of the journey.

We obtained at Ascension Island a number of live baby turtles, which I proposed to present to the Marine Biological Laboratory at Plymouth. On its staff are two old shipmates of mine, Messrs

Hodson, of the *Discovery*, and Clark, of the *Endurance*. We placed the turtles in one of the waterbutts on the after deck, where Wilkins fed them on small pieces of flying fish. They spent the whole day diving for pieces and fought with each other for possession of them. They are curious little creatures.

One of the men brought off a small rabbit, of which a few run wild on Ascension Island. It became a great pet and was most extraordinarily tame.

We arrived at St Vincent on 18 August, where we completed our coaling. Here, as on our outward trip, we received kindness from the members of Messrs Wilson, Sons & Company, Limited, and were entertained by the Eastern Telegraph Company mess.

Douglas and Wilkins carried on their investigations. Macklin, Jeffrey and Green, our fishing enthusiasts, went off to bring in a supply of fish, but returned with a small result, their time having been spent apparently in sailing the surf-boat out to Bird Rock and in bathing.